Collecting
Stories

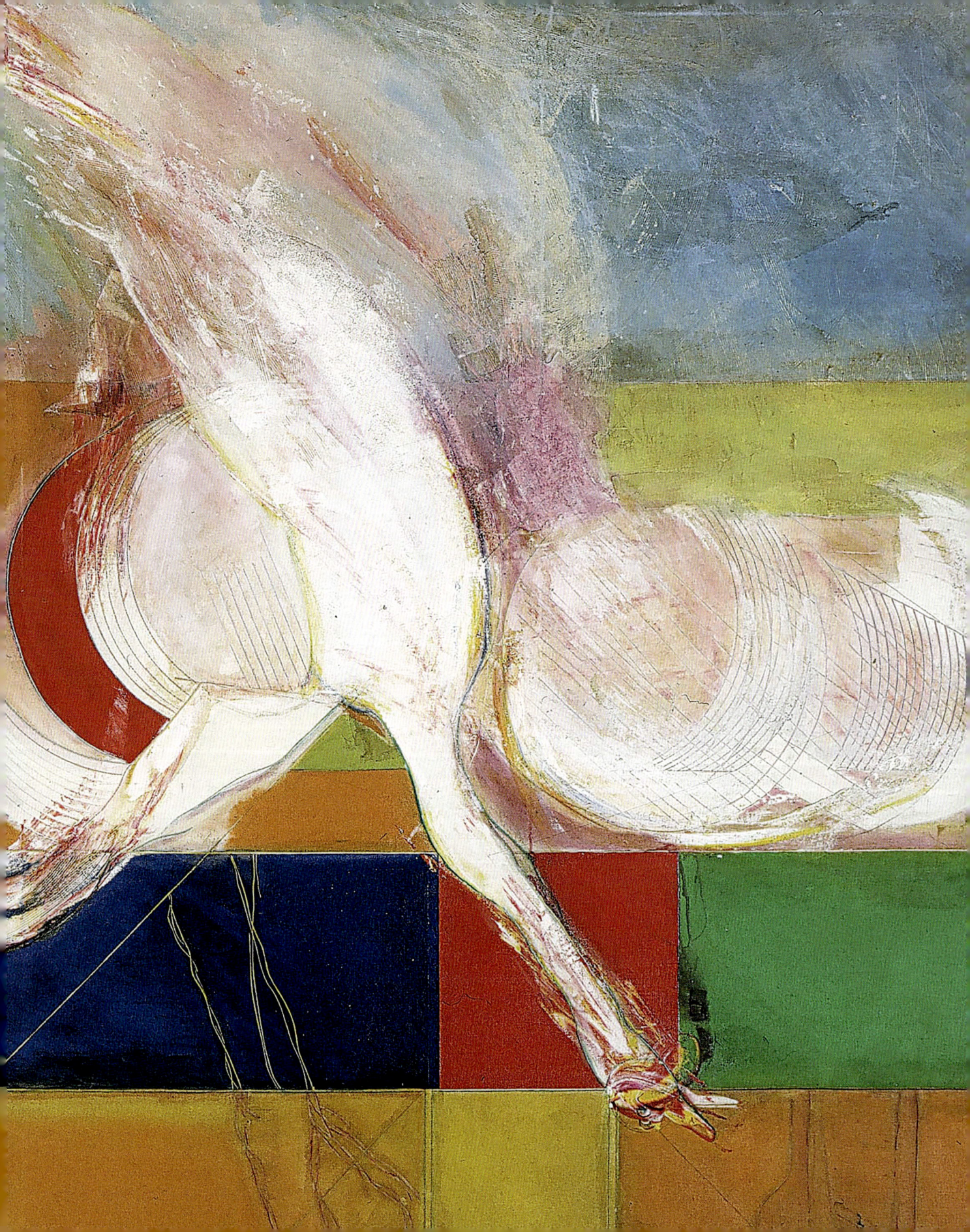

Collecting Stories

The cultural collections of the University of Liverpool

Edited by
Katy Hooper

LIVERPOOL UNIVERSITY PRESS

First published 2025 by
Liverpool University Press
4 Cambridge Street
Liverpool
L69 7ZU

British Library Cataloguing-in-Publication data
A British Library CIP record is available

ISBN 978-1-83624-008-2 paperback

Typeset by Carnegie Book Production, Lancaster
Printed in the Czech Republic via Akcent Media Limited

The manufacturer's authorised representative in the EU for product safety is:
Easy Access System Europe, Mustamäe tee 50, 10621 Tallinn, Estonia
https://easproject.com (gpsr.requests@easproject.com)

Contents

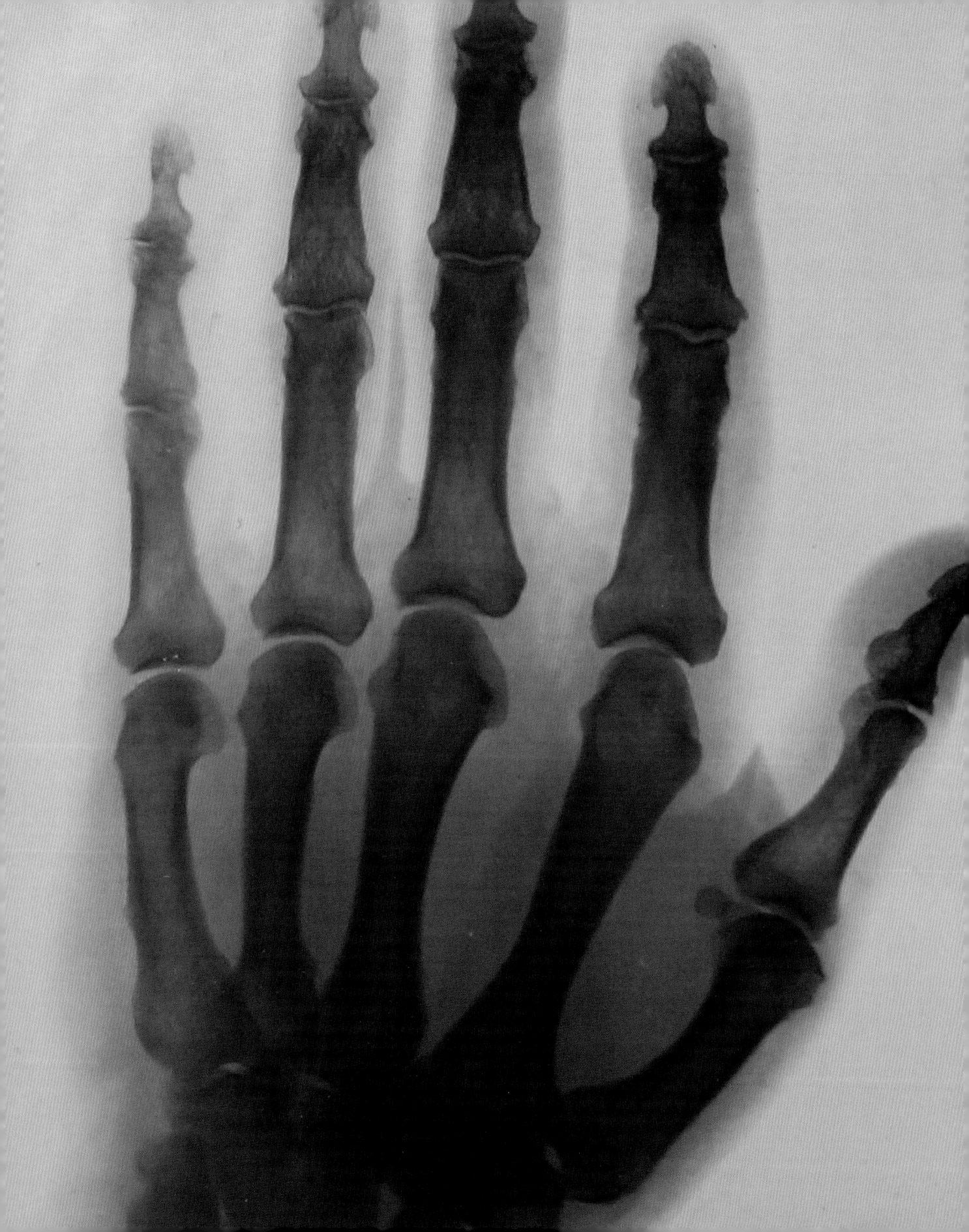

ACKNOWLEDGEMENTS

Production of this volume, made possible by a generous donation from Dr Geoffrey Eibl-Kaye, is the work of colleagues from across the University of Liverpool and beyond. The editorial board (Professor Georgina Endfield, Joanne Fitton, Katy Hooper, Emerita Professor Eve Rosenhaft, and Alison Welsby) would like to thank all those involved, especially the contributors who worked so enthusiastically to an exacting timescale, and Dr Amanda Draper, whose wise advice and wide knowledge shaped the volume well beyond her own contribution. We are grateful for the guidance of our steering group (Cilla Ankrah-Lucas, Professor Fiona Beveridge, Anthony Cond, Dr Matt Greenhall, and Mark Horne), and all those who reviewed the entries, including members of the Heritage, Arts and Culture committee and Emeritus Professor Dinah Birch, CBE. Colleagues across Libraries, Museums and Galleries gave their time and expertise to help speed the book towards publication: facilitating access to objects in our stores, liaising with academic contacts, advising on copyright, and sharing a wealth of professional knowledge and experience. They are too numerous to mention individually, but their collective endeavours have taken this book from idea to reality. Ben McGrae from the Centre for Innovation in Education, student partner Maisy Rooth Corder and student volunteer Bethany Ray all helped us respond to reviewers' questions. We are grateful for the insights on decolonisation and inclusivity of the DeCoL-SoLS-Advocates in the School of Biosciences – Alice Cairns, Kavitha Cronin, Isobel Diaz, Freddy Larsen, Kodie McDonald, Obimobi Onyeukwu-Onyenso, Eva Teodorescu, and Shuxian Zhou – and to Dr Stephen Kenny and Professor Emeritus Bernard Brabin (Liverpool School of Tropical Medicine).

The photography is the excellent work of Katie Clugston and Simon Critchley, with additional images supplied by Julia Thorne, Lyndsay Roberts, Ness Botanic Gardens, Max Rossell, and Stephanie Wynne and Steve McCoy of McCoy-Wynne. Thank you to Dr Anna Chen and Gwen Baines, whose language skills enabled us to seek copyright permissions in China and Japan, and to all the copyright holders who engaged so generously with the project.

PREFACE

This volume presents 52 items from the University of Liverpool's diverse and significant cultural collections, charting the development of these as a reflection of the University's own growth. From the fledgling University College Liverpool of 1881 to the global University of Liverpool of today, this volume depicts many of the key milestones in the University's history, embodied through its archival, special, and cultural collections.

These collections are large and diverse. They include over a million books, thousands of artworks and cultural artefacts, miles of archives and special collections, and diverse examples of art and sculpture across campus. These items are cared for by expert and passionate colleagues who use their knowledge and skills to preserve, present, and curate them for the enjoyment of thousands of people every year. The items depicted here are part of a working and evolving collection, used and seen every day by our students, academics, and visitors, and they are integral to teaching, learning, research, and enjoyment.

This volume reflects this, and the articles are written by collection experts, academic researchers, and our students. The authors convey their passion and expertise, and they depict how these items tell the story of the University, the city, and the centrality of human curiosity to education and discovery.

I would like to thank all of those people who have contributed to this volume and who have so willingly shared their expertise and passion through their articles. I would also like to thank the many people who have supported this volume in other ways, from selecting content to digitising items. Particular thanks go to Katy Hooper, our Special Collections Librarian, for her role as editor and for bringing her insight, skill, and determination to the selection and collation of items for inclusion. Thank you to the wider Editorial Board for their attention to detail, guiding hand, and oversight, and to Liverpool University Press for their support and partnership.

Special thanks are owed to Dr Geoffrey Eibl-Kaye, Liverpool graduate and physicist, whose generous donation has made this volume possible. He is a passionate bibliophile, philatelist, and longtime supporter of the University, and we hope that this volume is a fitting tribute to his generosity and lifelong love of the printed word.

Finally, thank you to the countless generations of curators, archivists, librarians, academics, and students who have preserved, used, and cherished our university collections, making them accessible to all for the 'advancement of learning and ennoblement of life'.

Dr Matt Greenhall
Director of Libraries, Museums and Galleries,
University of Liverpool

FOREWORD

This is a timely publication as the University of Liverpool gears up to celebrate its 150th anniversary in 2031. Over the course of the storied history of the University, the inquisitiveness and curiosity of its faculty, staff, and students have compelled them to ask difficult questions about the world around them and encouraged them to experiment to uncover hidden truths. They have tested their own and others' pre-existing ideas. The inspiration for their work has come from many directions, including the University and the surrounding city: its landscape and institutions, its facilities and buildings, its people, its characters, and its heroes. The process has been and continues to be innovative and challenging in equal measure – a hallmark of an institution dedicated to the discovery and advancement of human knowledge.

Their work not only relies on, but has also shaped, the cultural and heritage collections of the University showcased in this publication. These collections, carefully maintained by the University, are astonishing: artworks, artifacts, detailed historically significant chronicles alongside small but precious ephemera (some famous and some obscure), as well as material culture cutting a wide swath through place, time, and history. They cover and reflect across disciplines, helping us to understand the modern University and its place as a leading global institution in a thriving and proud city. They contain the records and stories of the thousands of people who have passed through the University, from Nobel Laureates at the peak of their careers to students just beginning to find their way in the world.

In short, the University's collections contain stories that are both powerful and personal, transformative and quotidian. As a former student at the University my own story, like countless others, appears in the University archives. As editor of the student union newspaper, the *Guild and City Gazette*, I hadn't considered that my articles would be joining a body of archival material stretching from the thirteenth century to the present day; that my voice would feature in some small way in the collections, which continue to grow and evolve as a living resource.

As Chancellor, I would like to express my gratitude and appreciation to everyone who has contributed to this publication and to those who continue to care for and curate the University's collections. As indelible marks of human aspiration, these items will continue to inform, to underpin, and to empower the academic mission. This publication showcases only a small sample of the fascinating manuscripts, objects, and artworks that the University possesses.

I hope that reading about them here brings you pleasure and provides insight into the remarkable collections. More importantly, I hope that they spark your curiosity and kindle a desire to learn more – perhaps by visiting the University and its collections in person and, as our digitisation program grows, by exploring them online.

As a university community, our collections contain our story. We couldn't be more excited to share them with you.

Wendy Beetlestone
Chancellor of the University of Liverpool

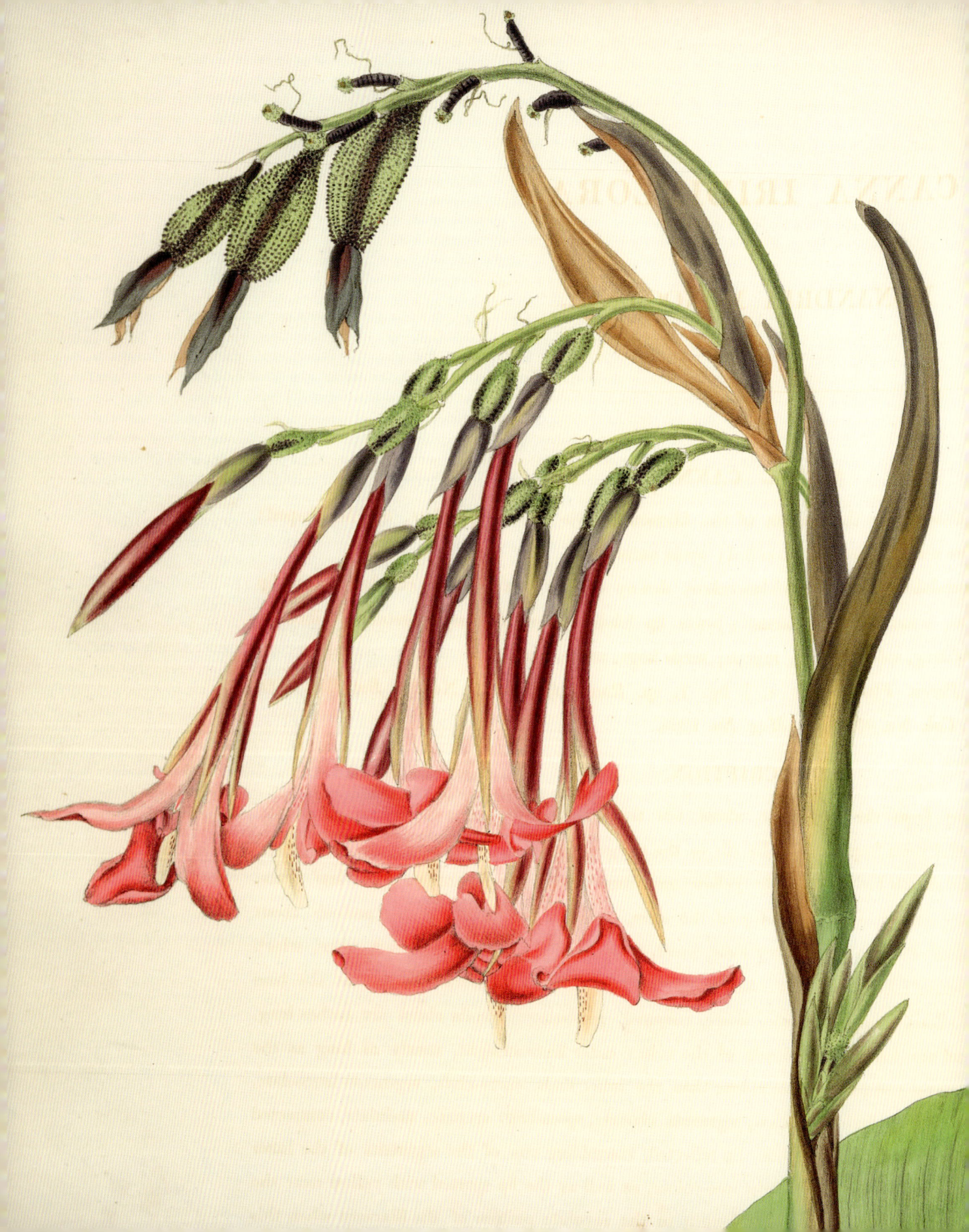

INTRODUCTION

Collecting Stories showcases more than 50 of the most striking items acquired over fifteen decades of collecting by the University of Liverpool's Libraries, Museums and Galleries and Botanic Gardens. It explores a range of objects representing each decade from the foundation of University College in the 1880s up to the 2020s via short articles and full-page photographs. The arrangement is broadly chronological by date of acquisition, telling the story of the growth of the University's cultural heritage collections by donation, purchase, bequest, and commission. Some decades are naturally more heavily represented than others: the 1900s, as University College Liverpool became the fully fledged University of Liverpool in 1903; the 1940s, as Liverpool responded to its wartime battering with a spirit of renewal and generosity; and more recent periods of active collecting in new genres and commissioning of public art. It eschews a conventional arrangement by date of creation – these items range from a 5,000-year-old ivory label (**10**) through to the current season's growth on the *Sorbus bulleyana* specimen at the University's Botanic Gardens (**52**) – for a kaleidoscopic snapshot of the collections.

The collecting history of the University is mapped onto the buildings the collections occupy and is partly the story of the development of the campus. The earliest College buildings no longer exist. The books, apparatus, and objects acquired as part of teaching and research activities were initially housed in departments and only gradually brought together, alongside the archives created by these endeavours. Even items designated cultural heritage on their acquisition have moved home as the Victoria Building's Tate Library was succeeded by the Harold Cohen Library and the Sydney Jones Library. Artwork retains a significant campus-wide presence.

The objects have been selected by curators and researchers familiar with the riches of the University's cultural heritage that are housed in the Library's Special Collections and Archives, in the Garstang Museum, in the Victoria Gallery and Museum, on campus in

the form of public sculpture, and in the Ness Botanic Gardens in the form of notable plants. They highlight the University's ongoing research engagement with artefacts of all periods: from the ancient world through the disciplines of Archaeology and Egyptology; from the medieval world, thanks to the Liverpool collectors who endowed the new University with fine manuscripts and the earliest printed books; from the intellectual explorations of the Renaissance and Enlightenment periods; from its own Victorian foundation leading to scientific and medical discoveries then and now; from twentieth-century cultures of popular music and science fiction; and with art created for the twenty-first century.

The range of the collections reflects the University's global reach and the diverse traditions it celebrates, in collaboration with its cultural partners. Ongoing research with National Museums Liverpool and international colleagues addresses the complex challenge of colonial acquisition practice and legacies to make the distributed Garstang archaeological excavation collections globally visible and accessible in both Arabic and English, with their countries of origin, Egypt and Sudan, at the core. Highlighting the date at which artefacts became part of the University's collections uncovers the cultural ties and networks that lay behind, for example, the 1945 gift to Professor Percy Roxby and his wife of an album of Chinese paintings and calligraphy (**23**) by Guo Youshou, Department of Education Chief for Sichuan Provincial Government. Other objects reflect the University as an institution in a globally connected city with diverse cultural and linguistic communities, including Arabic, Hebrew, Irish, and Romany. The life of Liverpool itself as a place of cultural happenings and creativity is celebrated in objects commissioned, created, designed, manufactured, written, printed, painted, photographed, published, bound, built, and grown in the city.

Each object's place in the institutional narrative is complemented by a brief description of the physical item, including its size: this matters for material objects designed to be handled, such as the silver coin (**7**);

handed out, such as Adrian Henri's painted paper hearts (38); or hand-held, such as the Islamic prayer book (17), Hebrew scrolls (28), or the portable sundial (16). The human scale and tactile qualities of these small objects is complemented by the towering scale of the largest, a polished steel sculpture (47) standing ten metres tall. The Piers Plowman manuscript (20) is almost exactly the size of the book you are holding.

Serendipitous connections have emerged in the arrangement of the images, juxtaposing the X-ray (9) of Lord Lister's hand with the delicately hand-coloured engraving (8) of the hand of the dairymaid, Sarah Nelmes, from whose cowpox sore the first inoculation against smallpox was made. This pairing also speaks to the conscious intention to highlight stories of hidden, unrecognised, or suppressed figures as well as the famous. So the contributions of women behind the scenes are celebrated in entries on the nineteenth-century authors John Gould (4) and William Roscoe (5). Refugees from and witnesses to war, persecution, and prejudice are highlighted by new research that aims to recover their stories, including those enslaved on plantations in the path of the volcanic eruption depicted by Turner (26) and individuals encountered by Edward Rushton (21) on Liverpool-financed slave ships.

Other themes and names recur across entries, including researchers, creators, and benefactors such as Oliver Lodge (9, 45); Dora Yates (18, 28); C.J. Allen (43, 45); generations of Rathbones (21, 30); and Charles Sydney Jones (14, 24) – but all those mentioned in this book are part of a community that has built up the University's intellectual, cultural, and financial capital and continues to build its future.

The contributors to *Collecting Stories* include current undergraduate and postgraduate students, research and teaching staff across all faculties, staff in curatorial and wider roles, partners from communities and cultural institutions in Liverpool and beyond, alumni and honorary staff, artists, and donors. Some contributors created the object they write about (41, 50); others were encountering 'their' object for the first time, responding to the challenge with enthusiasm and insight and forging new connections between the Libraries, Museums and Galleries, the wider University, and its cultural and creative collaborators. The riches of the different genres of the cultural heritage collections – archaeological finds, archives, artworks, biological specimens, books, cassettes, ceramics, coins, dental models, LPs on vinyl, manuscripts, maps, metalwork, medical X-rays, posters, photographs, plans, prints, pamphlets, press cuttings, sculpture, telegrams, timelines, typewriters, and trees – have enabled us to write a story that will continue into the next decade and beyond the University's 150th anniversary in 2031.

Katy Hooper
Special Collections Librarian, University of Liverpool

Selected items from the collection

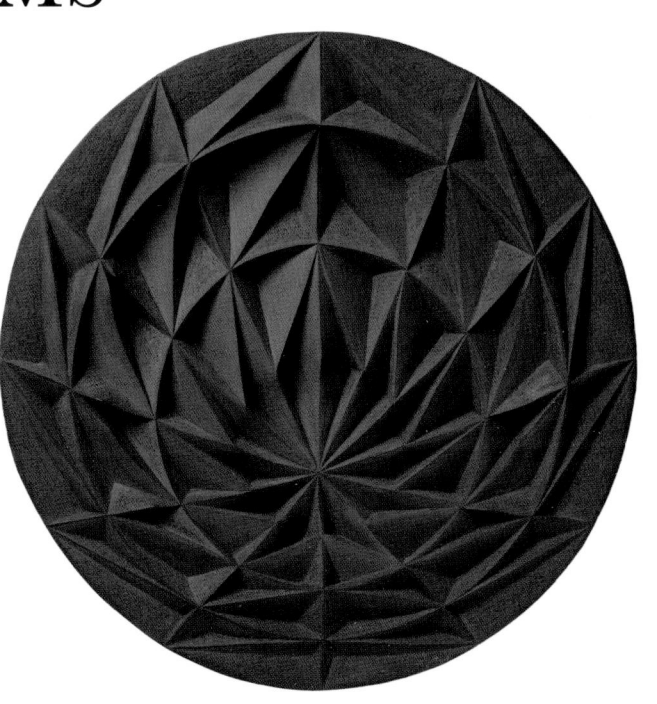

The nucleus of the library (1880s)

Front cover of *Keramic Art of Japan*, by George Ashdown Audsley, Architect, and James Lord Bowes, President of the Liverpool Art Club. Liverpool: published for the subscribers by the authors; London: Henry Sotheran & Co, 1875. Two volumes, printed in Liverpool. 41 × 31 cm.

The bequest of Abraham Hume, 1884.

A quality library is the cornerstone of any university, and this was appreciated by the Council of newly founded University College Liverpool in 1881. The Council reported that 'The nucleus of a College Library has been formed by a gift from the Rev. Canon Hume of about 1,000 volumes.' Abraham Hume later bequeathed his entire library. Within his donations the *Keramic Art of Japan* stands out today, with its fine red goatskin binding and gilt tooling depicting bamboo, a crane in flight, and a volcano (probably a representation of Mt Fuji). Inside, the bookplate of the Liverpool University College Library, depicting a tree of knowledge and the familiar liver birds, is pasted onto marbled endpapers.

Our donor, Irish-born Rev. Canon Abraham Hume, was a teacher and Anglican priest. He taught English and Maths at the Liverpool Mechanics Institute and was a founding member of the Historic Society of Lancashire and Cheshire. A strong supporter of learned societies and writer of over 100 publications, it seems fitting that he was an early benefactor of the University, and particularly the library.

Keramic Art of Japan is testimony to the fascination with Japanese art and design termed 'Japonisme' that quickly followed the forced reopening of Japanese ports to Western trade in the mid-1850s. Many private collectors, including James Bowes (1834–99), made purchases at the Paris Exposition of 1867, at which Japan had a pavilion. Bowes' collection of Japanese ceramics was exhibited in 1872 at the first ('Oriental art') exhibition of the Liverpool Art Club, an elite private gentleman's club for art lovers that held semi-public exhibitions. Only three years later, *Keramic Art of Japan* would feature Bowes' collection alongside other public and private collections described as the best examples of their time. It included the Imperial Keramic Collection Dresden (today in the Zwinger Palace) and South Kensington Museum (now the V&A), alongside dominant names in Liverpool art patronage, such as Sir A. Barclay Walker (of the Walker Gallery) and Philip H. Rathbone (influential in the establishment of the first professorship in Art at the University).

The essays in the book describe the use of imagery in Japanese decorative art and the cultural significance as understood by the authors. Audsley (1838–1925) wrote multiple essays on the subject and offered lectures, and Bowes would go on to be the first foreign-born Japanese Consul in Great Britain (1888). The fine coloured plates help to visualise the narrative descriptions, with examples of geometric patterns, flowers, trees, animals, birds, fish, insects, dragons, mountains, and more.

A review in the *Examiner* (22 January 1876) noted that the coloured plates were 'probably as perfect as chromolithography can make them'. Indeed, the colours are stunning and capture a sense of light hitting the 3D object. This technique was criticised as a 'serious blunder' in that it attempted to depict the solidity of the object rather than leaving it to the imagination of the reader. This scrutiny is not lost on the work of photographers and technicians today, who are tasked with the digital imaging of heritage collections using the most advanced techniques and equipment. Photography can only tell part of the story of all these objects. Nonetheless, Bowes' collected works on Japanese art, including *Keramic Art in Japan*, have been selected by Aikiko Mabuchi of the National Museum of Western Art in Tokyo as part of a facsimile series of primary sources on the reception of Japanese arts in the West, continuing the cross-cultural exchange.

Joanne Fitton

KERAMIC ART

OF JAPAN

Liverpool University College
New Library Block & Jubilee Clock Tower.

Scale 8 feet to the inch

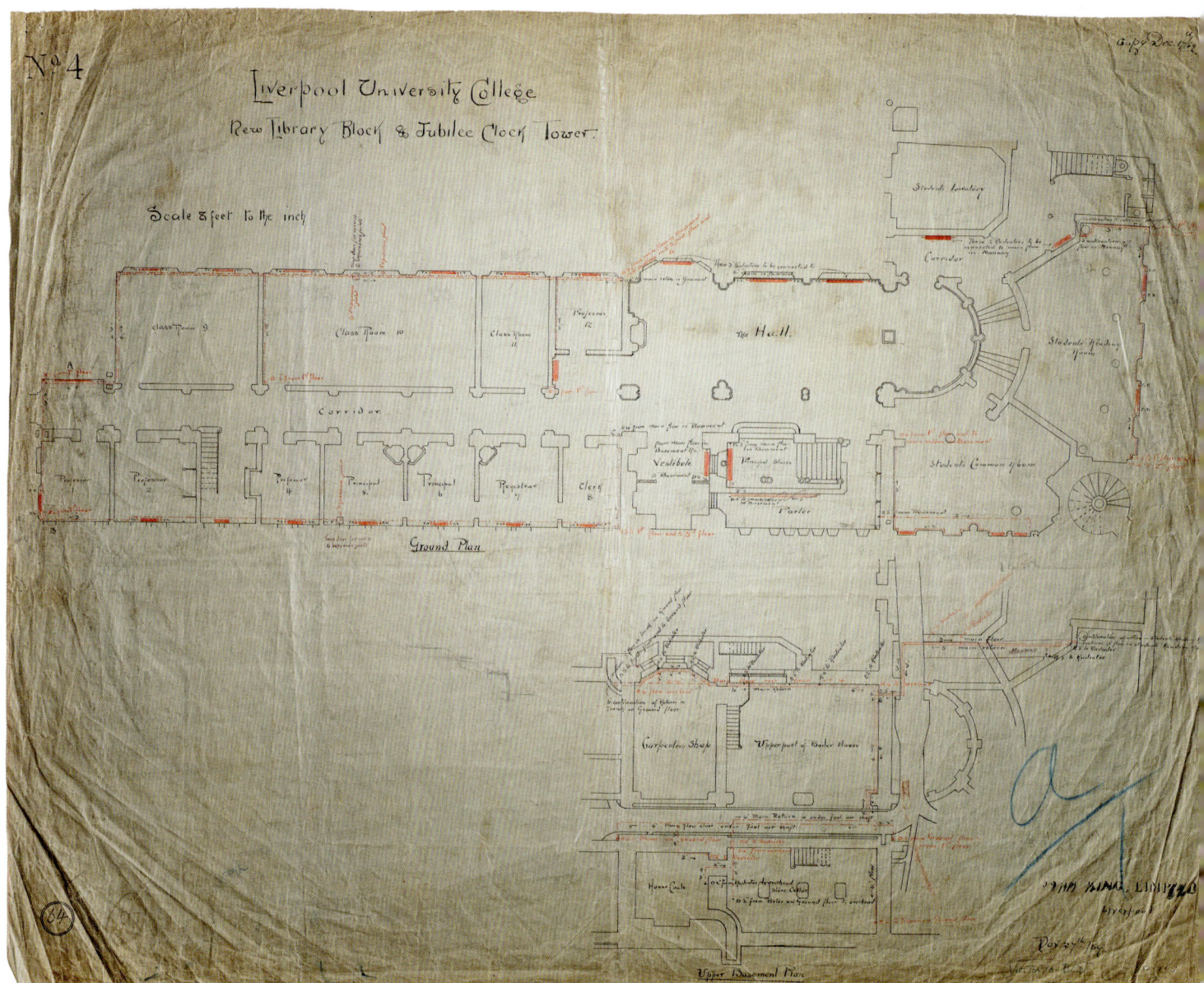

Ground Plan

Upper Basement Plan

Behind the red brick (1880s)

Victoria Building plan, 1889. Construction drawing in black and red ink and pencil on glazed fabric by John King Limited. 66.7 × 77.3 cm.

Commissioned by University College Liverpool, 1889.

This isn't the most seductive or accomplished drawing of the University's renowned Victoria Building. It tells us nothing of the ornamentation, glazed tiles, and double height spaces. The building's architect, Alfred Waterhouse (1830–1905), took exceptional care to produce refined drawings and was an accomplished draftsman, as other drawings in the University collections reveal – this is most certainly not one of his works.

Rather, it's one of the hundreds of diagrams, schedules, and details produced to help construct a major building of this stature – and, while this is only a construction drawing, it has an intriguing history. It shows a basic interior ground-floor plan, along with the basement. The external wall line is omitted, as are the ornate and splendid details; instead, the focus is on a rather banal but vital function – the central heating and ventilation system.

The aim of this system was to provide not only more comfortable interior temperatures and a means of heating large spaces more efficiently but also cleaner interiors. Air brought in through the ducts could be filtered before being piped throughout the building, while stale air was removed without having to open the windows – an essential requirement, as the building was located opposite an open railway cutting. Parts of Liverpool at this time held the unfortunate record for 'the tonnage of soot per acre deposited as a sort of sewage on people's heads, their buildings, their clothes and all they possess' (Reilly, 70).

The installation of a central heating and ventilation system, as well as the wider use of glazed tiles, faience, and terra-cotta, would all help to keep the building (both inside and outside) clean and free from grime. The architectural treatment was thus more than a stylistic response: it was a means of shielding the college from an external environment that was viewed as not only environmentally dirty but also socially problematic. Future campus planner Lord Holford labelled the district as a 'twilight area', while Charles Reilly painted a yet fuller picture, describing the district as a 'slum' lined with 'depressing shops and … noisy tram cars … between the Workhouse and the Lunatic Asylum, approached by the ghetto, in a third-class red-light district, this was the site chosen by the pious founders' (Reilly, 74). It was these narrow opinions that resulted in the subsequent erasure of the fine streets and architecture surrounding the Victoria Building to make way for what we now know as 'the campus'.

'Grim but Grand' was how a more charitable critic, Colin Rowe, described the city, and, if we look to the grandest building of them all, St George's Hall, we also find pioneering building services and 'air conditioning' installed by David B. Reid in 1851. On a much smaller scale, but even more radical, was the ventilation work of John Williams Hayward (1829–1914) at his 'Octagon House' in 1867, just a few streets away from the new College on Grove Street. Stemming from these pioneering schemes, the College too was to have the most up-to-date services set within its Gothick-revival cloak. Open coal fires were installed, although these features were more ornamental in nature, and heating was to be provided through the recent invention of radiators, supplied with hot water from the coal-powered boiler in the basement.

The radiators are marked up on the drawing in red pencil, along with the flow and return pipe work. Beneath the floor is a series of air ducts that supplied fresh air, with the foul air being discharged through a chimney in what is now the University quadrangle. It's a schematic working drawing that includes pencil sketches scribbled while on site by the engineers and contractors as they worked out the installation solutions. But who were these people, and why do we know so little about the important history of building technology and services? In this case we have an important clue, as the drawing reveals the name of the heating engineers, smudged but still legible: 'John King Limited'.

John King was based just a short distance from

the Victoria Building on Benson Street, off Mount Pleasant. From here they managed projects all over the country and built up a reputation designing heating and ventilation solutions for large buildings, including manor houses and churches. One of their leading engineers was Frederic William Barker (1862–1900), who was chief draftsman by the age of twenty and took responsibility for the services installations at the Victoria Building. He went on to invent a 'tubular automatic exhaust ventilator', perhaps testing out some of these ideas on the University project. He too lived just a few minutes' walk from the site on Mulberry Street and must have taken great pride in seeing the new college being constructed

in his own neighbourhood. His fiancé, Agnes Congdon, lived at Vine Street and they married at St Catherine's church on Abercromby Square in 1886, the same year he was promoted to manager of the firm.

Through this rather humble drawing, depicting one of the most quotidian building features, we can begin to explore the development of the campus and the people and opinions who shaped it. The drawing offers a glimpse beyond the 'red brick' into a history of technology, the increasing complexity of building design, and the pioneering structures of Liverpool that embraced these new inventions.

Iain Jackson

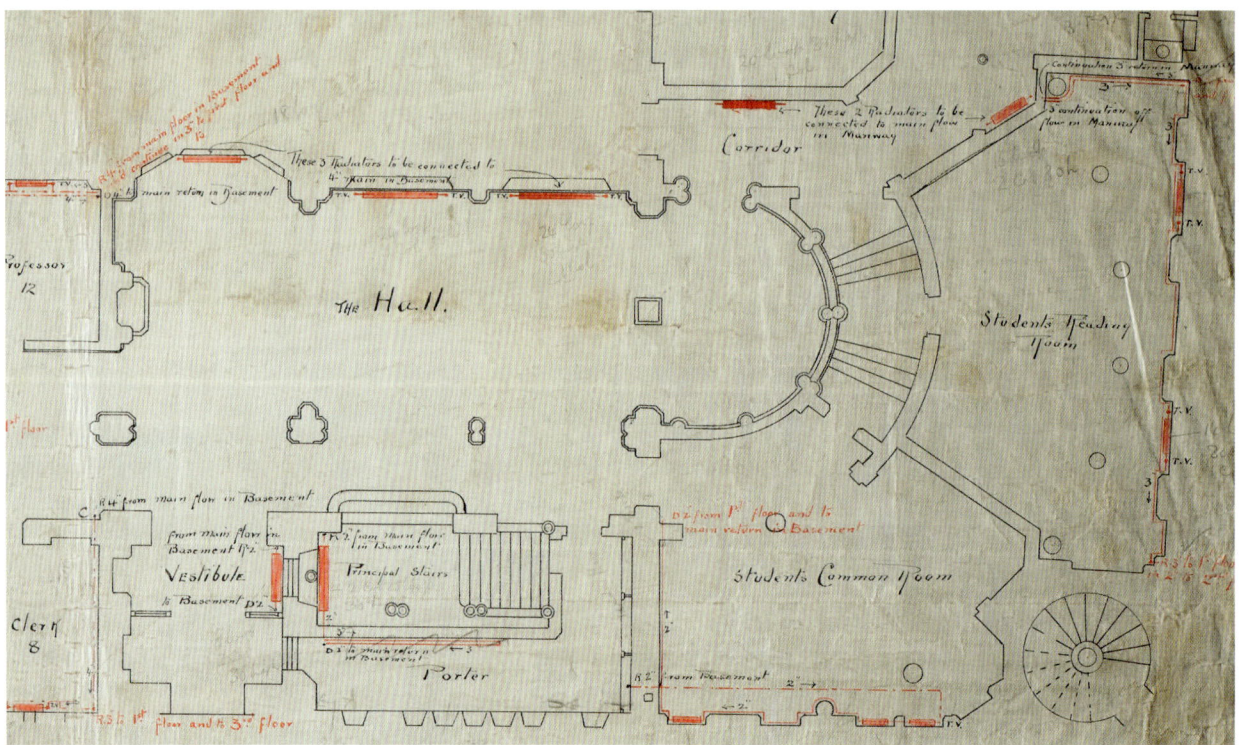

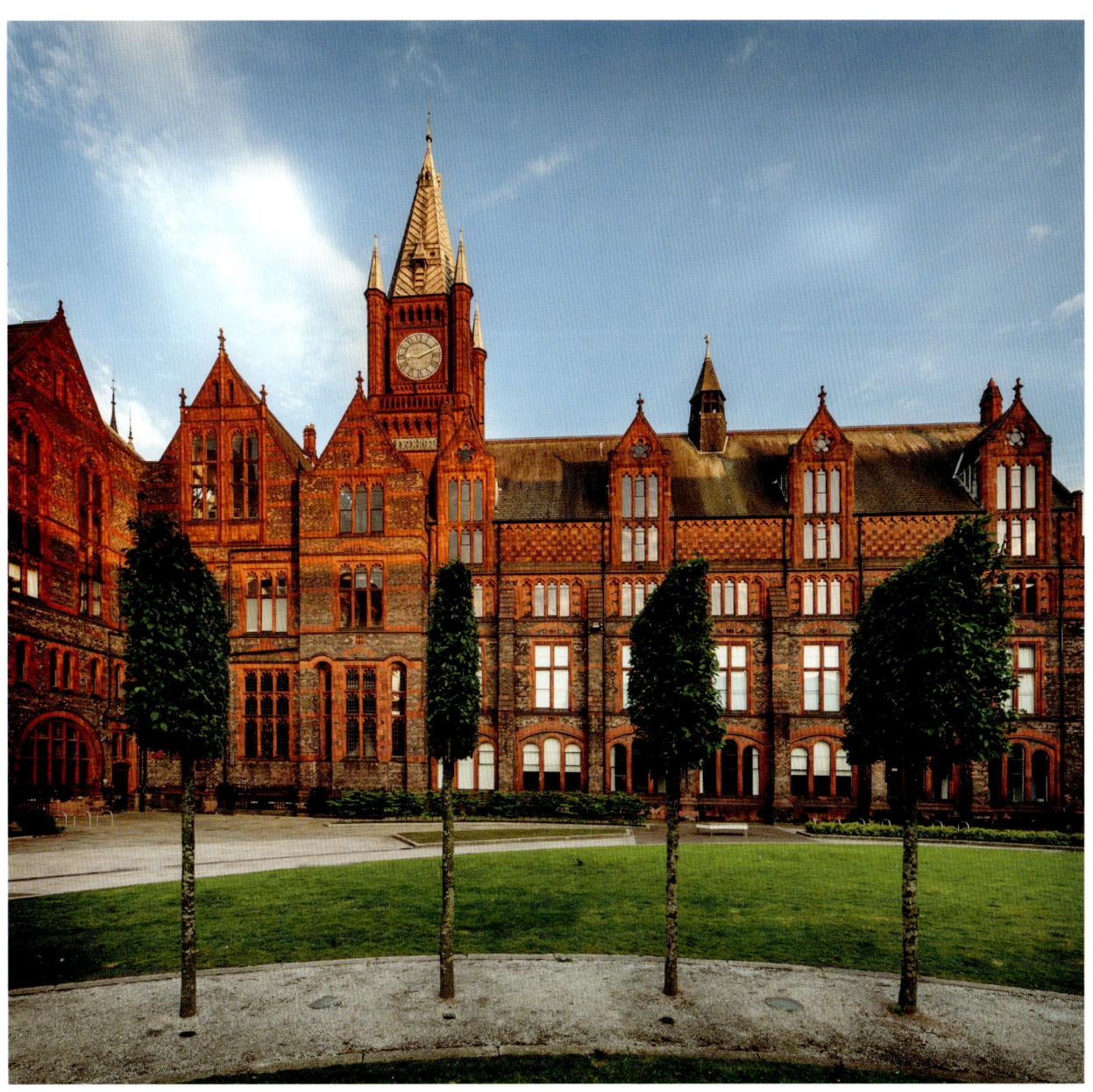

A VOYAGE THROUGH TIME: THE LEGACY OF *NEPHTHEIS FASCICULARIS* AND HMS *CHALLENGER* (1880S)

3

Specimen of *Nephtheis fascicularis*, collected by William Abbott Herdman during HMS *Challenger* expedition, southern Philippines, 1875; with scientific illustration commissioned in 2025. 18 × 4.5 cm.

Herdman collections, acquired 1880s. Specimen reidentified as Challenger syntype by Leonie Sedman, VGM (2024).

It is a rare privilege to narrate the story of an object that serves as a bridge between our scientific past, present, and future. Yet, one fascinating specimen used to establish the description of *Nephtheis fascicularis*, a lollipop-shaped sea squirt, continues to illuminate both the history of marine exploration and the future of Earth's oceans.

Even a brief inspection of the 150-year-old specimen reveals its unmistakable otherworldly appearance. The common name for *N. fascicularis*, the Lollipop Tunicate, reflects its blue-green stalked colony structure, which branches into a cone of clustered individual polyps. Other common names for the species include the Lollipop Coral or Blue Palm Coral, although *N. fascicularis* is not related to true corals. The species does, however, live among corals, and is mainly found in shallow warm-water reefs across the Indo-Pacific area. The species was first described in the mid-nineteenth century as part of a widespread naturalist movement to catalogue global biodiversity.

The specimen is one of a dozen syntypes (specimens of equal importance in the description of a newly discovered species) collected during the historic HMS *Challenger* expedition. This groundbreaking journey was the first true oceanographic expedition. The ship travelled more than 127,000 km between 1872 and 1878. The expedition's findings, which documented nearly 5,000 species new to science, continue to serve as a baseline for climate change research today. They also contribute to current teaching through the university's broader collection of specimens.

The discovery was made off the coast of a southern Philippine island on 30 January 1875 and was later described by Professor William Abbot Herdman

(1858–1924), a specialist in tunicates and the first professor of Natural History at the University of Liverpool (previously University College Liverpool). In 1886 Herdman named the species *Colella thomsoni*, after the expedition leader Sir Charles Wyville Thomson (1830–82). However, it has since been renamed *Nephtheis fascicularis* as it had been described earlier by Austrian researcher Dr Richard von Drasche in 1882. This species has been known by many names, with variant spellings, reflecting our evolving understanding of taxonomy over time.

While being associated with humanity's early exploration of ocean life, the specimen's significance extends into the present day. Ongoing research continues to reveal the role of the species in evolution, biomedicine, and ecology. Tunicates such as *N. fascicularis* greatly interest evolutionary biologists because of their close relation to vertebrates. This unlikely relationship has helped unravel the evolutionary trajectory of complex life on Earth through the study of tunicate characteristics and genetics. The invertebrate group is also of research interest for pharmaceutical applications owing to the bioactive compounds they contain, which are potentially useful for human medicine.

In addition to its interest to evolutionary and biomedicine studies, the species plays a role in the overall health of tropical reef ecosystems. Individuals contribute to maintaining water quality and supporting biodiversity. As filter feeders, *N. fascicularis* consume microscopic marine creatures and organic matter, which maintains healthy water quality. Furthermore, because individuals feed on organic matter, they can be utilised as bioindicators of pollution in marine environments. They also provide vital habitat for other marine

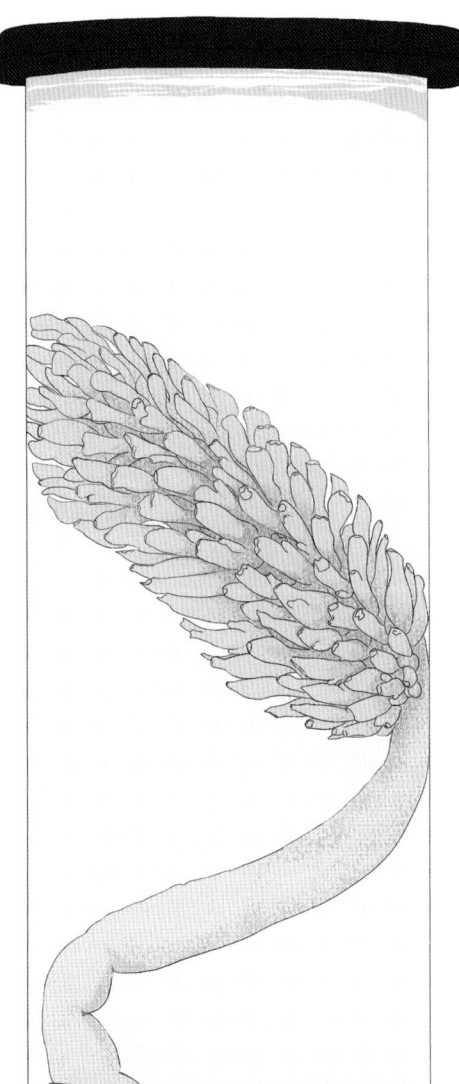
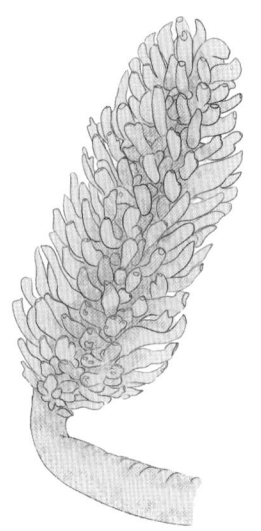
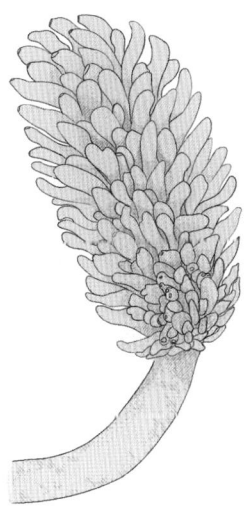

LIVERPOOL   UNIVERSITY
ZOOLOGY MUSEUM

PHYLUM CHORDATA
SUB-PHYLUM .... UROCHORDATA
CLASS.... ASCIDIACEA

ORDER ENTEROGONA

GENUS Colella

SPECIES thompsoni

LOCALITY 6°55' ,22°15'   10-20F.
                                        30:1:1875
CATALOGUE NO. 17-6A.

species, including fish and other invertebrates, enabling biodiversity to flourish.

Looking ahead to the future of Earth's oceans, responses of tunicates to environmental change can help identify patterns of resilience and vulnerability in marine ecosystems, guiding future conservation efforts. Historical specimens from the *Challenger* expedition act as unique snapshots of a time when oceans were substantially less impacted by human activity. Therefore, historical specimens serve as important ecological baselines for understanding impacts of global change.

N. fascicularis, alongside many other species previously unknown to science, embodies scientific progress by forever changing humanity's fundamental understanding of the world. The story of this sea squirt is an ongoing narrative that mirrors our evolving relationship with nature. Through preserving specimens such as *N. fascicularis* we not only maintain the legacy of the *Challenger* expedition but continue to learn from its contributions to our understanding of life on Earth – in both the present and the challenging future ahead.

Dina-Leigh Simons

In modern scientific illustration, detailed shading and specimen housing are omitted in favour of clear, defined lines only to mark biological edges. However, tunicates do not fare well when preserved because of their very high water content: what were once tiny, fragile zooids have lost much of their definition. I think the age of this specimen, still in good condition by tunicate standards, is worth celebrating. Thus, I married artistic illustration techniques such as the use of point and hatch shading with scientific illustration techniques to try to capture the history behind this specimen.

Lauren Aylward

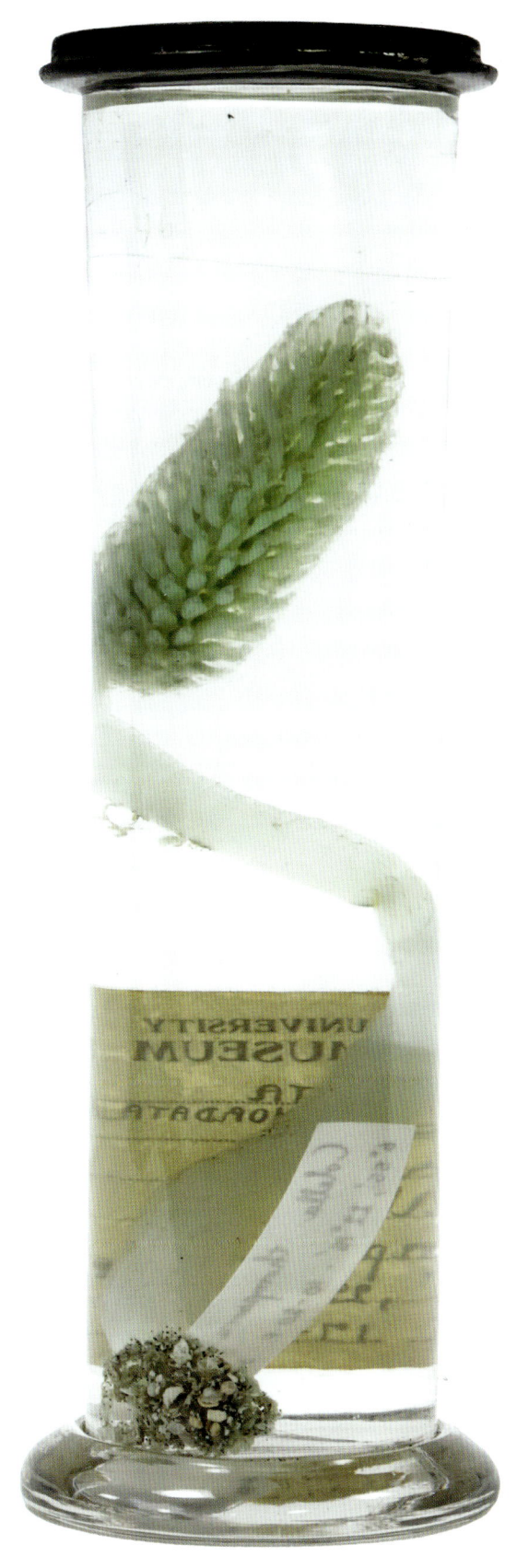

JOHN GOULD, BIRD MAN (1890s)

4

John Gould, *The Birds of Asia* (London: the author), plate 72 issued with part 17 in April 1865. 35 parts, 530 plates purchased as issued on subscription by the Liverpool Royal Institution. 58 × 40 cm.

Liverpool Royal Institution library; transferred to University College Liverpool in 1894.

When his father became foreman of the Royal Gardens in Windsor, the young John Gould (1804–81) swiftly combined his childhood fascination for birds with teenage entrepreneurial spirit and began stuffing birds and selling them to the scholars at Eton. Aged 21, Gould set up a taxidermy shop in London, which from 1828 onwards he juggled alongside a job as preserver at the Zoological Society of London. Work at the Zoo exposed Gould to both a growing market for accurate yet artistic illustrations of birds and a hotbed of natural history enthusiasts. When an assortment of birds from Brian Houghton Hodgson (1800–94), the East India Company's resident in Nepal, arrived in London around 1830, Gould set about self-publishing the collection in a series of imperial folio-sized hand-coloured lithographs.

Rough sketches and scribbled notes by Gould were transformed into plates by a collaborating artist, the first being his wife Elizabeth Gould, née Coxen (1804–41). Thus began a production model that would be replicated over six decades and 21 titles.

The Birds of Asia, in seven volumes, was one of Gould's most ambitious books. Richard Bowdler Sharpe (1847–1909), the British Museum's bird curator, explained in the introduction how Gould viewed Asia through its political divisions: *The Birds of Asia* reflected the close entanglement of European science with imperialism. Of the 530 species in the book, representing 14 per cent of the birds now known from Asia, many had never been illustrated in European literature before. Royalty, museums, the East India Company (to whom the book

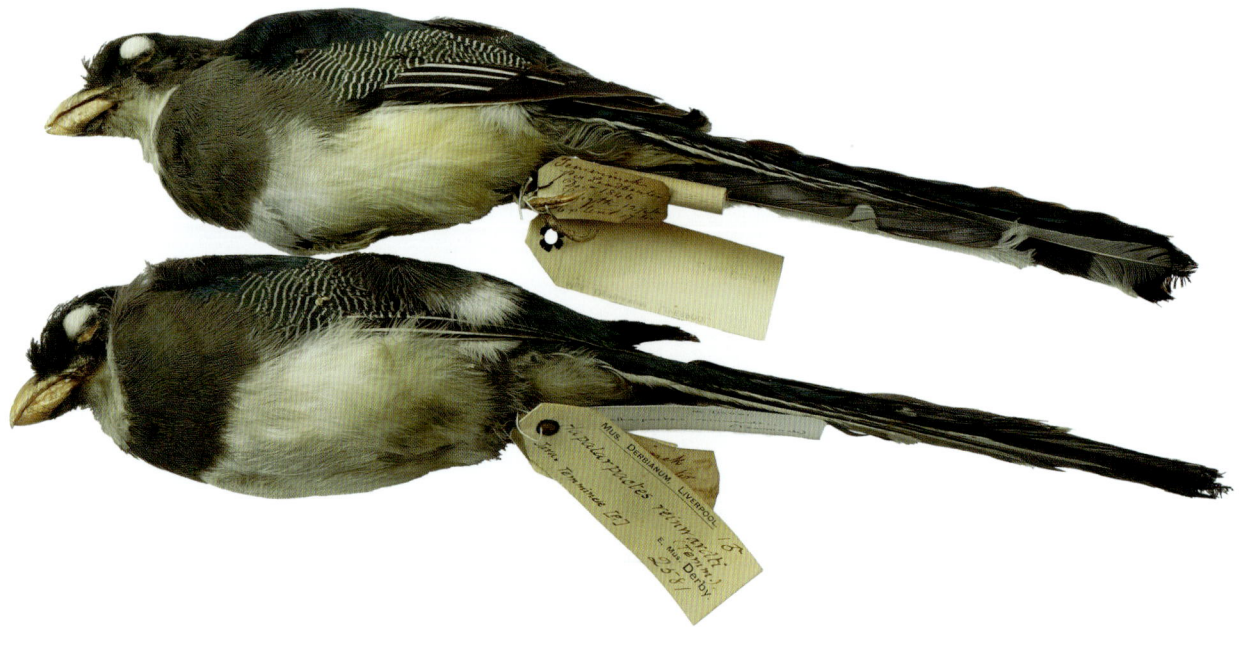

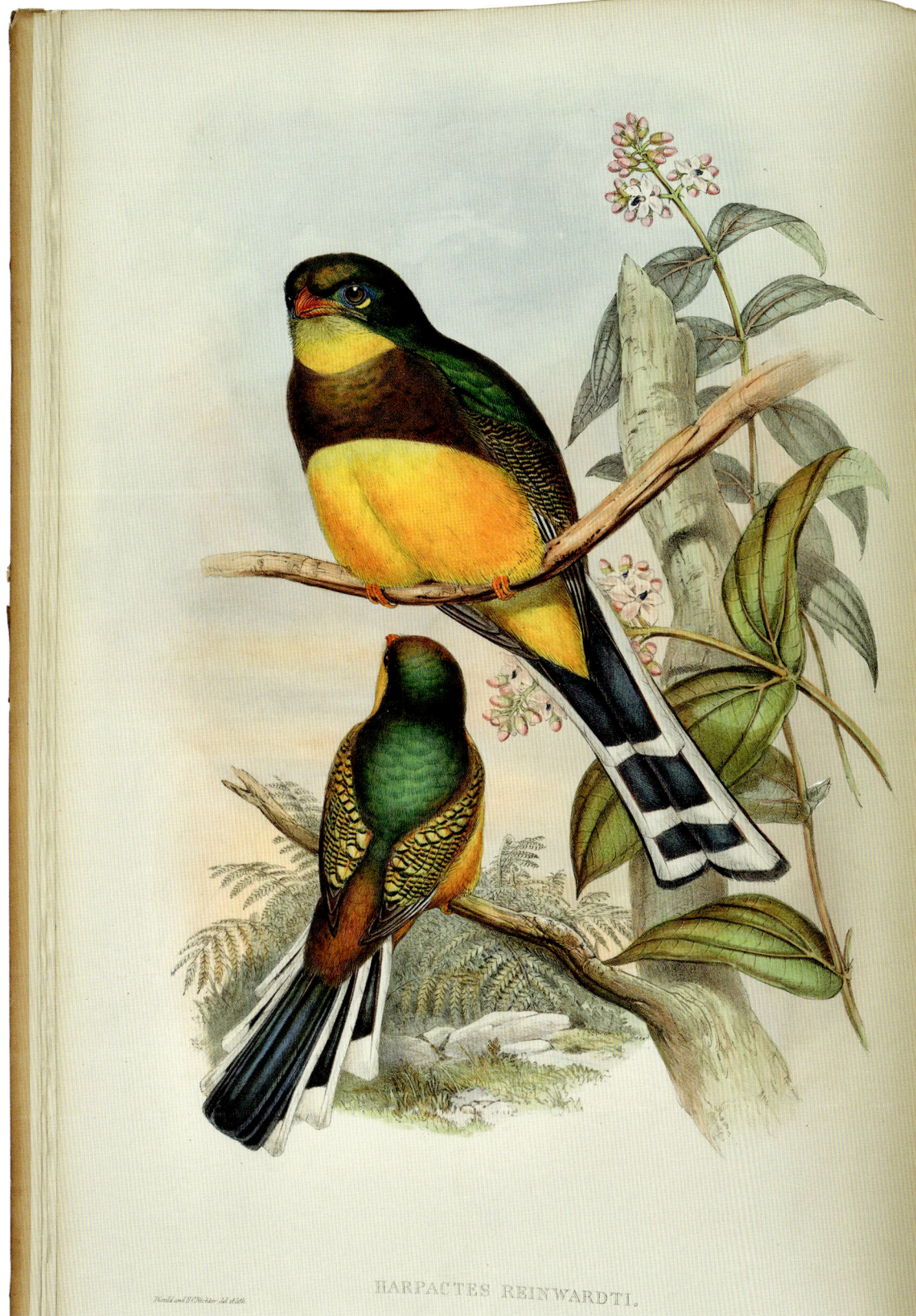

HARPACTES REINWARDTI.

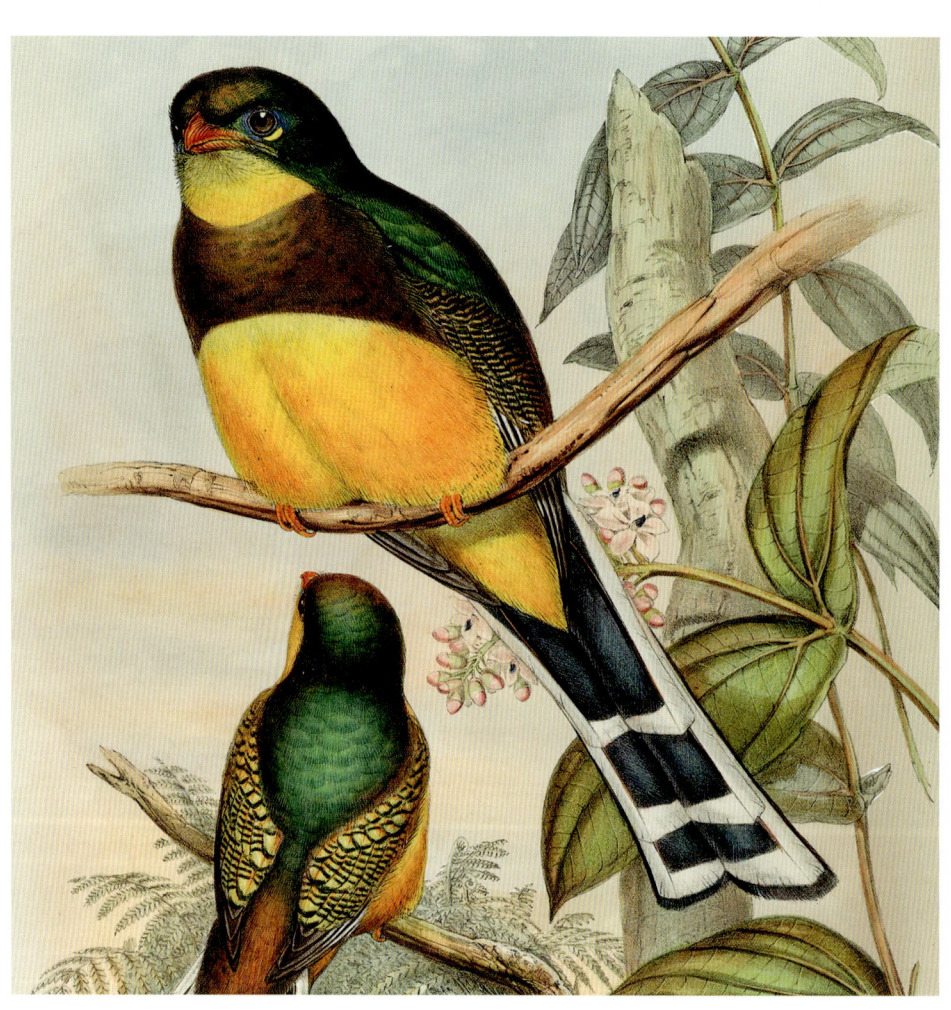

was dedicated), the Liverpool Library, the Liverpool Free Public Library, and the Liverpool Royal Institution (founded in 1814 by a group of local professionals and merchants) were among 165 subscribers. The first plates were distributed in January 1850.

Zoologist and museum director Coenraad Jacob Temminck (1778–1858) gave the Javan Trogon its scientific name, *Trogon reinwardtii*, in 1822 after Caspar Georg Carl Reinwardt (1773–1855), founder–director of the Dutch East India Company's botanical gardens at Buitenzorg (now Bogor). An adult male and juvenile were illustrated by Elizabeth Gould for *A Monograph of the Trogonidae, or family of the Trogons* (1835).

The Javan Trogons in *The Birds of Asia* is an unusual second plate of a species by Gould (it was also used in *A Monograph of the Trogonidae or Trogons* issued by Gould between 1858 and 1875, suggesting that it was his preferred version). Specimens previously owned by Temminck were borrowed from the Derby Museum in Liverpool. Gould knew the collection well, being a visitor to the 13th Earl of Derby (1775–1851) at Knowsley Hall, whose bequest of specimens had founded the Museum. The specimens studied by Gould were already faded and the famous traveller Alfred Russel Wallace (1823–1913) helped to correct the colours. The two adult male specimens (illustrated) borrowed by John Gould are extant in National Museums Liverpool (formerly the Derby Museum). They were bought by the 13th Earl of Derby from the dealers Leadbeater in December 1846 and bequeathed to the people of Liverpool on the Earl's death in 1851. There were only adults in the Derby Museum, so the juvenile was probably reworked from the Goulds' earlier illustration. Henry Constantine Richter (1821–1902), the artist Gould turned to after his wife's death, completed the illustration.

The Javan Trogon has been found on only six mountains in West Java. The small range was predicted by Gould based on the lack of specimens from Stamford Raffles (1781–1826), who governed Java during the East India Company's occupation and later founded the Zoological Society of London, and Raffles' friend Thomas Horsfield (1773–1859), zoologist for the Dutch East India Company and later curator of the East India Company's Museum in London. The species is currently vulnerable to extinction as the small population faces further habitat loss.

The final plates of *The Birds of Asia* were dispatched in August 1883, two years after Gould's death, his exquisite books building a legacy unmatched in Victorian natural history. Eleven years later the library of the Liverpool Royal Institution was transferred to University College Liverpool. The University of Liverpool collections consequently include Gould's *The Birds of Australia* (1840–69), *The Mammals of Australia* (1845–63), *A Monograph of the Trochilidae or Hummingbirds* (1849–61), and *Handbook to The Birds of Australia* (Vol. 1) (1865), among other natural history art that includes paintings by John James Audubon (1785–1851). Many of the members of the Liverpool Royal Institution, whose subscriptions underpinned the Institution's purchasing power, made their fortunes through transatlantic slavery.

John James Wilson

An adult male Javan Trogon *Apalharpactes reinwardtii* sits on a branch facing the viewer, with a juvenile below facing away. *Medinilla* flowers from Java and an unidentified fern are in the background. Illustrated and lithographed by John Gould and Henry Constantine Richter.

Made in Liverpool (1890s)

5

Canna iridiflora from *Monandrian Plants of the order Scitamineae: chiefly drawn from living specimens in the botanic garden at Liverpool, arranged according to the system of Linnaeus with descriptions and observations,* by William Roscoe (Liverpool: George Smith); bound by H.D. Keating, Liverpool; 168 pages, 112 leaves of plates. 56 × 43 cm.

Liverpool Royal Institution library, transferred to University College Liverpool in 1894.

The year 1828 saw both the publication of this Liverpool-authored, Liverpool-published, and Liverpool-bound botanical work by William Roscoe (1753–1831) and the death of Roscoe's friend and contemporary, the founder and president of the Linnaean Society, Sir James Edward Smith (1759–1828). The coincidence came at a time of transition from the Linnaean sexual system of botanical classification (focused on the number and arrangement of male and female organs in the flowers of plants) to the more structured taxonomy-based approach of today. This shift was particularly associated with John Lindley (1799–1865), first Professor of Botany at the University of London, whose inaugural lecture in 1829 also took aim at a peculiarly British tendency, as he saw it, to regard Botany as 'an amusement for ladies rather than an occupation for the serious thoughts of man' (Shteir, 33).

William Roscoe had many occupations and interests throughout his life: he worked as a lawyer in the late 1700s and was a vocal slave trade abolitionist, poet, and banker before his retirement in 1820 due to bankruptcy. He and a small group of Liverpool botanists created Liverpool Botanic Garden, the first botanic garden developed by public subscription to a private society, which was opened in 1803 on a site adjoining Myrtle Street. This collection of plants included exotic specimens from all over the world and boasted more than 4,000 different kinds of plant by 1807. Access to the garden gave Roscoe a rare opportunity for close study of specimens from the order *Scitamineae* (now known as *Zingiberales*), many of which were collected from Brazil, Myanmar, India, and other tropical regions. This order contains spices such as ginger, turmeric, and cardamom alongside the recognisable flowering house plant the 'Bird of Paradise'. These plants were of particular interest to Roscoe because of their perceived uses as medicines, fibres, and food, and his *Monandrian*

Plants of the order Scitamineae was the result of nearly thirty years of work on them.

The book consists of 112 coloured, engraved illustrations with descriptions, drawn in the most part from specimens held in Liverpool Botanic Gardens. The concluding paragraphs of Roscoe's Introduction accredit many people for the beautiful artwork, with significant recognition given to Miss Rebecca Miller and Roscoe's daughter-in-law Mrs Edward Roscoe, alongside several other women and uncredited individual Indian artists at Lucknow. The illustrations bring Roscoe's words to life, but formal recognition of the work of women artists was uncommon in publications of this time. Welcome efforts have been made recently to highlight their contributions, including Roscoe's contemporaries Catherine Blake (1762–1831), wife of William, and Elizabeth Gould (1804–41), wife of John, whose work is well represented in the University's collections.

The book is laid out in two sections: *Cannæ* and *Scitamineæ* proper, Roscoe's divisions of the tribe of plants formerly known as *Scitamineæ*. These distinctions fit loosely into subdivisions of the modern-day order *Zingiberales*, although many changes and additions have been made since the publication of Roscoe's work. After an introduction outlining some characteristics and classifications of these divisions, tables of genera and species are shown. The individual species pages are categorised again by genus, including descriptions and observations from Roscoe about the genus at the beginning of each new section. Each individual species has a full-page illustration and accompanying information, including name, general description, previous names and their literature references (with many of the specimens being previously undescribed), with further observations, and references. This information was used by Roscoe, alongside the collection of his own physical specimens, to create the most up-to-date and comprehensive

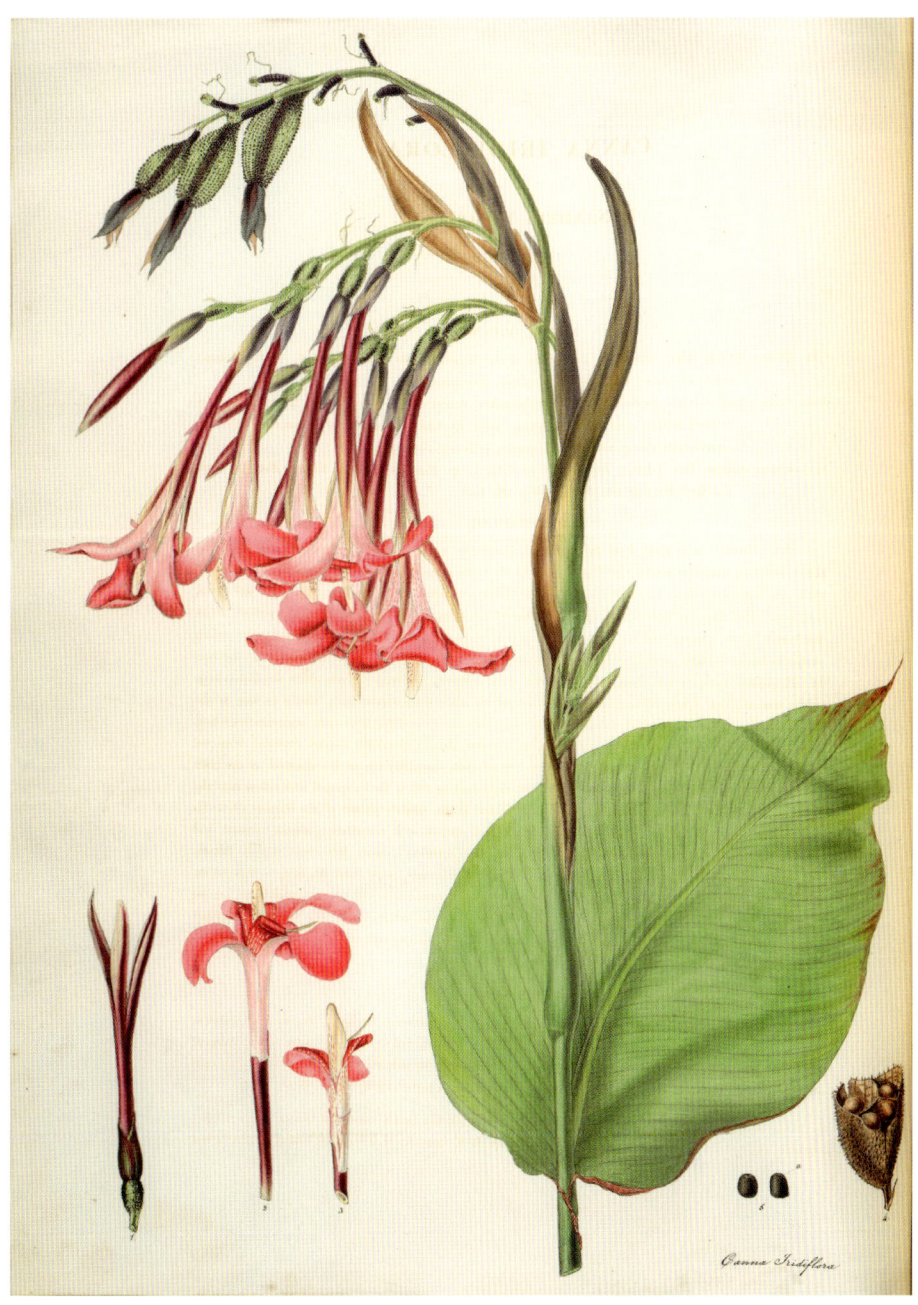

scientific text on these single-stamen plants (the first use of the word 'monandrian' is attributed to Roscoe). The language used in the descriptions and observations is simultaneously poetic and scientific, including phrases such as 'stoles as thick as a man's finger' and 'its fine crimson flowers being a great ornament to the Conservatory'.

One of only 150 copies printed, this volume has strong ties to Liverpool's history and its significance in the world of taxonomy. Its preservation allows people to learn from Roscoe's passion for botany and inspires future generations of taxonomists and botanists.

Aiden Ireland

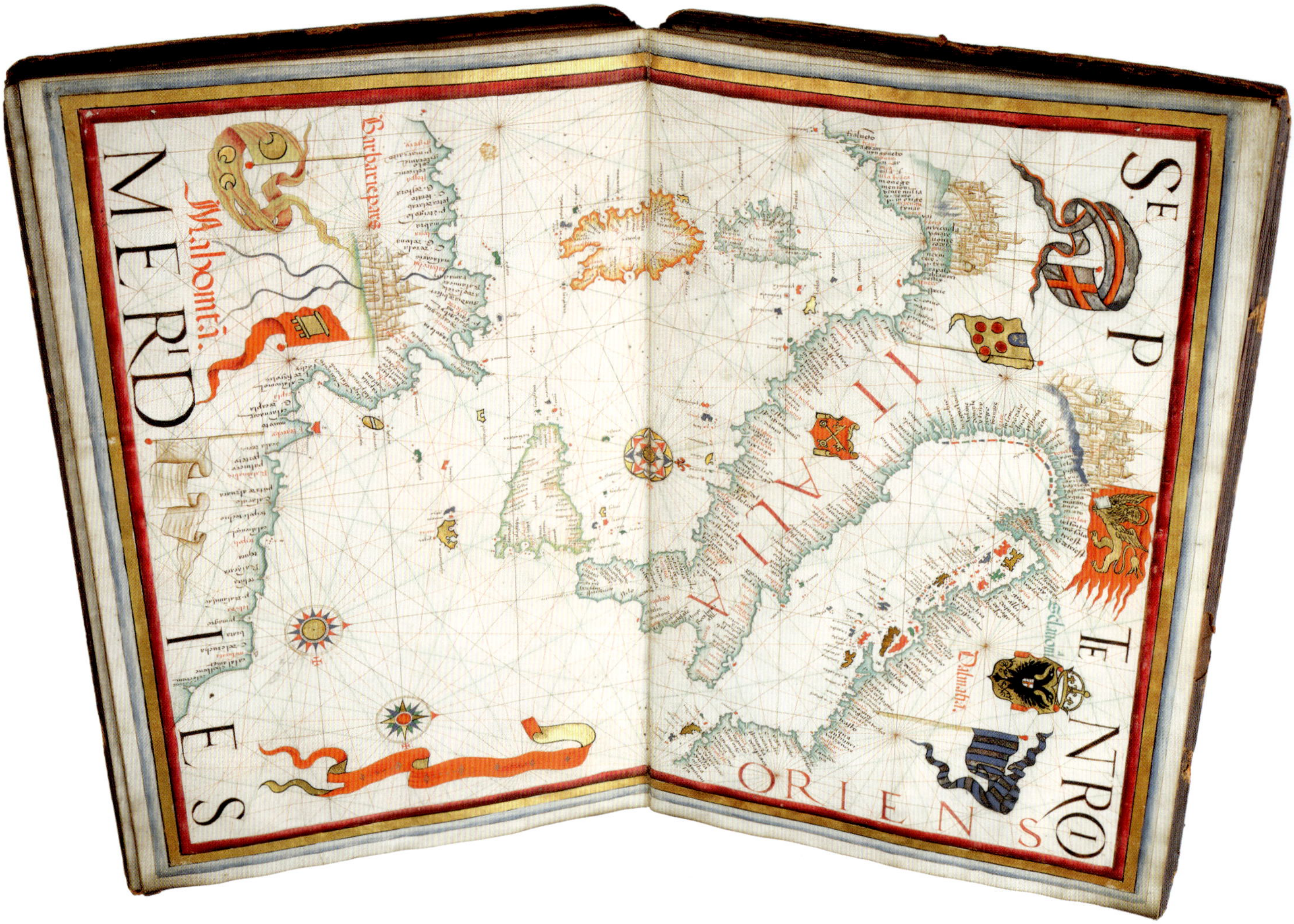

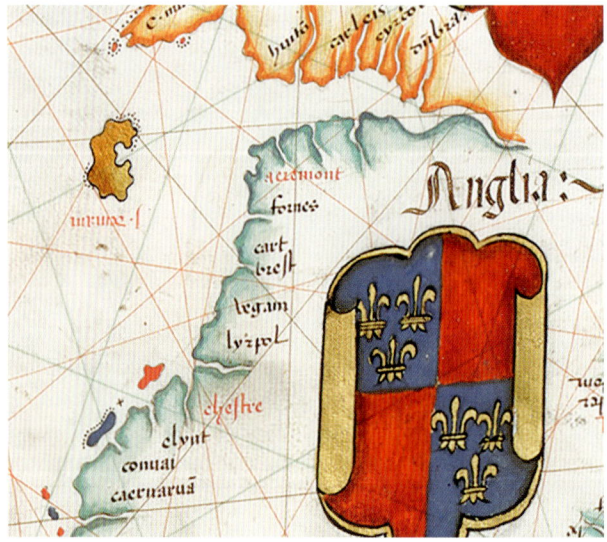

MERIDIES

SEPTENRO

ORIENS

ITALIA

Mahometi

Barbaricus

Dalmatia

Anglia

acomont
fornes
cart
brest
legram
lyspol
chestre
clynt
conual
caernarua

Sixteenth-century navigational aid (1900s) 6

Diogo Homem, Atlas of portolan charts. Portugal, 1561? Folio 3, Central
Mediterranean, Italy and the Adriatic. Illuminated atlas on parchment; seven charts
and astronomical table in a contemporary gold-tooled binding. 45 × 29 cm.

From the bequest of T.G. Rylands, 1900.

The appearance of portolan (nautical) charts in the thirteenth century is one of the most revolutionary developments in the history of cartography. Older maps, such as the medieval *mappaemundi* (world maps), gave a schematic interpretation of the world, whereas these charts were a practical wayfinding aid to help sailors' navigation. They emerged from the experience of the sailors themselves as they moved around the Mediterranean, forming a visualisation of accumulated knowledge and a valuable navigation aid for longer journeys.

None of these earliest working charts survive; they would have been used until worn out, but from them emerged a profession of chart making, initially in Genoa and Venice, then spreading to Majorca and beyond. The charts developed both with nautical innovations (for example, the first compass rose *c.*1375) and geographical extent (the Portuguese exploration of the Atlantic in the fifteenth century increased the scope south, west, and even to the far east). On the map shown, the seafaring centres of Genoa and Venice are embellished with cityscapes for emphasis. *Septentrio* indicates north and *Oriens* east.

This atlas's creator, Diogo Homem, came from a map-making family. His father became master of the Portuguese king's navigation charts in the early sixteenth century, and at least one of his brothers also produced charts. When he produced this atlas Diogo had progressed from simply copying his father's work and was including new discoveries. It is known he was working in England in 1547, and that he passed through Dieppe and spent his latter years (1569–76) in Venice, but further details are lacking. This is surprising, as his surviving attributed work marks him out as one of the most prolific Portuguese cartographers (producing thirteen atlases and eleven separate charts) who achieved a particularly high level of artistry.

This atlas was not intended for use at sea. Such a sumptuous edition would have been commissioned either by a collector themselves or as a high-status gift. For example, King Manuel I of Portugal commissioned a portolan atlas from Lopo Homem (the father of Diogo) and the only other Diogo atlas in Britain was probably commissioned by Mary I. Although this Liverpool atlas was not signed scholars do not doubt its provenance, as it is almost identical to his 1559 atlas now held in the Bibliothèque nationale de France.

Each sheet of the atlas, like all portolan charts, is criss-crossed by coloured lines radiating from a series of centres near the edge of the chart. These are rhumb lines, which indicate the 32 compass directions and were used by sailors as an aid to plot their course. The eight primary are in black, the secondary in green, and the 16 tertiary in red, a long-held colour convention that allowed the sailors to follow the lines more easily. The rhumb lines are not accurate over longer distances, a problem not solved until the invention of Mercator's projection (which happened about eight years after this atlas was created). In the detail shown, the shape of Britain is less accurately portrayed as it lies in an unenclosed waterbody and would have been less familiar to the sailors and chart makers. Liverpool is shown (Lyrpol), but the more important port of Chester (Chestre) is highlighted in red.

This atlas came to the University of Liverpool as part of the rich bequest from Thomas Glazebrook Rylands (1818–1900), a Warrington wire manufacturer with a wide range of interests that included early cartography (he wrote and privately published *The Geography of Ptolemy Elucidated* in 1893). His gift of 2,700 items is still the most generous that the library has received as a discrete collection.

Tinho da Cruz

THE FACE OF AUTHORITY IN ANCIENT EGYPT (1900s)

7

Silver tetradrachm coin of Ptolemy I Soter, minted in Alexandria 323–304 BCE. Silver. 2.7 cm; weight 14.59 g.

Accession date not recorded.

Ptolemy (who later became King Ptolemy I Soter) was an ancient Macedonian Greek general who served under Alexander the Great. He was part of Alexander's inner circle, which, after his death, took control of different parts of his empire.

Ptolemy was born in 367 or 366 BCE in Macedonia to a respected local family with maternal connections to the royal family. During his time in Alexander's army Ptolemy participated in several crucial battles and was also present in the Siwa Oasis in Egypt's Western Desert when the oracle of Amun proclaimed Alexander to be the son of Zeus and the legitimate ruler of Egypt.

After Alexander the Great died in 323 BCE, Ptolemy became satrap (governor) of Egypt. He started minting coins quite early on in his satrapy, and the images on those were used as a propaganda tool to help Ptolemy justify his position. The coins minted were in gold, silver, and bronze, with the silver coins being the prevalent ones. The obverse image on those early coins depicts Alexander the Great and underlines Ptolemy's right to the satrapy of Egypt. Ptolemy eventually became king of Egypt in 311 BCE (his coronation was not until 304 BCE) and, shortly after that, the Egyptian mints started producing coins with his image on the obverse of his coinage.

This coin from the Garstang Museum is a silver tetradrachm minted during Ptolemy's satrapy of Egypt. It depicts Alexander the Great with an elephant headdress on the obverse, and the ancient Greek goddess Athena holding a shield and a spear, a legend and a monogram to the left and an eagle in the lower right field on the reverse.

The Garstang Museum of Archaeology's numismatics collections number approximately 1,500 ancient coins. The largest corpus of coins comes from the Roman Empire, and some of these Roman silver coins were scientifically analysed by a member of staff from the Department of Archaeology, Classics and Egyptology (ACE). This was done as part of a large project that concluded with the publication of a seminal work on the Roman economy (*The Metallurgy of Roman Silver Coinage*). These coins were sampled by drilling into their cylindrical edge and the samples obtained were analysed using inductively coupled plasma emission spectrometry. The aim of this analysis was to establish the level of debasement (the lowering of the precious metal content) in Roman silver coinage.

The same innovative sampling was done on this coin (CC.299), but this time the analysis was conducted in-house at the University's Professor Elisabeth Slater Archaeological Laboratories using a microwave plasma atomic emission spectrometer. This was done as part of a funded PhD project that investigated the debasement of silver and bronze Ptolemaic coinage. In addition to CC.299, the Garstang Museum has thirteen bronze coins from the reign of Ptolemy and his successors that were similarly sampled and analysed by these methods.

This coin illustrates the collaboration between the Garstang Museum and the staff and students from ACE, and demonstrates that the University of Liverpool is a hub of innovation when it comes to archaeological science.

Diana T. Nikolova

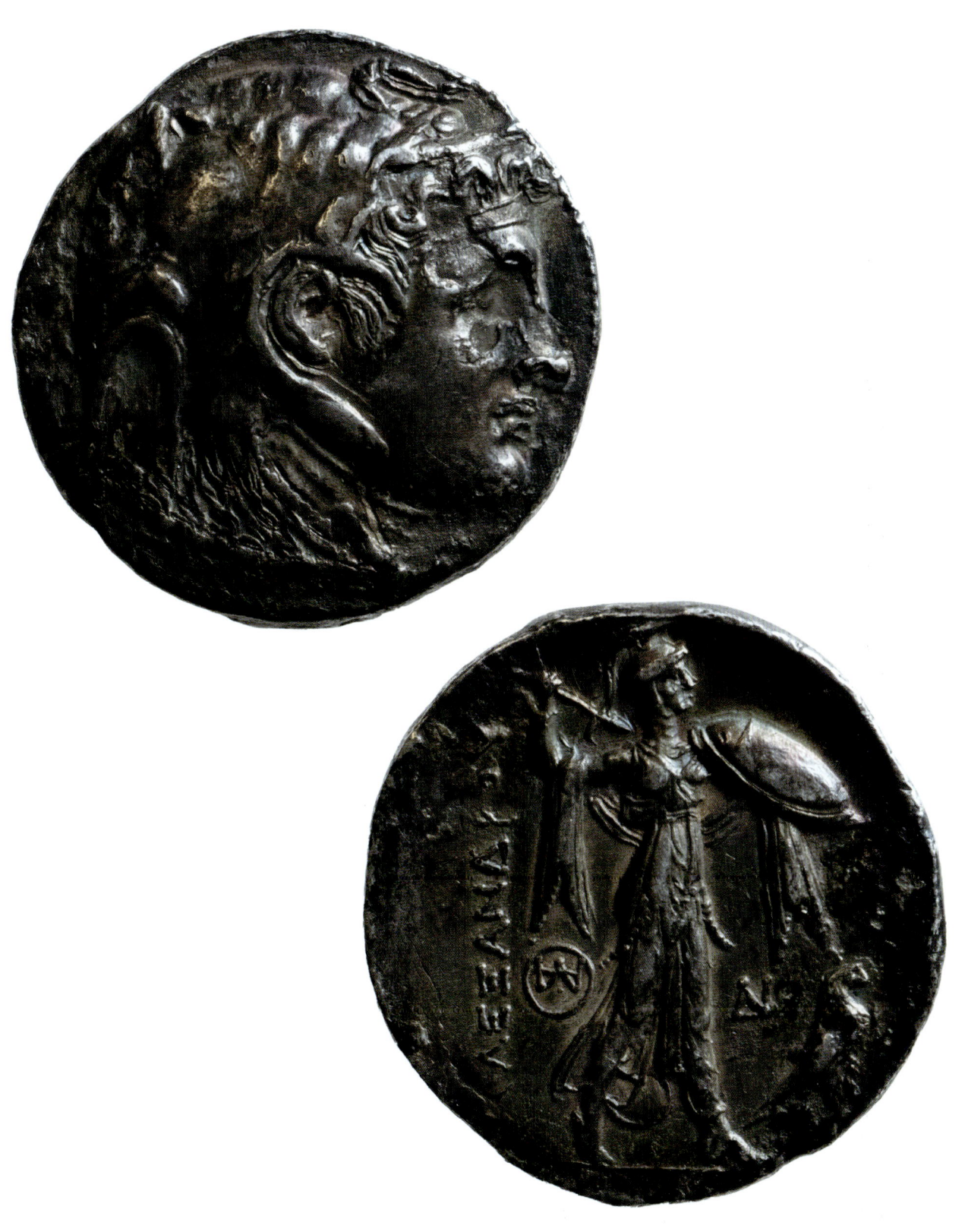

THE CONTRIBUTIONS OF ONESIMUS, LADY MONTAGU, AND DOWNIE IN THE FIGHT AGAINST SMALLPOX (1900s)

8

An inquiry into the causes and effects of the variolae vaccinae, a disease ... known by the name of the cow pox, by Edward Jenner (London: printed for the author, 1800). Engraving by William Skelton, coloured by W. Cuff, of cowpox sores on the hand of dairymaid Sarah Nelmes, from the second edition. 182 pages, 4 plates. 29 × 23 cm.

Blind stamp of Thompson Yates Laboratories; accession date to library of the Faculty of Medicine not recorded.

One of history's deadliest viruses, smallpox is estimated to have killed more than 300 million people since 1900. In the eighteenth century smallpox was a widespread and deadly disease that claimed the lives of many, leaving survivors with severe scarring and sometimes blindness.

The official eradication of smallpox 44 years ago stands as a triumph of modern medicine, but the journey to this achievement is marked by a complex history characterised by exploitation, bioethical transgressions, and marginalisation. Amidst the acclaim of figures such as Edward Jenner (1748–1828), who pioneered vaccine inoculation, or vaccination, which was based on the long history of effective but riskier variolation, two lesser-known individuals played pivotal roles in shaping the course of smallpox history. Onesimus (late 1600s–1700s), an enslaved African man, and Lady Mary Wortley Montagu (1689–1762), an English aristocrat, both made significant contributions that deserve greater recognition.

Onesimus was an African man enslaved by the Puritan minister Cotton Mather (1663–1728) in colonial America; as with many enslaved people, we do not know his birth name or place. Onesimus played a crucial role in introducing the concept of inoculation to the Americas. In 1716 he shared his knowledge of variolation, a traditional African practice, with Mather, who subsequently promoted it in Boston during the smallpox epidemic of 1721. Variolation, a precursor to the modern concept of vaccination, involved deliberately infecting individuals with smallpox (e.g., from pustules, by scratching the material into their arm or inhaling it through the nose) to induce a mild infection and subsequent immunity.

As a result of the white medical profession's suspicion of African medicine smallpox continued to prevail, however, and the last major outbreak in Liverpool (1901–03) was imported from Boston. It arrived via commercial shipping in December 1901, killing 160.

Lady Mary Wortley Montagu, an influential figure in eighteenth-century England, played a pivotal role in popularising variolation in Europe. Having observed the practice during her travels in the Ottoman Empire, where it was used to combat smallpox, Lady Montagu became an advocate for inoculation. In 1721 she had her own children inoculated, championing the procedure's safety and efficacy. Her advocacy helped pave the way for the acceptance of variolation in Europe, ultimately leading to widespread smallpox vaccination.

By the 1960s smallpox was still killing up to ten million people each year, yet not a single natural case has occurred worldwide since 1977. This achievement would have been impossible without the research of Professor Allan Watt Downie (1901–88), who held the chair of Bacteriology at Liverpool from 1943 until 1966, a post previously combined with that of City Bacteriologist, which now became a separate but closely linked appointment.

Downie's laboratory at 126 Mount Pleasant became the world centre for the study of smallpox, and it was under his guidance that in 1966 the World Health Organisation launched the smallpox eradication programme. His retirement in 1966 served only to give him more time to devote to the promotion and development of the programme, which was declared successful in 1979.

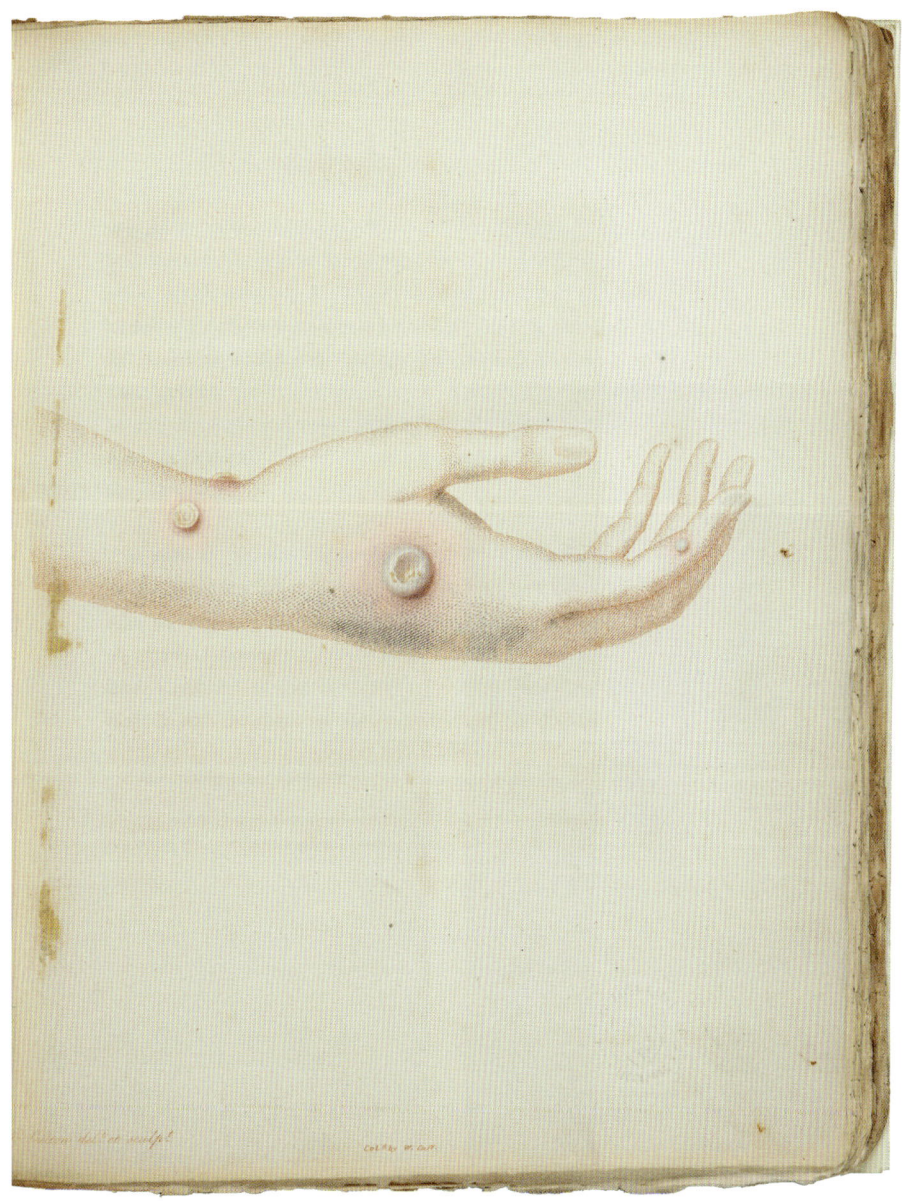

Downie's research, in both the laboratory and the field, provided solid factual back-up for the concept that patients were not infective until the rash appeared, despite becoming ill on the 12th day of their fourteen-day incubation period. This demonstrated that an outbreak could be contained if all contacts could be vaccinated and isolated by the time their fever became apparent. This knowledge gave the necessary time for contact tracing. The concept was simple and its execution by the WHO was instrumental in the success of the programme.

Because of the lack of any technology for total containment, Downie insisted that absolutely everyone who entered the lab – or the building itself – was vaccinated. This included himself and all his colleagues, including window cleaners and people making deliveries.

His contribution to world health cannot be overestimated, yet we should not forget that his work was built upon the foundations created by unsung pioneers such as Onesimus and Lady Montagu.

Carl Larsen and Leonie Sedman

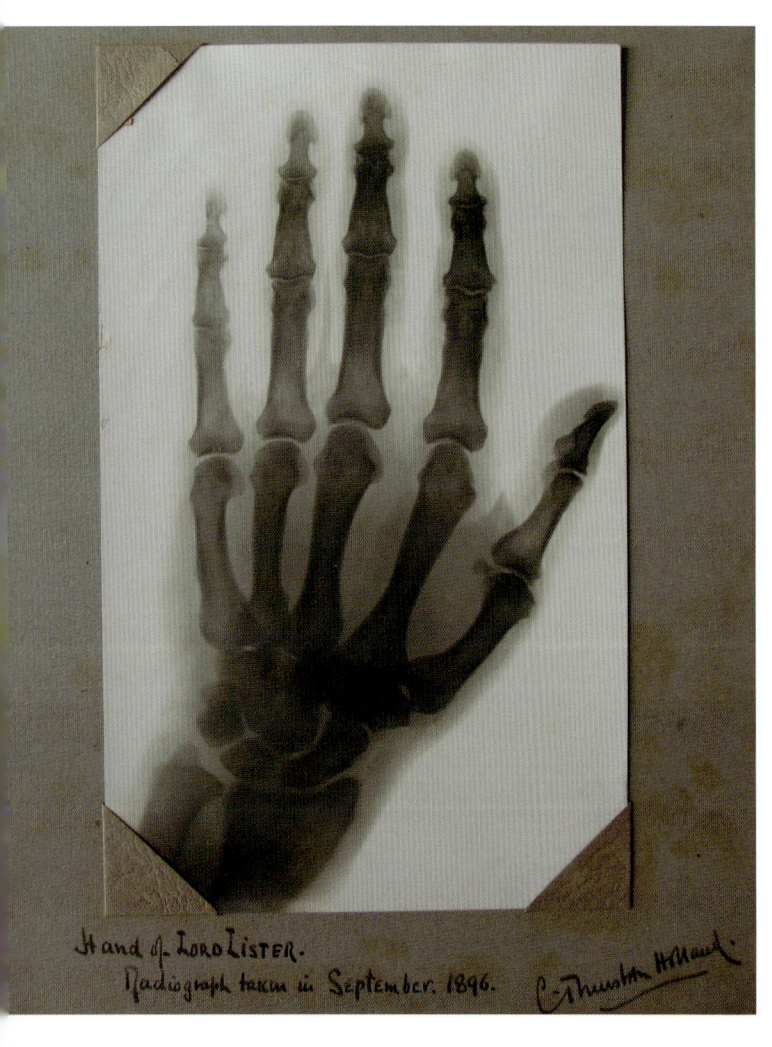

Hand of LORD LISTER.
Radiograph taken in September. 1896.   C. Thurstan Holland.

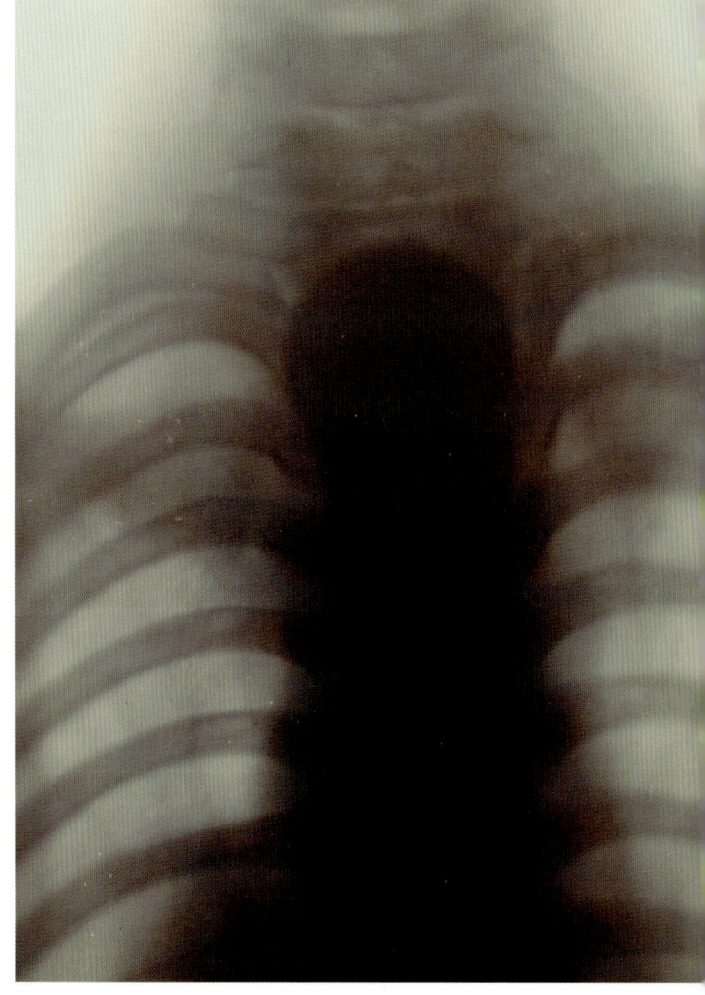

DISCOVERING X-RAYS (1900s)

9

Collection of X-rays associated with Charles Thurstan Holland, including Lord Lister's hand (1896) and swallowed penny (1898); print on photographic paper. 25 × 16 cm, mount size 30 × 25 cm.

Part of Medical Faculty collections, transferred to Heritage collections in 2005 from the University's Medical Imaging Department.

On 7 February 1896 a Liverpool general practitioner called Charles Thurstan Holland (1863–1941) persuaded a young boy who had accidentally shot himself to sit still for 90 minutes with his hand and wrist positioned on a photographic plate. The location was the laboratory of Professor Oliver Lodge (1851–1940) in the Department of Physics in Liverpool's University College, where the surgeon Sir Robert Jones (1857–1933) was waiting to see the results of this radical experiment. Jones, Thurstan Holland, and Lodge had learned of the discovery of X-rays by Willem Roentgen in Germany the previous year, and Lodge had purchased a primitive apparatus – an induction coil and Grove cells (a type of battery, fuelled by nitric acid) that produced X-rays. The faint image that developed on the plate showed the location of the bullet, enabling Jones to remove it. This was one of the first uses of radiology in the UK. Within a few months an X-ray tube was developed, allowing a focused beam of X-rays to be used to produce a clearer image from a shorter exposure period.

In May 1896 Jones bought Thurstan Holland an X-ray tube and he experimented on himself with different periods of exposure and strengths of X-ray to develop a reliable methodology and means of application. Later that year Liverpool's Royal Southern Hospital employed Thurstan Holland to set up the first radiology department, in which X-rays were used for simple diagnostic purposes such as bone fractures.

Thurstan Holland persuaded the pioneer of antiseptic surgery, Lord Joseph Lister (1827–1912), to have his hand X-rayed during a visit to Liverpool, as shown here. One of Thurstan Holland's enduring research interests was in the use of X-rays to locate foreign bodies which could then be surgically removed. Another X-ray, from 5 February 1898, shows a penny in the oesophagus of a twelve-year-old boy who had swallowed it on 8 November 1897. The penny was successfully removed on 10 February, three months after it had been swallowed and only five days after the X-ray was taken.

Over the course of his career Thurstan Holland published the results of his new imaging technique in over 100 papers in leading medical journals. He became recognised as one of the founding fathers of the speciality of radiology, which was quickly adopted in most large hospitals. He later moved to work at the Liverpool Royal Infirmary and from 1920 to 1931 was also a lecturer in radiology at the University of Liverpool, where he created a diploma course in 1922.

Sally Sheard

Fragments of Egyptian history (1900s) 10

Inscribed ivory label bearing the name of King Hor-Aha, from the Naqada Royal Tomb, Dynasty 0/1 (*c*.3100 BC). 3.8 × 4.3 cm.

From the site of Naqada in Upper Egypt. Excavated 1904.

The mother of King Hor-Aha, first ruler of a united Egypt, Neith-hotep was buried in a large tomb at the Upper Egyptian site of Naqada. The quality of her tomb and the goods buried with her indicate that she was an individual of extreme wealth and importance. A member of Egypt's first royal family, living over 5,000 years ago, she is the earliest historically recorded woman in the world.

The items buried with Neith-hotep provide an insight into the world of Egypt's elite at this time. Many of the items were produced by highly skilled craftsmen. Objects such as flint tools, obsidian vessels, and ivory figurines would have been time consuming to produce and the raw materials would have been procured through an extensive trade network. The closest sources of obsidian (volcanic glass), for example, were found in Asia Minor, Greece, and Ethiopia.

A particularly important innovation in the years preceding the unification of Egypt was the development of writing. The earliest uses of written symbols relate to power and status. By Neith-hotep's lifetime written inscriptions also served an administrative function, labelling objects, places, and possibly events.

The incised ivory tablet from the tomb of Neith-hotep in the Garstang Museum collections fits into this category. In 1904 John Garstang, who founded the Institute of Archaeology in Liverpool that year, visited the Naqada Royal Tomb and uncovered hundreds of objects left behind by previous excavations, around 500 of which are now housed in the Garstang Museum. This tablet was one of two identical copies found at the site, both badly damaged. The orange colouration and warping of the Garstang Museum tablet are evidence of exposure to the extreme heat of a fire in another section of the tomb.

The inscription, which sits at an intermediary stage between writing and picture, is arranged in three rows. We know from the other tablet (now in Cairo) that the top row contained the name and title of a king – Hor-Aha – and the image of a boat. The name of King Hor-Aha appears frequently in Neith-hotep's tomb, probably because he provided many of her burial goods. A small hole in the top corner would have been used to attach the tablet to an object, so that it acted as a label.

The second row features a large vessel on a stand in the centre, flanked by two people, one of whom appears to be stirring the contents of the pot. To the right is a depiction of an enclosure containing three figures, behind another individual pictured with a staff to express his authority. Above him another person bows in the direction of the enclosure. Above the central figures and on the left side of the label are hieroglyphs,

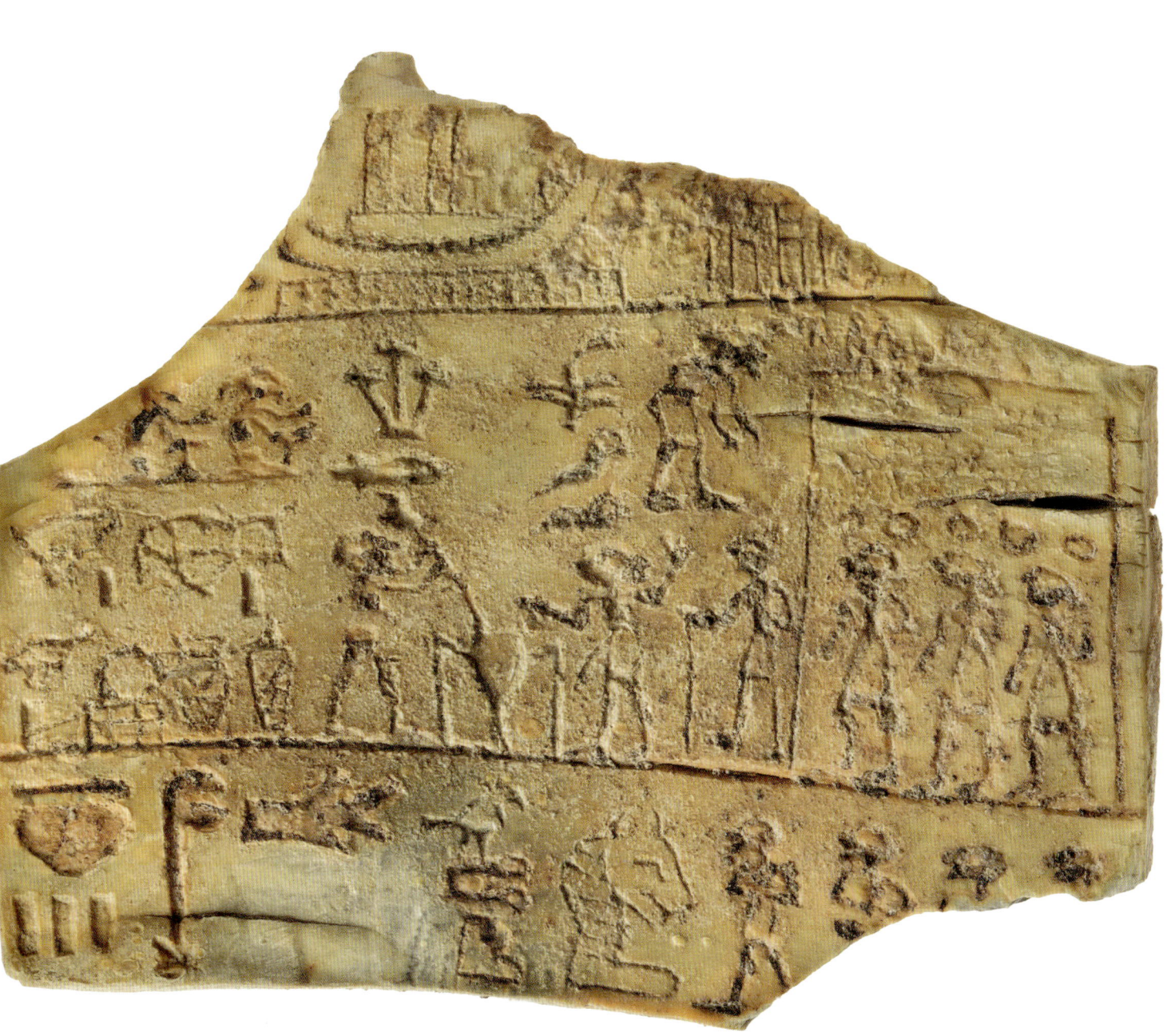

although it is very difficult to interpret the message conveyed by symbols from this early date. The third row shows four individuals on the right facing another hieroglyphic inscription. Again, the meaning of the text is unclear.

There is evidence that substantial damage was done to the tomb in ancient times. Broken and misplaced objects in the outer chambers suggest that the tomb was robbed, while some objects, such as this warped and discoloured ivory tablet, provide evidence for an extremely intense fire. A number of Dynasty 1 royal tombs at Abydos were damaged and burnt during civil unrest in the First Intermediate Period (*c.*2100 BC). It is possible that the Naqada Royal Tomb was similarly attacked.

Gina Criscenzo-Laycock

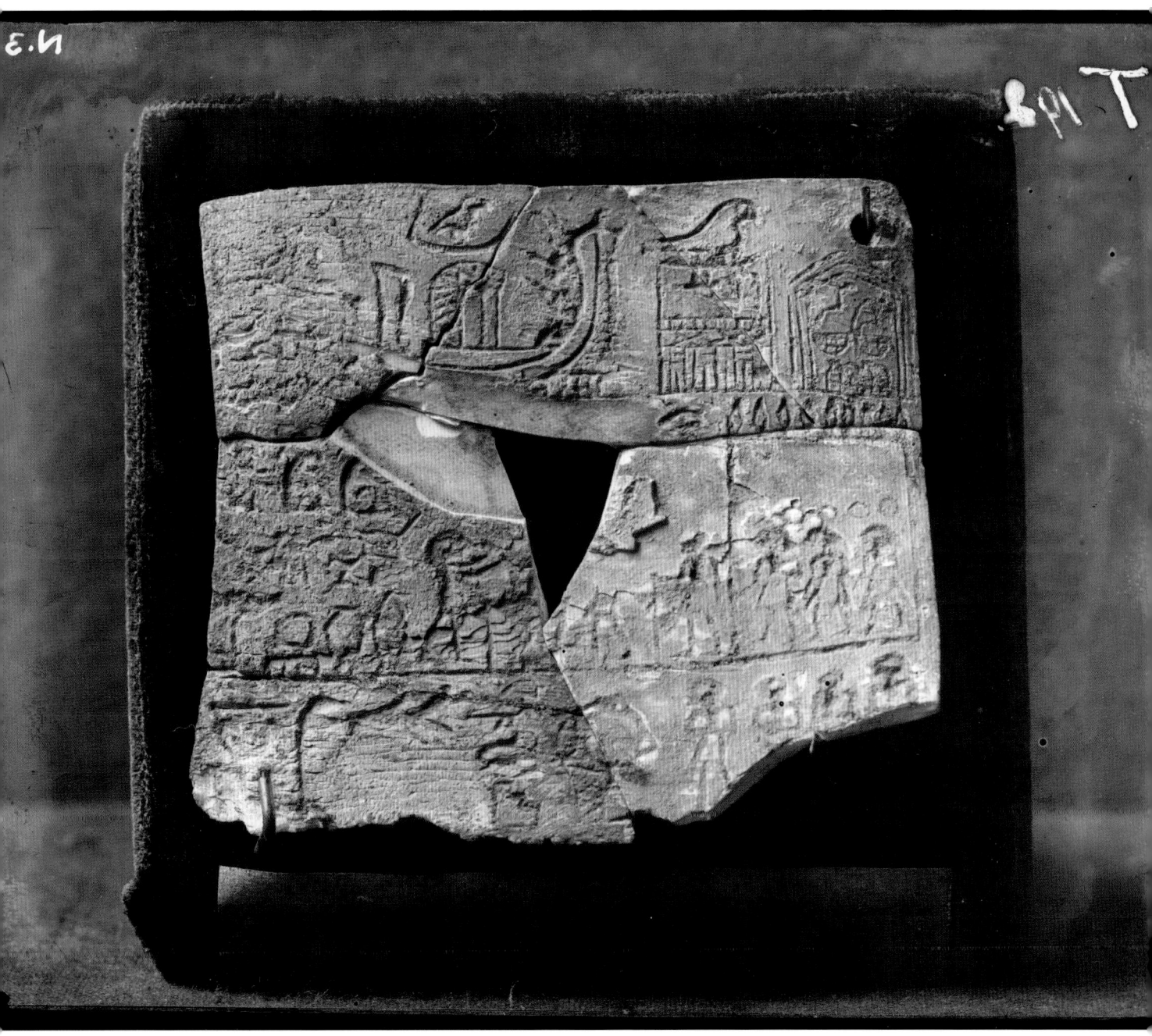

Photograph of second, more complete, ivory label from the Naqada Royal Tomb, now in Cairo. Four pieces of the object were excavated by Jacques de Morgan (1857–1924) in 1896; the final piece (lower right) was found by John Garstang (1876–1956) in 1904.

A BRAND NEW LIBRARY ON BOLD STREET (1900s)

11

Catalogue of the Liverpool Library; to which are prefixed the Laws of the Institution and a
List of the Proprietors (Liverpool, 1801) in printed volume of catalogues of the Liverpool
Library, 1801–11, bound in gold-tooled parchment by John Jones of Liverpool in
1813, with a fore-edge painting of the Lyceum on Bold Street by William
Ball. 21.5 × 13.5 cm.

Presented by Matthew Gregson to Mary Earle, Lady Patroness of Liverpool Public Library, 1813;
Gregson Institute collections given to the University in 1906.

Libraries are generally seen today as a vital public good, but this has not always been the case. The idea of the modern public library – funded by the taxpayer and providing free access to books – dates back to the 1850s. Before then, numerous types of lending library were built not by the state but by individuals and groups acting autonomously. Sometimes they did so in pursuit of profit, but in other cases they were motivated by faith, philanthropy, or education.

Founded in 1758 as one of England's first subscription libraries, the Liverpool Library played an important part in this history. Reading became increasingly important to a growing number of people during the 1700s. No longer the preserve of aristocratic elites, books were used for pleasure and for education, providing access to self-improvement and social mobility in the absence of systematic schooling. Yet many books were also prohibitively expensive, meaning that most would-be readers relied on borrowing books rather than buying them. Subscription libraries were an innovative – though generally expensive – solution to this problem. They were private membership clubs in which members paid annual membership fees to acquire more books than each could afford individually.

This copy of the Liverpool Library's 1801 printed catalogue is unique. Bound in gold-tooled parchment and decorated with an evocative fore-edge painting of the Library's newly built home on Bold Street (the Lyceum), it reflects the scope for self-expression when every part of a book was still made entirely by hand. The painter is named as William Ball, who may have been employed by John Jones (1771–1831) in his Liverpool

book bindery and may have been related to the ceramics decorator of the same name who was active in the city in the 1760s.

A handwritten inscription helps to explain why this book attracted such lavish attention:

> *Presented*
> *To Miss Mary Earle*
> *as Lady Patroness*
> *of the*
> *Liverpool Library*
> *By Her*
> *Obedient Humble Servant*
> *Matthew Gregson*
> *President*

Although subscription libraries were generally dominated by men, women were rarely forbidden from joining. Borrowing records, in the very few cases where they survive, help us to access the thoughts and interests of ordinary women about whom we know virtually nothing else – women such as the Bristol haberdasher Mary Adams or the New York innkeeper Catherine Bradford. Both can be found in the C18th Libraries Online database compiled by researchers at the University, which makes available information on book holdings, membership, and book usage at subscription libraries in Britain and North American in the years 1731–1801.

We don't know what women borrowed at Liverpool, but we do know that it was one of the very few libraries – perhaps the only one – to create a formal role specifically

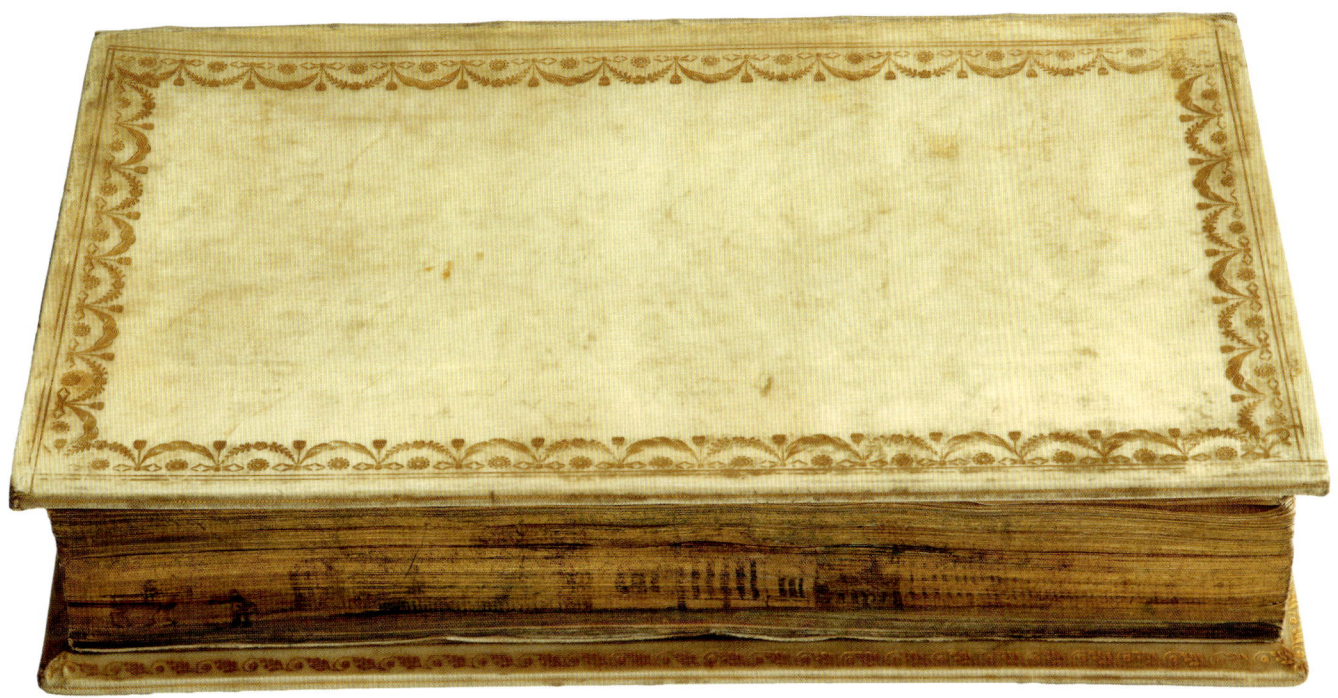

for them. Unlike the role of President (always a man), the role of Lady Patroness was purely ceremonial. Selected annually, she was presented with a richly bound copy of the latest catalogue (like this one) and encouraged 'to enjoy the privilege of reading'. The recipient was usually young and unmarried, and often related to members of good standing. In this case the awardee was probably Mary Earle (1794–1854) of Spekeland House, who turned 19 around the time this catalogue was presented in 1813.

While this book reveals the hidden role of women in Liverpool's cultural development, it also points to a much darker history. The Earle family, like many investors in Liverpool's subscription libraries, gained their wealth and social status from the trafficking of enslaved Africans. Mary's father was Thomas Earle (1755–1822), a one-time mayor of Liverpool who, along with his brother William, trafficked at least 19,000 Africans into slavery, of whom at least 3,000 died on the voyage across the Atlantic. The Lyceum building – like so many of Liverpool's exceptional surviving Georgian buildings – was built upon the backs of millions of African people stolen, trafficked, abused, and enslaved for centuries of free labour.

Sophie Jones and Mark Towsey

SONGS BY BEN JONSON.
A SELECTION FROM THE PLAYS,
MASQUES, AND POEMS, WITH THE
EARLIEST KNOWN SETTINGS OF
CERTAIN NUMBERS.

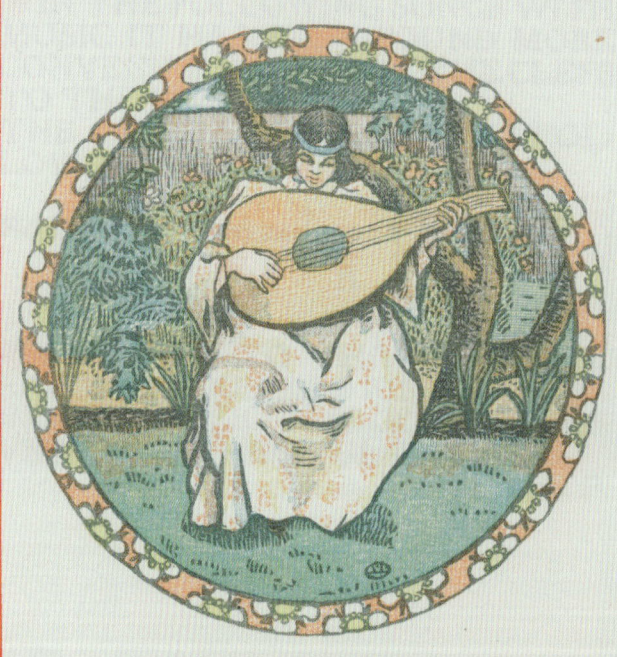

THE ERAGNY PRESS, THE BROOK,
HAMMERSMITH, LONDON, W.

The book beautiful (1910s)

12

Songs by Ben Jonson; printed volume published by the Eragny Press, 1906. 59 pages with frontispiece and music. 21 × 14 cm.

Bequeathed as part of the William Noble collection, 1913.

The William Noble collection contains over 1,000 books, the majority of which are finely printed and limited editions published in England in the late nineteenth and early twentieth centuries as part of the private press movement. *Songs by Ben Jonson: a selection from the plays, masques, and poems* is one of these fine volumes. They were bought as they appeared by William Noble (1838–1912), Treasurer of the Mersey Docks and Harbour Board, and formed 'his personal collection of rare and beautiful books'. Many still contain correspondence between the book collector and the books' authors, printers, and booksellers.

The collection is a significant part of Noble's bequest to the University, which comprised the bulk of his considerable estate and valuable possessions: 'I bequeath the whole of my collection of books and the bookcases containing them in the expectation that the books shall not be sold or dispersed and that they shall be used with clean hands' (University Archive P6/30). His will stipulated that the residue of his estate be used for the foundation of a scholarship or fellowship. A century later, the William Noble Fellowship still provides the time and funding for an early career researcher in the Department of English Literature to forge their own connections with books.

The book-makers associated with the private press movement shared a keen interest in every step in the production of a book. They sought out the best-quality paper and ink and personally designed or commissioned the type, page layout, ornaments, and illustrations of each of the editions that they made. Some private press publishers even printed the pages and engraved the woodblocks themselves. Through such close attention to quality and detail they aimed to create works that were original, beautiful, and pleasant to read.

This approach to book-making was in part a reaction to the Industrial Revolution, which private press printers felt had brought about a damaging decline in the dignity of the worker, and in the aesthetic and functional qualities of the products made. The trade-off was that both making and buying private press books were expensive activities. As the Noble Collection makes apparent, the books these publishers painstakingly produced immediately became highly sought-after collectors' items.

William Morris (1834–96) is undoubtedly the most famous name to be associated with the private press movement, and the Noble Collection includes copies of every edition printed at his Kelmscott Press. But Noble collected across a wide range of presses and his library also contained all but one of the books printed at Lucien and Esther Pissarro's Eragny Press during Noble's lifetime. The Pissarros came to London from France, bringing a continental connection to an otherwise English movement. The Eragny Press is perhaps best known for introducing colour printing to the private press movement, and it was also the only private press to use music type. When it was produced in 1906 *Songs by Ben Jonson* represented a high point in the output of the press: a showcase of the Pissarros' skills across the book arts, which were remarkably wide-ranging, even among private-press publishers. The title-page colour illustration was designed and engraved on wood by Lucien (1863–1944), and the borders and initials designed by Lucien and engraved by Esther (1870–1951). The types used to produce both the letters and music were designed by Lucien and the book's complicated printing in multiple colours was undertaken in part by the couple themselves. Lucien also designed the decorative printed papers used to bind the book, while the ink was sourced from Germany and the paper from France.

Despite the attractiveness of the finished product, *Songs of Ben Jonson* did not sell well and, in a clear indication of the difficulty involved in opting to produce high-quality, beautiful books in a commercialised, mechanised world, the couple, who could rely on neither private means nor a wealthy backer, lost money making it.

Niamh Delaney

The spirit of philanthropy at the University of Liverpool (1920s)

13

University of Liverpool Appeal poster (1920). Printed in colour on paper, 1920.
33.7 × 22.4 cm.

Commissioned for the University Appeal, 1920.

In 1920 the University of Liverpool conducted a major fundraising effort with the goal of raising £1,000,000. By 1922 £407,000 had been raised thanks to the financial support of 9,993 donors. Images of the University campus were used on the campaign's promotional poster and postcards: a series of 36 postcards with etchings by Ernest Coffin depicting existing and proposed University buildings was sold in aid of the appeal. These not only encouraged donations but also reflected the charitable spirit that has been known to thrive in the Liverpool community. This culture of support and giving has been crucial in increasing access to education and opportunity for students from all backgrounds, creating an atmosphere that encourages aspiration and development for all. In the words of the Appeal's Manifesto, the University 'can be classed high among the most prosperous and the most modern universities of Great Britain, yet it is unable to extend the work of vital importance, for which it was founded, without the means required immediately for expansion'.

In the immediate post-war period there was a surge in student numbers, largely as a result of men returning from war service. Women student numbers also increased, accounting for more than one-third of the total student numbers at the University of Liverpool by the mid-1920s. The campaign's slogan, 'Help youth to realise ambition – therein lies efficiency and the nation's destiny', was significant in this post-First World War society. The importance of education in helping societies recover and succeed was largely recognised as the world experienced significant social and economic changes. In Britain, a post-First World War financial crisis in higher education led to the foundation of the University Grants Committee in 1919 to coordinate state funding, but it could not meet all financial needs and universities turned to philanthropy to increase access

and improve their facilities. The slogan emphasised that educating the next generation would not only help them achieve their own goals but also advance the nation. It reaffirmed the idea that having an educated and skilled population was crucial to a nation's future stability and development. This campaign sought to invest in young people to create a more effective and productive society.

That message is still relevant today – perhaps even more so. In the twenty-first century, where technological breakthroughs, climate change, and international crises demand individuals who are well educated and flexible, the belief that personal ambition influences national efficiency and destiny is especially important. Even though, since 1920, access to education has greatly increased, continued investment in youth and higher education is still essential for determining a country's destiny. The slogan, both then and now, captures the reality that a country's development depends on maximising the potential of its youth.

In 1920, acquiring £1,000,000 to support the then 1,600 students was a significant financial hurdle. With less than 1 per cent of the population attending university, such funding highlighted the limited access to higher education at the time, which was mostly reserved for wealthy students. This investment was critical for supplying necessary resources (such as teachers, libraries, and basic campus amenities) at a time when universities were smaller and less dependent on the sophisticated infrastructure that characterises modern institutions. Growth and investment also acted to increase access to higher education. By the mid-1930s the student demographic was beginning to change, with greater availability of grants and scholarships. In their 1936 report the University Grants Committee noted that at least half the students in provincial universities came from public elementary schools.

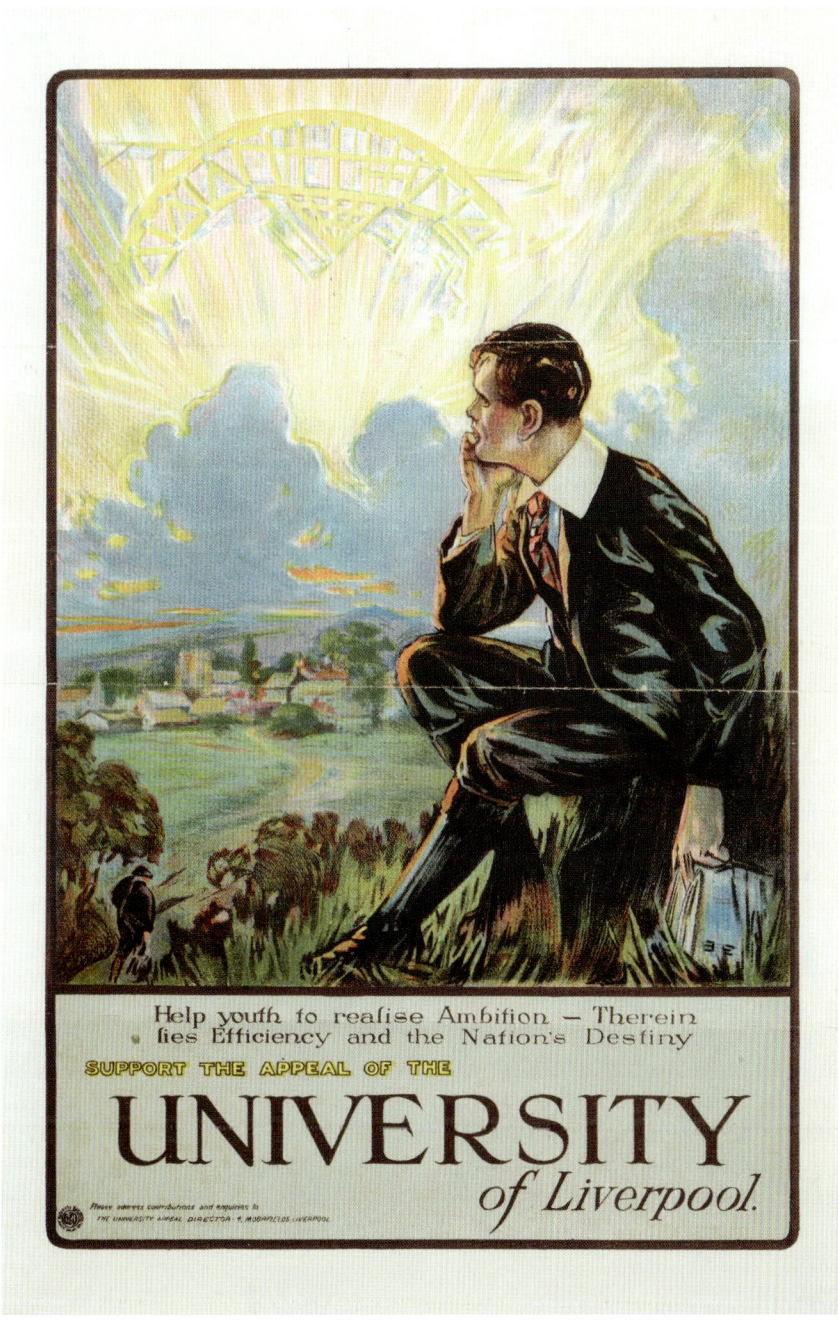

Today, over half of young people pursue higher education, demonstrating a huge increase in availability. For comparison, to support the University's current 33,000 students the equivalent funding would be £1.1 billion, which indicates both the expansion of university education and the growing costs associated with current expectations. The 1920 funding campaign helped shape the future of education at the University by opening doors to education and creating a framework for the expansive, inclusive University that we see here today.

Rowan Bradbury

An early edition of Ranulf Higden's *Polychronicon* printed by William Caxton (1482) (1920s)

14

Printed volume (incomplete, with repairs) on paper, in later pastiche binding by Rivière & Son of leather over uncovered beech boards, brass clasps with leather straps. 25.4 × 16.8 cm.

Bought from Henry Young, bookseller, Liverpool, presented by Charles Sydney Jones. Accessioned 4 October 1921. Earlier ownership records at Young's South Castle Street premises destroyed during the Liverpool Blitz.

Some books preserve a legacy even greater than the texts that they contain. They capture a way of thinking about the world that inspires their readers and allows them to remain relevant as subsequent generations encounter them. One such volume, the University of Liverpool's copy of William Caxton's 1482 edition of Ranulf Higden's *Polychronicon*, stands as testament to the lives and achievements of four influential men, united across six centuries by a love of books and a passion for making knowledge accessible to their peers.

Higden (*c.*1280–1364), a Benedictine monk at St Werburgh's Abbey, now Chester Cathedral, wrote the first of several versions of his universal history around 1327. Satisfying his community's desire for a text that placed England's past within the greater framework of world history, he drew on the works of chroniclers who had come before him, shaping and adding to what he found. The result was an encyclopaedic account of the world's geography and history, from Creation to the reign of Edward III, which was an instant hit with

ecclesiastical and secular readers alike. Over the next four decades Higden continued expanding his 'Historiam Polychronicam' (or 'Chronicle of many times') and after his death others went on to copy, expand, translate, and abridge the text, bringing it to new readers throughout the fourteenth and fifteenth centuries.

The first and most notable translation was made in the 1380s by John Trevisa (*c.*1342–1402), a prolific scholar and translator of medieval texts, who painstakingly converted Higden's lengthy Latin text into Middle English and extended the history down to 1360 for his patron, Thomas, fifth baron Berkeley. As well as supplying the English laity with unprecedented access to a universal history, Trevisa's translation gained further traction throughout the fifteenth century for making various biblical paraphrases available at a time when English translations of the Bible were forbidden.

Eighty years after Trevisa's death, England's first printer, William Caxton (*c.*1422–91), used Trevisa's translation as the basis for his 1482 edition of the

Britons dwellyd first in this Ilond the .xviij. yere yere of
Hely the prophete the vj yere of Siluius postumus kyng
of latyns, xliij yere aftir the takyng of Troye to fore the
buyldyng of Rome four honderd and xxxij yere ¶ Beda libro
primo· They come hether and toke her cours from armorik that
now is that other bryptayn, they helde long tyme the south contre,
yes of the ylond. ¶ Hit befel afterward in vaspasianus tyme
duke of Rome that the Pyctes shiped out of Sacia in to Oce,
an and were dryuen aboute with the wynde and entred in to the
north costes of Irlond and fonde there Scottes and prayd to ha
ue a place to dwelle in, and myghte none gete. For Irlond, as
Scottes saide myght not susteyne bothe peple ¶ Scottes sente
the pyctes to the northsides of bryptayn. And behight hem helpe a,
yenst the Brytons that were theyr enemyes yf they wold aryse

And toke hem wyues of her doughters vpon suche a condicion
yf doubte fylle. Who sholde haue right for to be kynge they sholde
rather chese hem a kyng of the moder side than of the faders side,
of the women kyn rather than of the men kynde Gankt In
vaspasiane themperours tyme whan marius azuirag9 sone was
kyng of Britons. One Roderik kyng of pyctes cam out of Sa,
cia and gan to destroye Scotland, thenne marius the kynge sle,
we this Roderick. And yaf the northe partye of Scotland, that
het Cathenesia to the men that were come with rotherik and we
re ouercome by hym for to dwelle Inne, but these men had none
wyues ne none myght haue of the nacion of brytons, therfore
they saylled in to Irlond and toke to theyr wyues prysshmens
doughters by that couenaunt that the Moder blode sholde be put
to fore in succession of herytage. Giz c' IX. Netheles spring sup vir
giliu seith that pyctes ben agatyrses that had somme dwellyng
place about the waters of sacia, & they ben called pyctes of pyn
tyng and snytyng of woundes that ben seen on her bodyes, For
they hadde moche flewme and were ofte boyed and lete blood,
and had many woundes seen on her bodye So that they semed
as men were pynted with woundes, therfore they were called
pyctes as pynted men ¶ These men and the gothes ben
al one peple. For whan maximus the tyraunt was wente oute
of Bryptayn in to Frauce for to occuppe thempyre. Thenne Gra,
cianus and valentinianus that were brethern and felaws of
thempyre brought thyse Gothes oute of Sacia with grete pef,
tes with fflateryngе and fayre byhestes in to the Northe

94

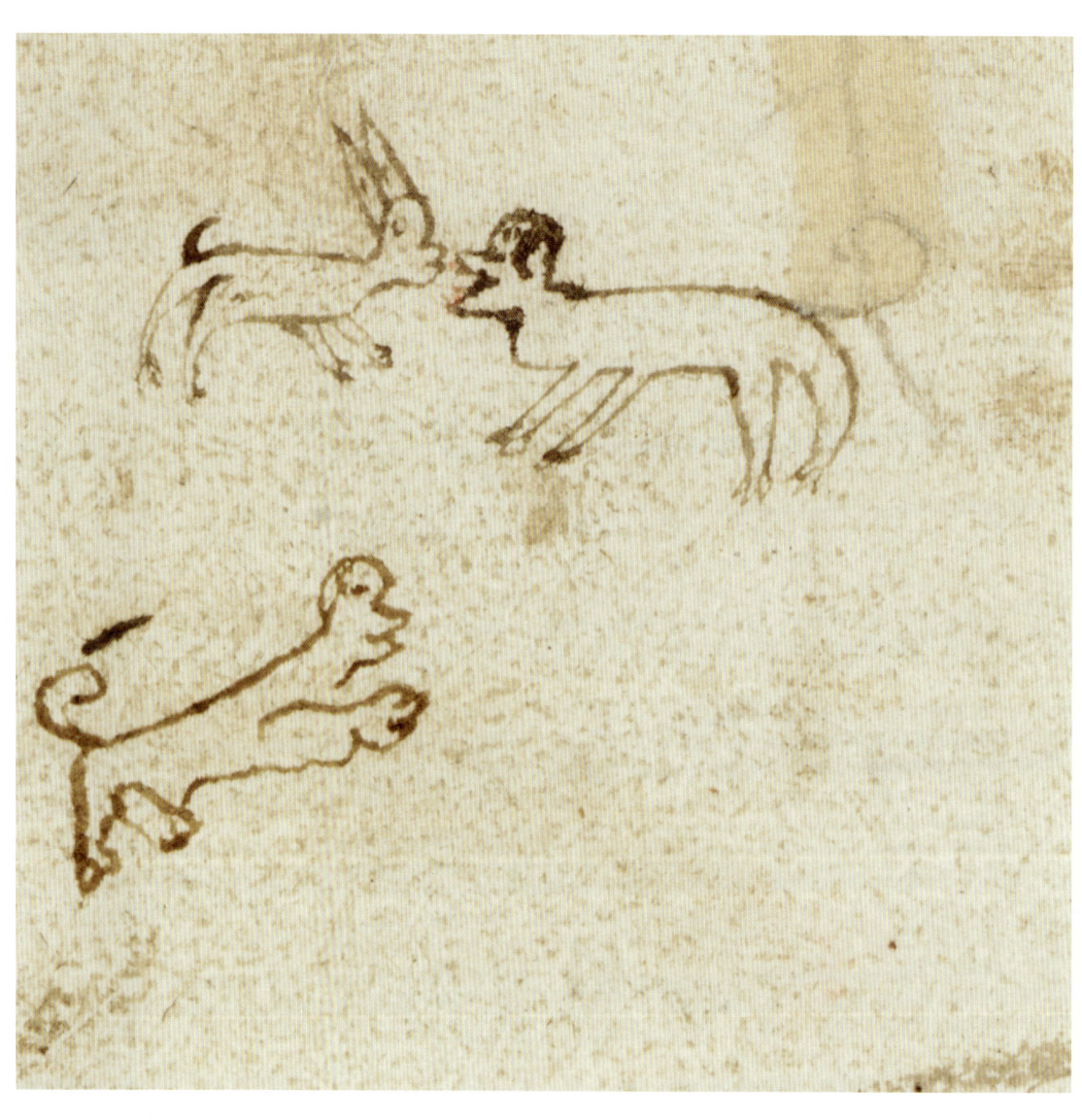

Polychronicon. Caxton made his own contribution to the history by modernising Trevisa's English and adding a continuation covering events up to 1461, which he named the 'Liber Ultimus' ('Last Book'). He also created a prologue, epilogue, and index to the work. The wider reach that Caxton's edition had through the new technology of print ensured that Higden's universal approach to history passed into the Tudor age, where it was utilised by antiquarians and historiographers.

The University of Liverpool holds two incomplete copies of Caxton's edition of the *Polychronicon*, which in its entirety was a chunky text of 450 folio leaves. The copy with reference number Inc.CSJ.D03 provides strong evidence for continued interest in the text beyond the fifteenth century, containing numerous underlinings, annotations, and sketches of rabbits and dogs in a variety of later hands, as well as marks of ownership by members of a family surnamed 'Richardson'. Such regular use by readers may explain why it is now significantly incomplete.

This copy was purchased for the University in 1921 by Sir Charles Sydney Jones (1872–1947). Jones, a successful businessman and politician who served as lord mayor of Liverpool (1938–42), had a lifelong interest in education. He assisted the University in various roles, including as President of the Council (1930–36) and Pro-Vice Chancellor (1936–42), and was one of its most important benefactors. The Sydney Jones Library bears his name today in honour of the generous funds he provided for books and the great gift that he made in 1945 when he donated his private collection of more than 200 volumes of medieval manuscripts, incunables (books printed in the fifteenth century), and other valuable books to the University. It is fitting that his copy of the *Polychronicon* now resides in the educational environment that he helped to foster and which, like the text itself, is dedicated to the pursuit of knowledge in a global context.

Sarah L. Peverley

Early astronomical texts: circles, wheels, and ellipses (1920s)

15

Diagram showing Earth's orbit around the Sun, from Copernicus, *De Revolutionibus* (Book 3, Chapter 20). In a volume of three illustrated printed works published 1533 and 1543, in Nuremberg and Basel, with a contemporary, mid-sixteenth-century Oxford binding of calf over wooden boards, with brass clasps and later red leather spine label with title 'Copernicus' tooled in gilt. 28 × 21.5 cm.

Date of accession not recorded.

This intriguing volume contains three mathematical astronomy texts, each purchased separately by a sixteenth-century owner and taken by that owner to a bookbinder in Oxford to be bound together in a beautiful and robust contemporary binding of decorated calfskin over sturdy wooden boards. The texts this binding protects are related: they include two of the most important works ever written in the history of mathematical astronomy, Ptolemy's *Almagest* and Copernicus's *De Revolutionibus*.

For about 1,400 years the most highly regarded astronomical text was the *Almagest*, written in Greek in Alexandria around AD 150 by Claudius Ptolemy. Its title comes from the Arabic for 'The Greatest'. Ptolemy's model of the Solar system had a stationary Earth in the centre, with the Sun, Moon, and planets orbiting around it on complicated paths. For example, the planet Mars moved on two circular wheels. The larger wheel rotates once every Mars year, carrying a smaller wheel (the epicycle) rotating once every Earth year. To account for observed irregularities in the motion of Mars through the sky the simple two-wheel picture had to be modified. The large wheel is not centred on the Earth but displaced slightly to one side (it is eccentric), and its motion is uneven, sometimes a little fast, sometimes a little slow. The *Almagest* gave explanations on how to use this model to calculate the apparent positions of the planets.

In the early Middle Ages European scholars relied on second-hand Latin translations of Arabic texts. In the Renaissance access to Greek texts became possible, and the German scholar Joannes Regiomontanus (1436–76) produced a shortened Latin translation from the Greek in 1462, which was first printed in 1496. This volume

contains one of our two copies of the 1543 printing of his text.

Also published in 1543, *On the revolutions of the heavenly spheres* by Nicolaus Copernicus (1473–1543) was the first major advance on Ptolemy's theories. Copernicus made the Sun the centre, instead of the Earth. Instead of Mars moving on two wheels, one with a period of one Earth year, one with a period of a Mars year, the motions were separated. All the motions with periods related to the Earth year were moved to Earth's orbit around the Sun; Mars's orbit involves only periods based on the Mars year. Copernicus was pleased with this separation: 'It is necessary above all … not to attribute to the celestial bodies what belongs to the Earth.' Copernicus rejected Ptolemy's variable speed wheels and insisted on using only wheels with a uniform circular motion. Though the ideas in Copernicus' heliocentric model were more modern, it did not lead to better predictions of the planets' motion, and errors were still about as large as in Ptolemy's model. Nevertheless, a later owner of this volume recognised the importance of Copernicus's work by adding his name on a spine label.

The third text in the volume is the 1533 edition of another work by Regiomontanus: 'On Triangles', an important book on triangles and trigonometry, considering both triangles on flat surfaces and on the curved surface of a sphere, which builds on the work of both Greek and Arabic geometers.

Building on the texts in this volume, the next big advance in astronomy came through three figures, all born after the year 1543: Danish astronomer Tycho Brahe (1546–1601), German mathematician Johannes Kepler (1571–1630) and Holy Roman Emperor Rudolf II (1552–1612). Working with data from Tycho's greatly

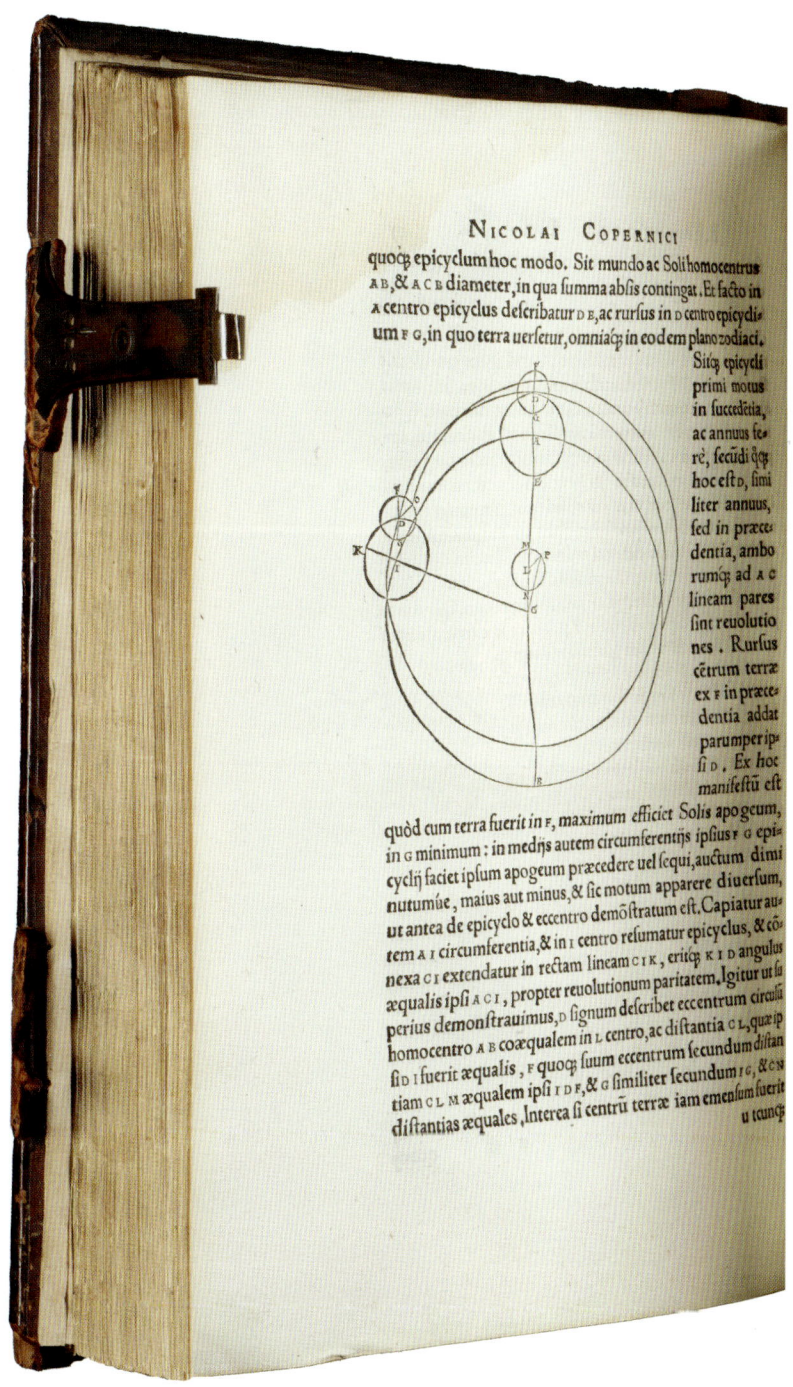

quôq; epicyclum hoc modo. Sit mundo ac Solihomocentrus A B, & A C B diameter, in qua summa abfis contingat. Et facto in A centro epicyclus defcribatur D E, ac rurfus in D centro epicycli um F G, in quo terra uerfetur, omniáq; in eodem plano zodiaci.

Sitq; epicycli primi motus in fuccedètia, ac annuus fe rè, fecûdi q; eq; hoc eft D, fimi liter annuus, fed in præce dentia, ambo rumq; ad A C lineam pares fint reuolutio nes . Rurfus cètrum terræ ex F in præce dentia addat parumper ip fi D . Ex hoc manifeftû eft

quôd cum terra fuerit in F, maximum efficiet Solis apogeum, in G minimum : in medijs autem circumferentijs ipfius F G epi cyclñ faciet ipfum apogeum præcedere uel fequi, auctum dimi nutumûe, maius aut minus, & fic motum apparere diuerfum, ut antea de epicyclo & eccentro demôftratum eft. Capiatur au tem A I circumferentia, & in I centro refumatur epicyclus, & cô nexa C I extendatur in rectam lineam C I K, eriéq; K I D angulus æqualis ipfi A C I, propter reuolutionum paritatem. Igitur ut fu perius demonftrauimus, D fignum defcribet eccentrum circûfiâ homocentro A B coæqualem in L centro, ac diftantia C L, quæ ip fi D I fuerit æqualis, F quoq; fuum eccentrum fecundum diftan tiam C L M æqualem ipfi I D F, & G fimiliter fecundum I G, & eû diftantias æquales ,Interea fi centrû terræ iam emenfum fuerit

u tcûcq;

improved observations of the planets, Kepler discovered that he could describe the planetary motions by using a Sun-centred model with elliptical orbits instead of multiple circles. The new model made predictions 20 times better than all the previous methods. Rudolf II commissioned Brahe and Kepler in 1600 to produce a new, better, table of planetary positions, the 'Rudolphine Tables' (1627) – but that is the story of a different remarkable book in our collections.

Paul Rakow

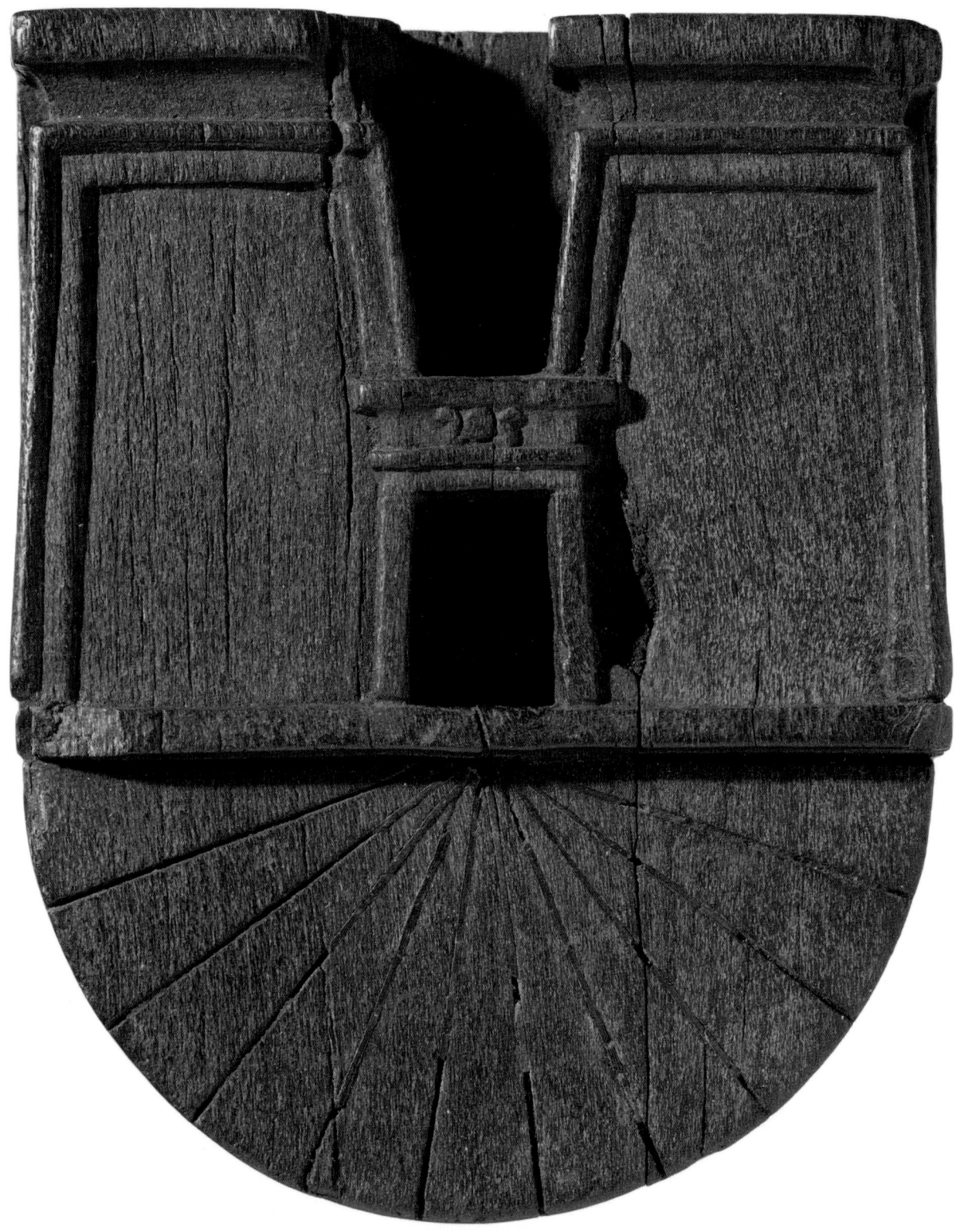

From the Lion Temple, Meroë, Sudan. Excavated 1909–10 by Professor John Garstang, founder of the Liverpool Institute of Archaeology. The sundial is the inspiration for the Garstang Museum logo.

Here comes the sun (1920s)

16

Wooden sundial from Meroë representing a temple gateway. A solar disc flanked by uraei (rearing cobras) can be seen on the door lintel. Reign of Tañyidamani (150–100 BC). 9.8 × 7.6 cm.

From the James and Elizabeth Smith Collections, 1927.

One hundred and twenty kilometres north of Khartoum lie the ruins of ancient Meroë. For almost a thousand years (*c.*700 BC–AD 330) Meroë was an important religious and administrative centre in the Kingdom of Kush. One of the earliest cities in Africa outside Egypt, Meroë was at the heart of a complex, literate culture. Abandoned in the fourth century, the ruins were reidentified as the ancient city of Meroë in 1772. Between 1909 and 1914 the site was excavated by Liverpool archaeologist John Garstang. Today the city and several surrounding temple and funerary complexes are part of the UNESCO World Heritage site Archaeological Sites of the Island of Meroe.

Garstang found many monumental structures at Meroë, including several buildings he identified as palaces and temples. The large temple of the Meroitic god Apedemak, depicted as a lion-headed man, was probably built after the middle of the second century BC. A wooden sundial was found in the ruins of this Lion Temple. At 9.8 × 7.6 cm in size, it was designed to fit into the palm of a hand. The upper part of the object is decorative, and represents the pylon gateway entrance of a temple – an architectural feature the Meroitic people took from their Egyptian neighbours.

The lower part of the object reveals its function: a semicircular surface with lines radiating from a small central hole. A small rod (now lost) would have been placed in the hole, and the position of the shadow cast in relation to the radiating lines used to calculate the time. In order to work correctly, the sundial would have to be held flat and pointed due north – not particularly convenient restrictions for a *portable* time piece!

The material excavated by Garstang at Meroë has been distributed widely. Much of it stayed in Sudan, at Meroë itself or in Khartoum at the Sudan National Museum, although a portion of the finds was brought to the UK. The largest individual collection of this material is housed at the University of Liverpool's Garstang Museum, but many other objects were distributed to museums across the UK and beyond. In 2024 a project called 'Reconstructing the ancient past: digital access and visibility of the Garstang distributed collection' was launched by the Garstang Museum and Liverpool's World Museum to locate material from John Garstang's early twentieth-century excavations. This will establish a network of partner museums and expertise starting in the north-west of England, with the intention of going global.

Funded by the Arts and Humanities Research Council, the project is part of a nationwide Research Infrastructure for Conservation and Heritage Science (RICHeS) programme to safeguard heritage for future generations. The project will collate objects now scattered worldwide with archival records and photographs held in the University. Garstang's use of photography as an archaeological method placed him at the forefront of heritage science in his day, and the artefacts and photographs from some of his excavations provide the only record of communities and landscapes that have since been destroyed. Researchers will be able to investigate lost places and cultures, and even objects destroyed in the events of the Second World War when an incendiary device dropped on Liverpool's World Museum. This is particularly pertinent for regions with ongoing political instability such as Sudan, with news reports of looting at major museums including the Sudan National Museum.

Ashley Cooke and Gina Criscenzo-Laycock

Overleaf Photographs of stone tablet from the same excavation. The sundial was found alongside a stone tablet depicting Apedemak on one side and King Tañyidamani on the other, giving a likely date for the earliest phase of the Lion Temple.

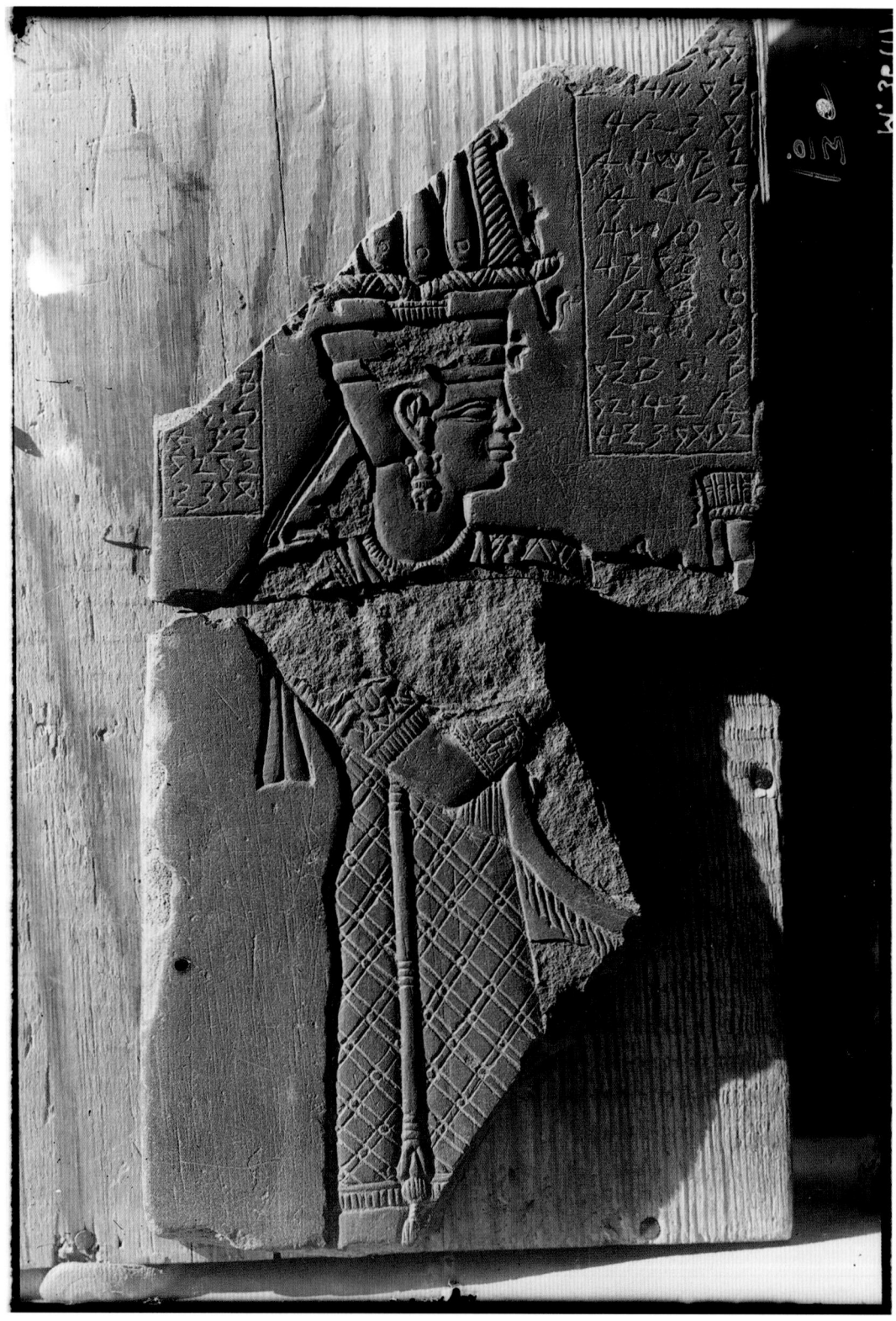

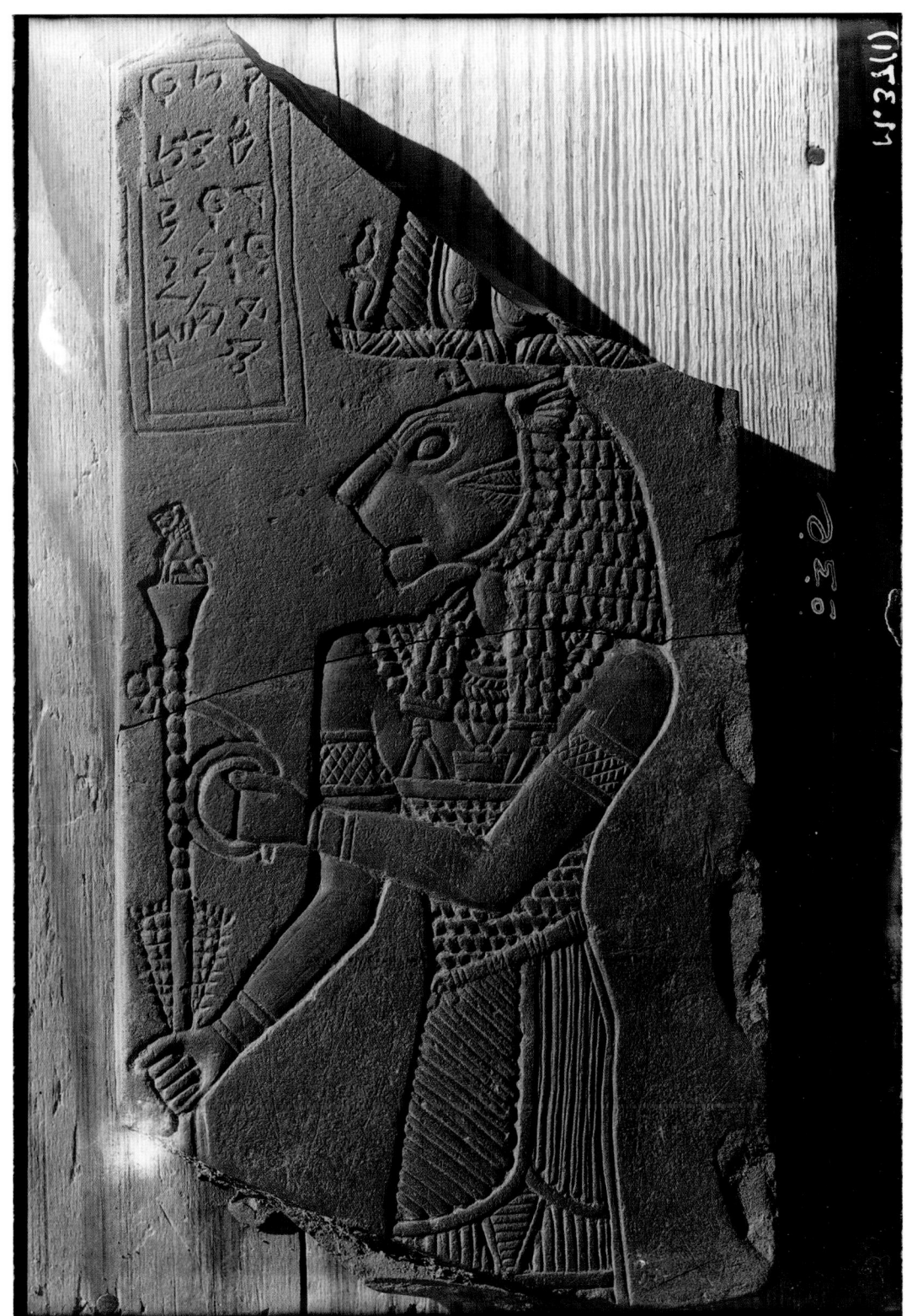

PORTABLE PRAYERS (1930s)

17

Qur'ān. Selections (Arabic and Turkish). Undated. Mid-nineteenth century? Sūras 1, 2, 36, 67, 78, 94–98, 100–14 and other passages; with prayers (du'a') in Arabic and Turkish, containing occasional passages from the Qur'ān, names of the Prophet and of God (al-asma al-husna), and magical formulae in Turkish. 136 folios; bound in brown leather with gold and silver tooling, in a braided brown cloth case. 13 × 9 cm.

Presented by Richard T. Golding.

Through its inclusion of Qur'anic passages and *du'a* (prayers) in both Arabic and Turkish, this manuscript highlights the linguistic and cultural blending that was a hallmark of the Ottoman era. Arabic, as the sacred language of the Qur'an and Islamic scholarship, held deep religious significance, while Turkish served as the administrative and everyday language of the Empire. By presenting these sacred verses and supplications in both languages, the manuscript reflects an Ottoman tradition of intertwining spiritual reverence with local linguistic accessibility. The manuscript's modest size and leather binding make it portable, suitable for both personal devotion and communal rituals. Its ornate gold and silver tooling, complemented by a separate leather case and finely woven cloth bag, underscores the reverence in which the text was held and the care taken in its preservation. This craftsmanship reflects a culture that esteems sacred texts as both spiritual and material treasures, viewing their beauty as an embodiment of divine harmony.

In addition to *du'a* (prayers), the text includes names of the Prophet and the *al-asma al-husna*, or 'most beautiful names', representing the 99 attributes of Allah, each embodying a divine quality, such as *Al-Rahman* ('The Most Merciful') and *Al-Hakim* ('The All-Wise'). A *sura* (Arabic: سُورَة, romanised: *sūra*; plural: سُوَر, romanised: *suwar*) is a chapter of the Qur'an, each containing verses addressing themes of faith and divine wisdom. The specific *suwar* featured in this manuscript were probably chosen for their association with sacred counsel, mercy, and protection: *Al-Fatiha* (*Sura* 1), known as 'The Opening', is a prayer seeking guidance and compassion, integral to both daily and personal devotions; *Al-Baqarah* (*Sura* 2) provides important theological guidance and ethical principles, including *Ayat al-Kursi* (Verse of the Throne,

2:255), frequently recited for protection; *Ya-Sin* (*Sura* 36), known as the 'Heart of the Qur'an', is traditionally recited for blessings and protection, especially during hardship or in remembrance of the deceased; *Al-Mulk* (*Sura* 67) emphasises Allah's sovereignty and the purpose of life, with themes of accountability that inspire personal reflection; shorter *suwar* (78–114) are commonly recited for their brevity and focus on themes of divine unity, guidance, and protection; *Sura* 112 (*Al-Ikhlas*) asserts Allah's oneness, while *Suwar* 113 and 114 (*Al-Falaq* and *An-Naas*), known as the 'chapters of refuge', are recited for protection from harm.

Donated to the University of Liverpool by Richard T. Golding, a notable figure in Liverpool's early twentieth-century musical community, the manuscript reflects both the University's academic interest in Islamic cultures and the city's deep-rooted connection to Islamic heritage. From the eighteenth to the twentieth centuries, maritime connections facilitated cultural and economic exchanges, with early Muslim sailors and traders establishing vibrant communities. Indeed, Liverpool's history as a port city has seen continuous influence from Muslim cultures, with communities from Türkiye, Yemen, Somalia, South Asia, North and West Africa, and across the Islamic world settling and contributing to the city's multicultural fabric.

Today, Liverpool is home to one of the UK's oldest mosques, the Abdullah Quilliam Mosque, established in the nineteenth century, which highlights the city's enduring Islamic heritage. These historical connections have made Liverpool a vibrant centre of cultural exchange, a legacy reflected in the University of Liverpool's teaching and research on Arab and Ottoman histories, cultures, and the Arabic language. This includes the Arabic strand of the MA in Translation offered by

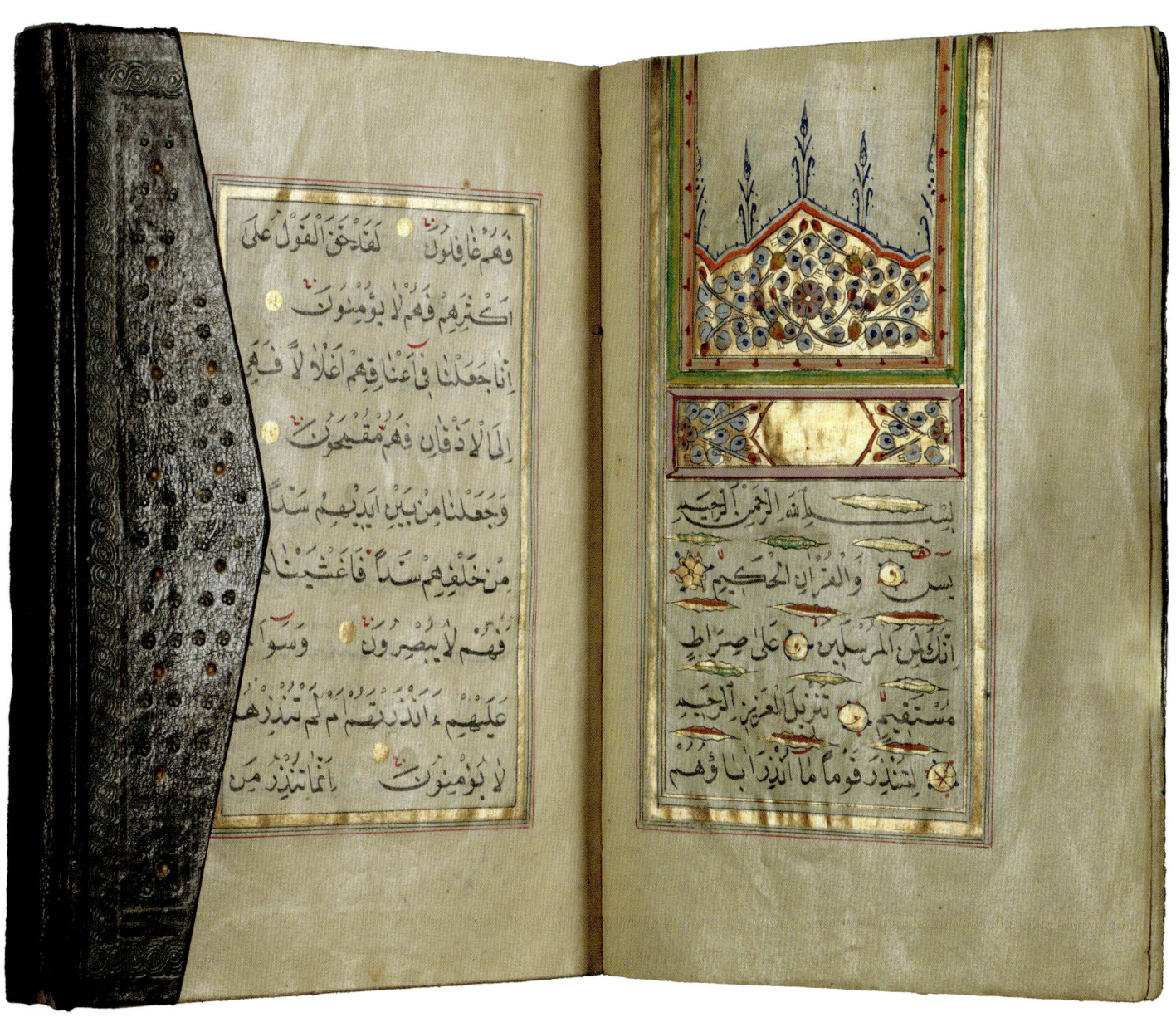

the Department of Languages, Cultures & Film, which prepares students to navigate the linguistic and cultural intricacies required for effective and culturally sensitive translation between Arabic and English. The University's commitment to this legacy is further demonstrated by its thriving Turkish, Arab, and Islamic Societies at the Liverpool Guild of Students, its active collaboration with the Liverpool Arab Arts Festival, and its dedication to preserving historic Islamic texts, both within its own collections and in partnership with National Museums Liverpool.

Şizen Yiacoup

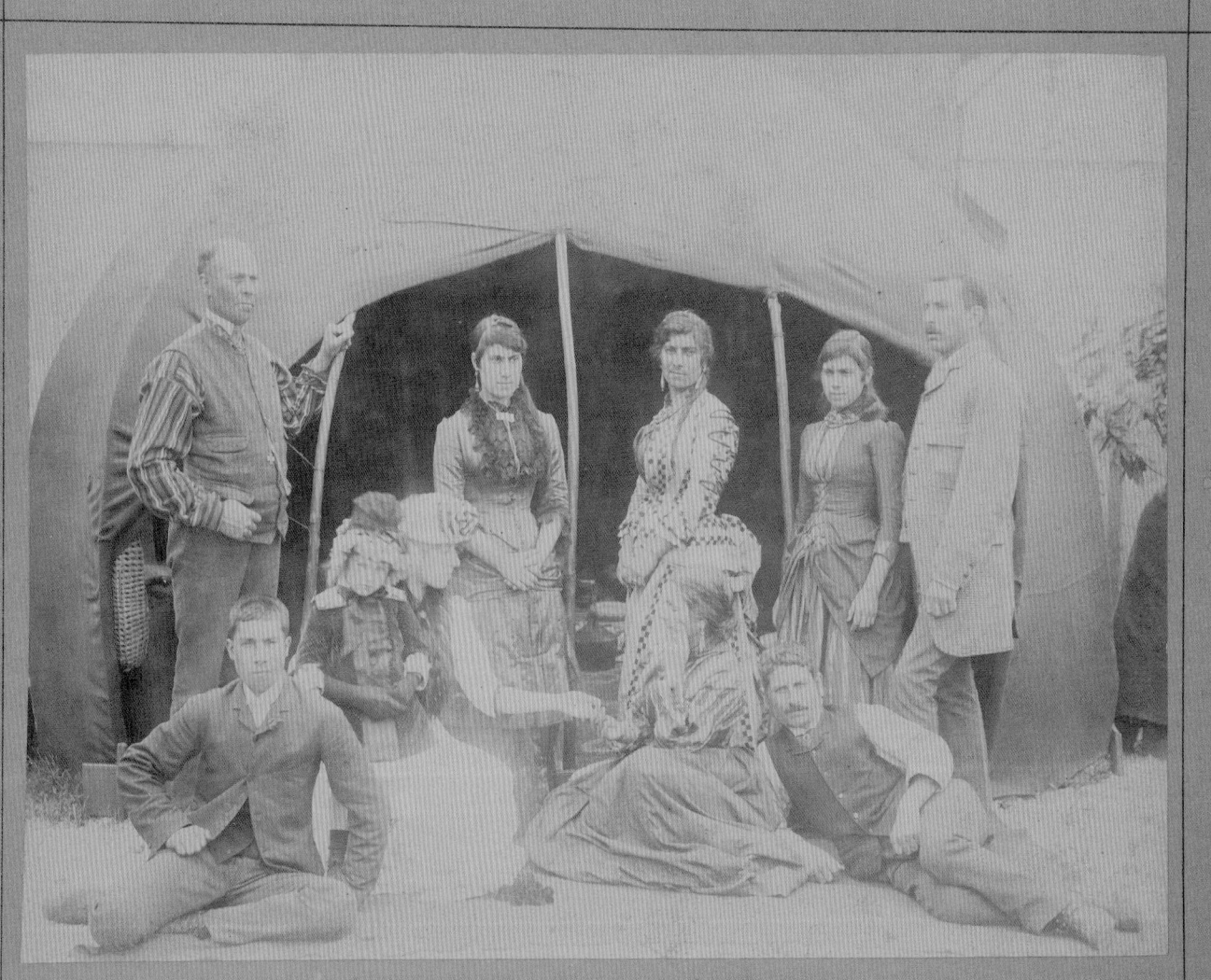

Margaret Smith Alice Smith 63, St Paul's Churchyard, London, E.C.

George Smith. Corinda Smith Cecilia Smith.

International Exhibition, Liverpool, 1886.

Ernest Smith. Nathan Lee. Wallace Boswell

International Exhibition, Liverpool, 1886 (Lazzy Smith and family) (1930s)

18

Photograph by London & County Photo Co., London. Reproduced in the *Journal of the Gypsy Lore Society* (3rd series, 16 [1937]). 24 × 27.5 cm.

Probably donated by Dora Yates as part of the Gypsy Lore Society archive and library, 1935. The University of Liverpool Special Collections and Archives houses one of the world's most important archives relating to Gypsies.

As a Romanichal youth I had known of the work of the Gypsy Lore Society (GLS) and had met many of its members, including Dora Yates (1879–1974), Walter Starkie (1894–1976), Richard Wade, Ferdinand Huth (1889–1984), and others. After graduating from Liverpool University, as the first Romani man to be awarded a degree from a British university, I emigrated to Australia. I completed master's and doctoral degrees, and was fortunate enough to be granted periods of study leave from the University of Newcastle, Australia, in 1998 and 2002 to work on the Scott MacFie Gypsy collections. After retiring, I continued to visit the Special Collections and Archives.

Spanning 136 years from 1888 to the present, the Scott MacFie Gypsy collection (named after Robert Andrew Scott MacFie, 1868–1935) comprises a wide range of materials. Although he ran a successful sugar-refining business in Liverpool, MacFie's real passion was administering the GLS and editing its journal. From 1907 to 1914 he was the secretary–treasurer of the GLS and chief editor of its journal, assisted by Dora Yates. MacFie stated: 'My ambition is to have in the G.L.S. one authority on every necessary subject, and to promote collaboration. Then I wouldn't need to know anything,

and all my duty would be to send postcards 'Consult Mr. —.'

During the years of MacFie's management, his recording of the GLS archive materials was an exemplar of meticulous record keeping. Every incoming letter was pasted in chronological order in an Incoming letterbook; each letterbook had a call number; and each page was numbered. The Incoming letterbooks had each letter individually numbered in pencil; sometimes there are multiple letters and/or postcards on one letterbook page; sometimes there are multiple pages of the same letter on the same letterbook page.

Every reply was copied on a Watt machine, a portable copying machine that was among the first widely used devices to successfully produce an exact copy of an original written work, and pasted in chronological order in an Outgoing letterbook. These had a separate letterbook page number for each page of letter and, at the front, an alphabetical list by recipient and by page.

More than 10,000 letters were arranged in the 24 volumes of Incoming letterbooks and nearly 8,000 letters in the ten volumes of Outgoing letterbooks. Macfie's arrangement of correspondence means that analysing material spanning years, and even decades, becomes possible.

MacFie also subscribed to a newspaper clipping service and maintained both a bound collection of newspaper articles about Gypsies and additional volumes of pictorial material.

These archives were written *about* Romani people, often from racialised and Romantic view points, but rarely *by* them. When this did occur, it showed how Romani people could generate counter-narratives that challenged the claims of the Gypsilorists. Examples in the Scott Macfie collections include Esmeralda Lock (1854–1939), a literate Romani woman who left a small but important trail of correspondence spanning 62 years, and the innovative Romani entrepreneur George 'Lazzy' Smith (1830–?1914), who toured extensively through the British Isles from the 1860s to the 1890s, presenting Gypsy Balls. He and his entourage even appeared at the 1886 Liverpool International Exhibition of Navigation, Travel, Commerce and Manufacture. He was also active in promoting the welfare of Romani people, and in fact directly challenged members of the GLS for their lack of sympathy for actual Romani people.

After the First World War MacFie ceased active work with the GLS, and following his departure, the quality of the record keeping was never the same. Nevertheless, the GLS continued to collect and retain material from the 1920s up to the present: an enormous store of information about Romani people, albeit of variable quality and fragmented time span.

Ken Lee

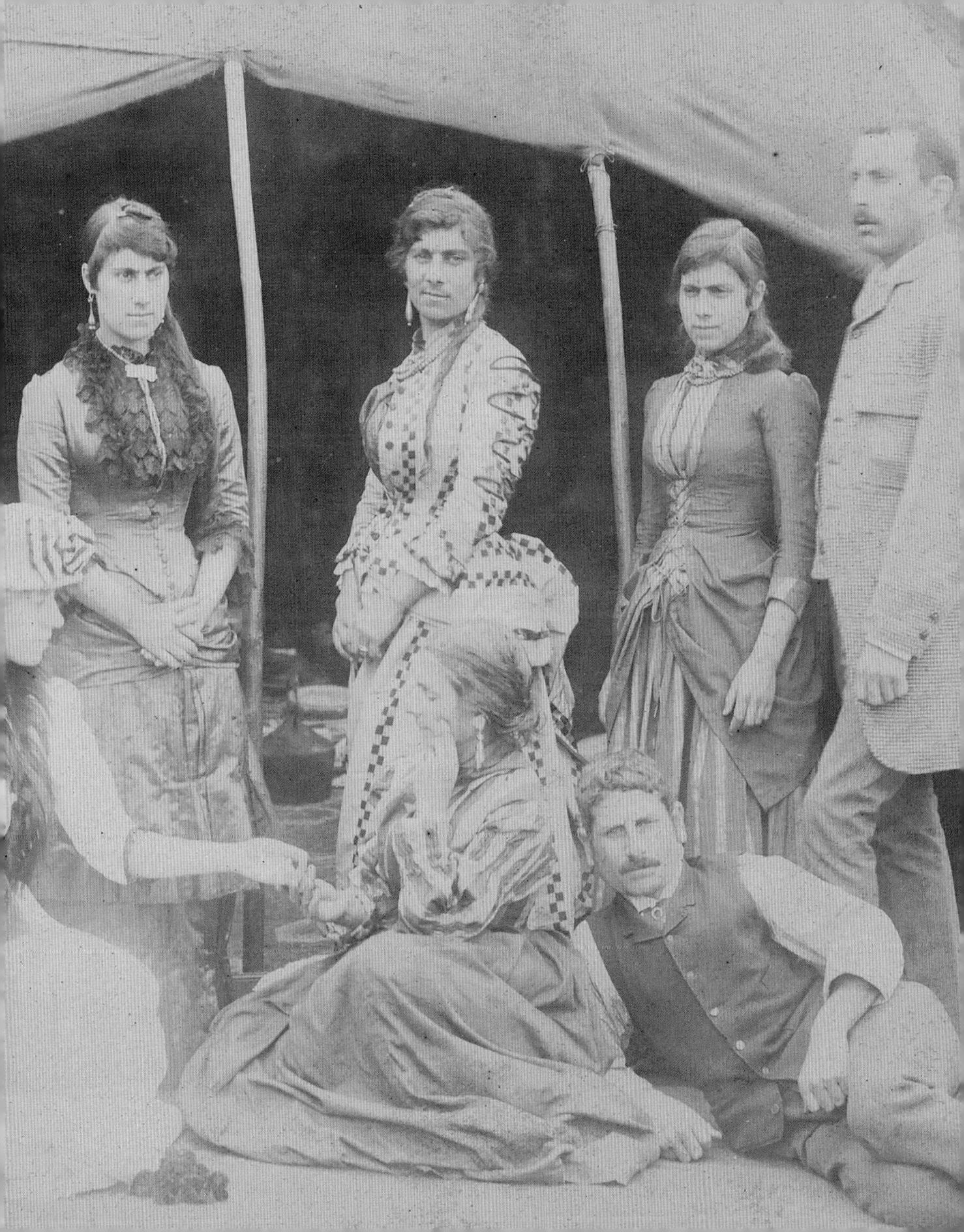

Improving Preston teeth (1930s)

19

Mould guide of the complete range of gum sections and teeth made by the Wilmington Dental Manufacturing Company, 1894. Porcelain in leather concertina folding case. 226 × 24.1 cm, folded to 37.5 × 24.4 cm.

Given to Mr Miller, dental surgeon, by the manufacturers; Mr Miller died in 1933, and the shade guide was subsequently donated to the museum by his son, 1930s.

In the late eighteenth and early nineteenth centuries dental health in the British Isles deteriorated markedly with the widespread availability of imported sugar. Early false teeth were the preserve of the wealthy and consisted of extracted human teeth (often teeth extracted from casualties of the Battle of Waterloo, the Crimean War, and the American Civil War) riveted onto a base of crudely carved 'ivory' of sea-lion or hippopotamus origin. These 'Waterloo teeth', as well as fitting poorly, were organic in origin and so would decay (like the teeth they replaced), and soon become both malodorous and unsightly. The development of porcelain false teeth in the late nineteenth century, which could not decay, concurrent with the widespread availability of relatively cheap and well-fitting Vulcanite bases (natural rubber, hardened by a process involving heat, pressure, and sulphur, to which the porcelain teeth were attached by small rivets) allowed much wider access to false teeth.

After the development of well-fitting and functional dentures and the removal of the threat of dental pain, the emphasis increasingly fell on the use of dentures to restore, or impart, a pleasing appearance. Accordingly, a demand arose for dentures that matched the patient's facial anatomy (and wishes). The guide pictured shows a large variety of shades and moulds (shapes) of porcelain teeth from which the dentist could select (even to mimic the appearance of 'Waterloo teeth').

This guide, produced by the Wilmington Dental Manufacturing Company of Delaware in 1894, captures a pivotal moment in the industrialisation of porcelain false teeth manufacture, demonstrating a response to a demand that extended well beyond the UK. It allows for the selection of porcelain teeth in 95 different shades and several hundred possible configurations of teeth and gums, for complete or partial dentures, with an immense number of resultant combinations. The guide was presented by the company to Mr Miller, a dentist from Preston, when he visited their stand at the great Chicago Exhibition because of the extremely high number of porcelain teeth he ordered from the company to meet his clientele's needs. This clearly illustrates the demand in just one town in the industrialised north of England.

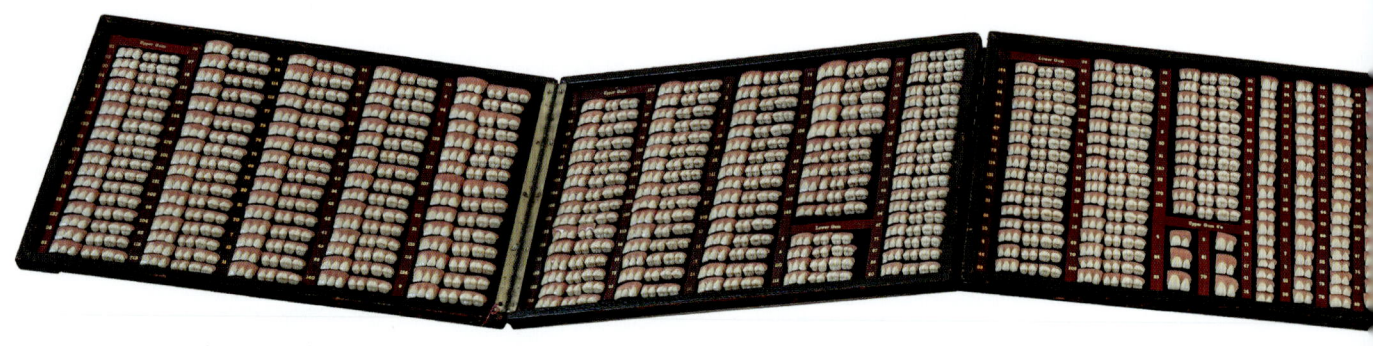

As well as being an alternative to having visible dental disease, or its consequences, dentures thus became a socially desirable commodity. Taking advantage of the early development of general anaesthesia, people could effectively insure themselves against the future expense of dental bills by having their all their teeth extracted (irrespective of their condition) under anaesthetic and replaced with complete dentures. In large parts of industrialised Britain this procedure was commonly given as a 21st birthday present, while brides-to-be would also have this carried out partly to improve appearance but, in the absence of a dowry, also to make them less of a future financial burden to the household. These practices extended well into the mid–late twentieth century in parts of the UK. Porcelain teeth and Vulcanite bases remained the clinical benchmark until the post-Second World War development of plastic (acrylic) teeth that could be bonded chemically to even better-fitting acrylic dentures. With the formation of the National Health Service in 1948, very simplified forms of this kind of guide illustrated here continued to be used extensively as a new generation of patients sought dental treatment.

In the latter half of the twentieth century in the UK, as generations had grown up with fluoride toothpastes, increased oral health awareness, and a wish to retain and restore their own natural teeth, the use of this form of guide became confined mainly to a small number of (usually elderly) patients. However, in the early twenty-first century a number of social and economic conditions have arisen that have resulted in many teeth now being extracted across all age groups. In Liverpool, where the Dental Hospital was founded in 1860 and Dental School in 1876, there is a long track record of graduates providing high-quality care to their patients. This care will continue in the future, with continuing use of a shade and mould guide when required, to help restore a patient's function, aesthetics, and self-esteem.

Callum Youngson

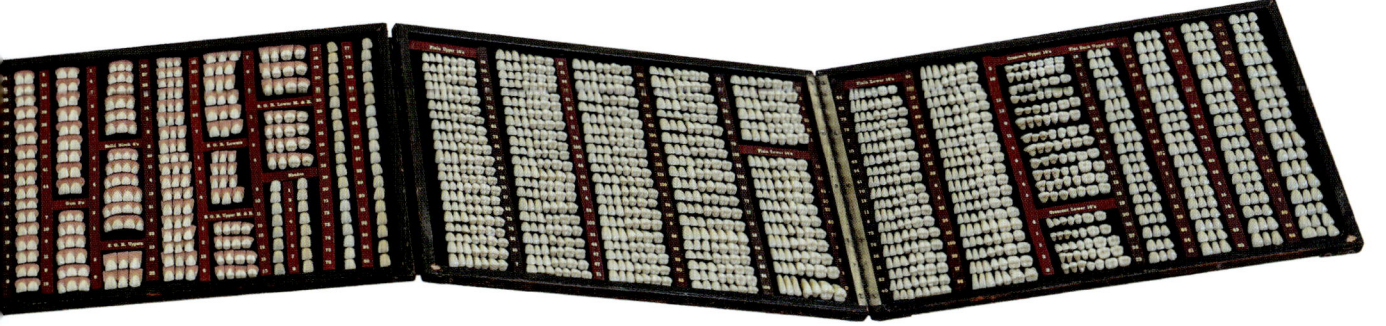

How to live well (1940s)

20

Manuscript of *Piers Plowman* by William Langland, fifteenth century; on parchment with decorated initials; iii + 103 + iv leaves. 26 × 20 cm.

Donated by Clara Hornby, 1944.

The work now commonly referred to as *Piers Plowman* is a work of social, religious, and political comment, a complex satire that takes as its theme the need for each person to live well and do not just well but better and best, in the hope of achieving a properly functioning society. These themes, the palpable urgency with which the presumed author, William Langland, writes, and the series of dream-visions and interlaced allegory he chose for the poem's structure have combined to make this one of the most significant and respected works in the English language, if not always the most easily understood.

Piers seems to have begun its existence sometime in the mid-1360s in a short draft version of about 2,500 lines, and was still being revised up to the late 1380s (when we presume the author died), by which time the poem extended to over 9,000 lines. It exists in three distinct versions: the A-, B-, and C-texts, plus that early draft (the Z-text), and it appears that Langland was responding to the way the poem was being received in his revisions, including the way Piers the ploughman, the poem's central figure, was adopted as a rallying call for the Peasants' Revolt (1381). Later versions sought to dampen such revolutionary connections, but the preoccupation with how to live well in personal and political terms remained and continues to resonate today.

Liverpool's manuscript of *Piers Plowman* is fairly plain, but its clear layout, neat handwriting, alternating red and blue coloured capitals indicating verse paragraphs, and added gold tracery marking the start of the sections (passus) into which this famously long work is divided make it visually appealing. This particular manuscript was copied during the early 1400s; it is an A-Text followed by a C-text, which picks up where A finishes. Such combinations are not uncommon and indicate a desire to represent the whole poem, where 'whole' means all the poem that is available, not just the finished but shorter version, which is what the A-text seems to be. Over 53 manuscripts of the poem exist, of which no two are identical; this creates 'the most tangled textual history of any great Middle English poem' (Eyler and Benson 2005) and our manuscript is part of that. For example, in all other copies the second line of the poem contains the word 'shroudes' (garments, shrouds), but in LUL MS.F.4.8 we find 'shregges' (shreds). Why, we don't know, but the change opens up intriguing possibilities from simple scribal error to deliberate substitution. The poetic and conceptual fluidity for which the poem is famed is thus represented early on in this copy, while the esteem in which it was held is manifested in its handsome eighteenth-century binding.

In 1944 this copy was offered for sale by Bernard Quaritch Ltd, who cannily sent it for inspection to J.H.G. Grattan of Liverpool University, an authority on *Piers Plowman*. Since the bookplate of Sir William Horton, Baronet of Chaderton, was pasted on the inside cover, Grattan referred to it as the Chaderton manuscript, Ch for short. His pleasure in the 'delightful coincidence' that this abbreviation also fitted the initials of the donor of the manuscript to the University is recorded in the first footnote in his article on the manuscript (Grattan 1947). That donor was Mrs Clara Hornby. She recognised that, as an aspiring university, Liverpool rightly desired a copy of this significant English poem, and so provided the first English medieval manuscript of the collection, which was, in the words of the Senate of the day, 'The most valuable single book the Library has ever received … extend[ing] by nearly two centuries our means of illustrating the history of English literature by contemporary books'.

This unassuming manuscript thus embodies many things: the often-forgotten work of women donors; the desire for wholeness innate to humans and institutions alike; and the continuing importance of a poem from the late 1300s, which is as full of variation as the kinds of appeal it exerts.

Jill Rudd

In a somer seson whan softe was the sonne
I shope me into schroudes as I a schepe were
In abite of an ermite vnholy of werkes
Went wide in þis worlde wonders to here
Ac on a may mornyng vppon maluarie hilles
me befelle a ferly of feirey me þouзt
I was wery of wandred and went me to reste
vnder a brode banke by a bourne syde
As I lay and lened and loked on þe water
I slomerd in to a slepyng it swede so mery
And þenne gan I mete a merueilouse sweuen
þat I was in wildernesse wist I neuer were
bot as I behelde in to the west an hie to the sonne
I saw a toure on a toft trieliche ymaked
A depe dale be neþe a dongeoun þer Inne
With depe diþes and derke and dredful of siзt
A faire feld ful of folke fande I þer bitwene
Of alle maner of men þe mene and þe riþe
Werchyng and wandryng as þe werld askey
Summ putt hem to the plow pleied ful selde
In settyng and sowyng swonke ful harde
Whom þat þes wastours with glotonye distroie
And summ putt hem to pruide apparailed hem þerafter
In comtenance of cloþyng comen disgised
In preiers and penance putt hem many
Alle for loue of owre lord lened ful streite
In hope to haue after heuen riþe blisse
As ankers and ermites þat holden hem in her celles
comen nouзt in contre to karien aboute
ffor no likerouse liflode her licam to plese
And summ chosen to chaffare þei cheuen þe better
As hit semeth to owre siзt þat suche men þriuen
And summ murþes to make as mynstralles conne
And gete gold with here gle giltles I trowe
Bot iapers and iangelers iudas childrin

THE FROTH AND VENOM OF PERSECUTION (1940s)

21

Poems, by Edward Rushton, 1806. Printed work bound in one volume with *The West Indies, and other poems*, 1810, by James Montgomery (1771–1854), in binding of leather over marbled paper boards. 160 pages. 16 × 11 cm.

Donated by the Rathbone family, accessioned 13 December 1945.

Among the books donated by the Rathbone family is *Poems, by Edward Rushton*, a small, plain volume, printed in London in 1806. The library has another copy, but this one tells some special stories. On the flyleaf there is a stirring, hand-written dedication:

> To Mr Willm Rathbone –
> – the Friend of Liberty, and of Man,
> who when the path of rectitude
> lay thro the froth and venom
> of Persecution
> turned not aside.
> This little Volume is presented
> By the Author
> with his best wishes and respects.

The 'Author' was Edward Rushton (1756–1814), a Liverpool-born sailor from the age of eleven, who had as a teenager signed up for one of the slaving voyages then generating much of the port's prosperity. Having contracted an eye infection while attempting to assist captives confined to the hold, he went blind. Back in Liverpool he managed a pub, edited a newspaper, and ran a radical bookshop. He also began writing poems supporting radical movements in America, Ireland, and France. He was among the Liverpool writers (William Roscoe, 1753–1831; James Currie, 1756–1805; Peter Newby, 1745–1827) fervently promoting the abolitionist cause, and the only one to have witnessed slaving voyages directly. Records identifying the ships he sailed on, and their Liverpool owners, have recently been located by researchers. Through 'the Roscoe circle', radicals from various professions, he knew William Rathbone IV (1757–1809), locally prominent for attempting to run a shipping business without trading in slaves: hence the dedication.

The book contained 45 poems, some previously printed by John McCreery (1768–1832), the Irish-born printer who produced the 1806 volume. 'Will Clewline', a ballad against the Press Gang, appeared in a high-quality illustrated broadsheet in 1801. Rushton could write sentimental marine ballads, but favoured a political edge ('The Neglected Tar'). There are elegies for lower-class poets neglected by the establishment (e.g. Hugh Mulligan, another abolitionist writer). Rushton's *West-Indian Eclogues* (1787), impassioned dialogues highlighting the experiences of enslaved Africans, were perhaps too shocking to republish when legislation to abolish the slave trade was proceeding through parliament, and were omitted. Instead, Rushton provided 'Briton and Negro Slave', dramatising the brutally oppressive nature of plantation life, and a rousing speech in the voice of Toussaint L'Ouverture (–1803), leader of the Haitian rebellion, by then dead in a French gaol.

'To a Redbreast' contrasted birdsong with the sounds of Liverpool as heard by a blind man. However, across the years 1805–07 Benjamin Gibson (1774–1812), a Manchester eye surgeon, undertook several operations on Rushton; while one eye was irremediably damaged (hence the eyepatch in the portrait held by the Royal Liverpool School for the Blind, which he helped to found in 1791), Gibson was able to restore enough sight in the other for Rushton to walk independently through a town he had experienced only aurally for 30 years, to read unaided, and to see his wife and children for the first time.

Once opened, the volume thus offers students and researchers a focal point between several histories, and our understanding of the transatlantic slave trade and its abolition, of Liverpool activism, and of the emergence of working-class and disabled writers is visibly the richer for this unshowy 'little Volume'.

Paul Baines

To Mr Willm Rathbone —

the Friend of Liberty, and of Man,

who when the path of rectitude

lay thro the froth and venom

of Persecution

turned not aside.

This little Volume is presented

By the Author —

with his best wishes and respects

———

SAFELY OVER BORDER

Member Of Party From Liverpool

OTHERS LIKELY TO HAVE LEFT SPAIN

Word was received by Professor E. Allison Peers late last night to the effect that the relatives of a member of the Liverpool University party of students who went to San Sebastian a week ago had received a cablegram from the French border.

The communication was from Miss Greig, who resides at Kirkcaldy, and simply stated "Safely over the border." She was one of those who went to attend the summer school of Spanish arranged by Professor Peers

LIVERPOOL BOYS' RETURN

EXPERIENCES IN SANTANDER

NEARLY EVERYBODY SEEMED TO BE ARMED'

The ten Liverpool boys from the Evered-avenue Selective School, Walton, who, in charge of Mr. J. MacDonald, the Spanish master of the school, were in camp on the coast near Santander at the outbreak of the revolution, arrived in Liverpool early this morning.

Much anxiety had been felt for their safety, as no news concerning them had been received until Tuesday, when a telegram from the civil governor of Santander was received by the Liverpool Director of Education (Mr. C. F. Mott) intimating that a party of schoolboys had been embarked on a British warship at Santander on the previous day. Mr. Mott immediately communicated with the Foreign Of the boys the School.

Motor Cars Commandeered

Mr. MacDonald narrated the experiences of the party to the *Daily Post* this morning. He said that the boys left Liverpool by the steamer Orduna on July 16 for a month's holiday in camp at Santander. "On the day of our arrival, Sunday, the 19th, revolution had broken out," he said, "and hardly had we settled in camp, four miles from Santander, when we were removed to what is known as the Old Pavilions, some little distance away, for safety. The town of Santander was soon in a state of pandemonium. Motor-cars had been commandeered, and, occupied by armed men, were dashing about in wild confusion.

"It was difficult to distinguish between the various factions—Popular Front, Fascists, Extreme Left and Right, Communists, and Republicans. Everybody seemed to be armed and ready to have a 'pop' at one another. The threatened danger from San Sebastian at length compelled the Consul to have us removed eight days after our arrival, and we were taken on board the warship Verity to Bilbao, together with 200 British refugees, many of whom had lost fortunes. Our party was conveyed to Bayonne, where arrangements were made for our transhipment to Dieppe and London.

"While in camp, the price of food rose to such an extent," said Mr. MacDonald, "that our month's expenses were more or less exhausted. The boys, however, have enjoyed themselves despite the inconvenience, and were particularly happy on the warship. They are all fit and well, and were thrilled by their experience."

The boys are:—Fred Buckley-Mellor, 89, Bowland-avenue; George Duncan, 79a, City-road; Kenneth Close, 25, Devonfield-road; Kenneth Clayton, 13 , of Huyton ngston-street ress is no 7, Clinton ning-street kfield-road Liverpool

Anxiety About Students

A party of forty Liverpool University students are also in Spain at the moment. They left London on Saturday to attend a summer school at San Sebastian. They arrived on Sunday, when a reassuring telegram was sent by the leader of the party to Professor Allison Peers, Professor of Spanish at Liverpool University. Since then, however, no word has been received, and in view of the heavy fighting in the San Sebastian area there is some anxiety as to their safety.

Among other Liverpool visitors to Spain is a schoolmistress, Miss Grace Coombs, who is on the staff of the Canterbury-street Elementary School, and who left Newhaven last Friday en route for San Sebastian. No word has been received from her since. Miss Coombs lives at 63, Upper Parliament-street.

Professor's Confidence

Professor Peers told the *Daily Post* that he now felt quite confident that all the members of the party were safe. "If it has been possible for Miss Greig to get across the border," he said, "I am sure that the road to France from San Sebastian, which is only twelve miles, is now in the hands of Government troops, and that being so the students should have all been able to get to safety together."

Professor Peers added that the relatives of another girl in the party had had a letter, posted on Tuesday, saying that the students had that day been given the choice of going over to France or staying on at San Sebastian. As it was then thought that the trouble had more or less finished they decided to stay on. The letter stated that they were being given every help by the officials at the British Consulate.

Sir H. Hetherington's Message

The Vice-Chancellor of Liverpool University (Sir Hector Hetherington) sent a telegram to the Foreign Office yesterday, asking for assistance on behalf of the party of students.

Though no reply had been received from the Foreign Office up to a late hour last night, the University authorities are satisfied that there is no cause for undue anxiety, especially in view of the arrival at San Sebastian of British destroyers.

Among the party are the following:—Miss C. Kolb, Central-road, Wrexham; Miss Amy Evans, Heatherbrow, Childwall-bank, Liverpool; Miss M. McLeroy, 14, Greasby-road, Wallasey; Mr. J. H. Mundy, 24, Ivernia-road, Walton (leader of the party); Miss Nora H. Bishop, 19, Park-road, West Kirby; and Miss Emily Louise Squire, 93, Avondale-

No News Of Students

No news has been received since Sunday from the forty Liverpool University students who went to San Sebastian, and in view of the heavy fighting in that area there is some anxiety as to their safety. Professor Allison Peers, Professor of Spanish at Liverpool University, has been in touch with the Spanish Consul, but the latter has heard nothing so far. Professor Peers has also communicated with the Foreign Office, and hopes to hear from them to-day.

Among the forty is Miss Grace Kolb, of Wrexham. Miss Kolb's uncle holds a post in the Liverpool Education Department

Mr. Henry McKenna, of 108, Kingsley-road, Prince's-avenue, an employee of Messrs. J. A. Kelly, Goree Piazzas, is awaiting news of his daughter, Miss Minnie McKenna, a dancing instructress, on holiday in Spain. An old girl of St. Malachy's School, Dingle, she has been visiting Paris and Spain with a Glasgow girl friend. Mr. McKenna received on Monday a letter she wrote from the Hotel Terramar Palace, Sitges. Since then nothing has been heard from her.

SUMMER SCHOOL OF SPANISH

Sir,—Now that our University students and other members of the University of Liverpool Summer School of Spanish are safely home again from San Sebastian, I should like to be permitted, in the name of the University and of the relatives of these members, to thank the *Daily Post* and *Echo* very cordially for its thoughtfulness in keeping us I

LIVERPOOL STUDENTS AND THE SPANISH CIVIL WAR (1940s)

22

Press cuttings relating to the Spanish Civil War collected by Edgar Allison Peers, 1936. Print column 5.8 cm × various lengths.

Donated in 1946 as part of the Peers collection of pamphlets, periodicals, and press cuttings relating to the Spanish Civil War.

Professor Edgar Allison Peers (1891–1952) bequeathed a substantial legacy in the form of the Edgar Allison Peers Collection, which contains around 300 books, pamphlets, and press cuttings mostly relating to Spain during the Civil War (1936–39) and its aftermath, lecture notes, and correspondence. The collection, particularly the press cuttings – some of which are annotated by Peer's own inscrutable handwriting – offer an invaluable insight into his much wider legacy as a catalyst for Hispanic Studies in the UK and as a stout defendant of the civic university.

A truly gifted researcher on the Spanish mystics and the medieval poet Ramon Llull (1232?–1316), Peers was appointed Lecturer in Spanish at the University of Liverpool in 1920 and Gilmour Professor of Spanish in 1922, while in 1923 he founded the *Bulletin of Hispanic Studies*. His research would produce dozens of books, but teaching was fundamental for him. As a lecturer he was very much aware of the need for close liaison between schools and universities, and every year he would embark on an exhaustive campaign to promote the subject in schools throughout the country; he would visit over a hundred schools each year, give lectures, and organise courses for teachers. His efforts over three decades bore fruit, and a large number of schools started offering Spanish. By the time of his death in 1952 he had consolidated the discipline as a university subject and nearly every major university in Britain had a department of Spanish or Hispanic studies.

The press cuttings in the Edgar Allison Peers Collection relating to the Spanish Civil War highlight his unflagging support for education and his commitment to teaching and the values of the civic university. Peers set up a Summer School of Spanish in the 1920s, with courses in Liverpool and Spain that aimed to enable those students who had not had the opportunity to learn Spanish in school to catch up with those who had, and offered sessions on Spanish grammar, syntax, and phonetics as well as literary and history classes, among others. When the Spanish Civil War erupted on 17 July 1936, 40 students from the University of Liverpool who had gone to San Sebastián for the Summer School were trapped in Spain. In the following days there would be news and reports in the *Liverpool Daily Post* and the *Liverpool Echo*, some of them written by Peers himself, keeping friends and relatives informed of the latest events and news regarding the students' whereabouts and the fighting in the Iberian Peninsula. The clippings stand now as a diary of key historical events seen through the lens of a university and a city concerned about their students and citizens. Throughout the ordeal, Peers was in touch with the Spanish Consul and the Foreign Office in an effort to get the students across the border as swiftly as possible. They managed to reach England safely, and on 26 July Peers offered to give free classes to the students who had had to return from the Summer School – and anyone else that had been prevented from learning Spanish in Spain due to the conflict – proving his unwavering commitment to teaching, to the community around Liverpool, and to the discipline more broadly. Peers continued to run the Summer School in the university throughout the Spanish Civil War and over the next decade he invited several exiled Spanish authors to the University of Liverpool to offer lectures to students.

The press cuttings are a true testament of his ethos, where a passion for teaching and civic allegiances came together to completely transform Hispanic Studies as a discipline in the UK.

Diana Cullell Teixidor

Liverpool in China in 1945 (1940s)

23

Album of paintings and calligraphy by 39 Chinese artists, in concertina-binding with fabric cover. No. 12 inscribed and signed by Feng Zikai, July 1945, with his seal. 42 × 39 cm.

Presented to Professor Percy Maude Roxby (1880–1947) and Mrs Roxby by Mr Gou Youshuo on 10 November 1945; given to the University in their memory in 1947.

This precious album comprises 39 paintings and pieces of calligraphy. The catalogue of the album demonstrates that all 39 contributors were significant contemporary Chinese painters and calligraphers. Some, such as Zhang Daqian (1899–1963), Wu Zuoren (1908–97), Feng Zikai (1898–1975), Zhao Shaoang (1905–98), and Guan Shanyue (1912–2000), are considered to be among the finest artists of the modern era. More than half of the same list of artists occur in a very similar 'sister' album presented to Joseph and Dorothy Needham, now in the collections of the East Asian History of Science Library of the Needham Research Institute, Cambridge. The Cambridge album was commissioned for Drs Joseph and Dorothy Needham in late 1945 by Guo Youshou, Department of Education Chief for Sichuan Provincial Government, and prepared by the artist Xie Wuliang. The introduction at the beginning of the Liverpool album was also written by Guo Youshou in 1945 and dedicated to Professor and Mrs Roxby, 'the virtuous couple'. Percy Roxby (1880–1947), Professor of Geography, had come to Chongqing in 1945 as British Council Representative.

Guo Youshou had family ties to the Chengdu art world at the time. This was a unique period in Chinese history, when many of the best Chinese artists moved west to Sichuan Province to escape the Japanese invasion. They mainly gathered in Chengdu, which was famous for its teahouses. As well as containing works by famous artists, the album includes ones by some artists whose works are less well known in the Peoples' Republic of China because they emigrated to Taiwan in 1949. As such, it bears witness to a flourishing but brief and largely unexplored period in Chinese art history.

In 1960 Feng Zikai was appointed as the first president of the Shanghai Chinese Painting Academy. With his noble artistic character and great influence, he played an important role in the establishment of the academy. In the 1950s and 1960s, when Shanghai painting circles were full of famous artists, Feng Zikai was like a banner, uniting many famous Chinese painters around the academy.

With his unique calligraphy and painting style, Feng Zikai is mainly famous for his cartoons, but he believed that calligraphy was far more important. He once said:

> Calligraphy is the highest art. One of the main principles of art is to receive with the senses. The purest senses are the eyes and ears. Among the arts that appeal to the eyes, the purest is calligraphy, and among the arts that appeal to the ears, the purest is music. Therefore, calligraphy and music occupy the highest position in all arts.

His calligraphy, which originated from the Northern Wei Dynasty, is grand and generous, and its romantic temperament is revealed in the shape and composition of the characters. It also included *zhangcao* (regulated cursive script). His works are undoubtedly of great research value to both professionals and amateurs interested in calligraphy, painting, prose, music, and literature.

The Chinese script reads:

> Mr Tian, an old man was dead drunk and dancing,/
> Two children helped him to board the boat.
> To Professor Luo Shipei, the virtuous couple. Please appreciate and correct.
> July 1945/Painted by Zikai
> Chinese characters: Poet: 宋伯仁 Poem: 《村田乐》
> Characters for first line:《田翁烂醉身如舞》
> (Note: The first sentence is from the poem 'Village Joy' by the Song dynasty poet Song Boren).

Anna Chen and John Moffett

62

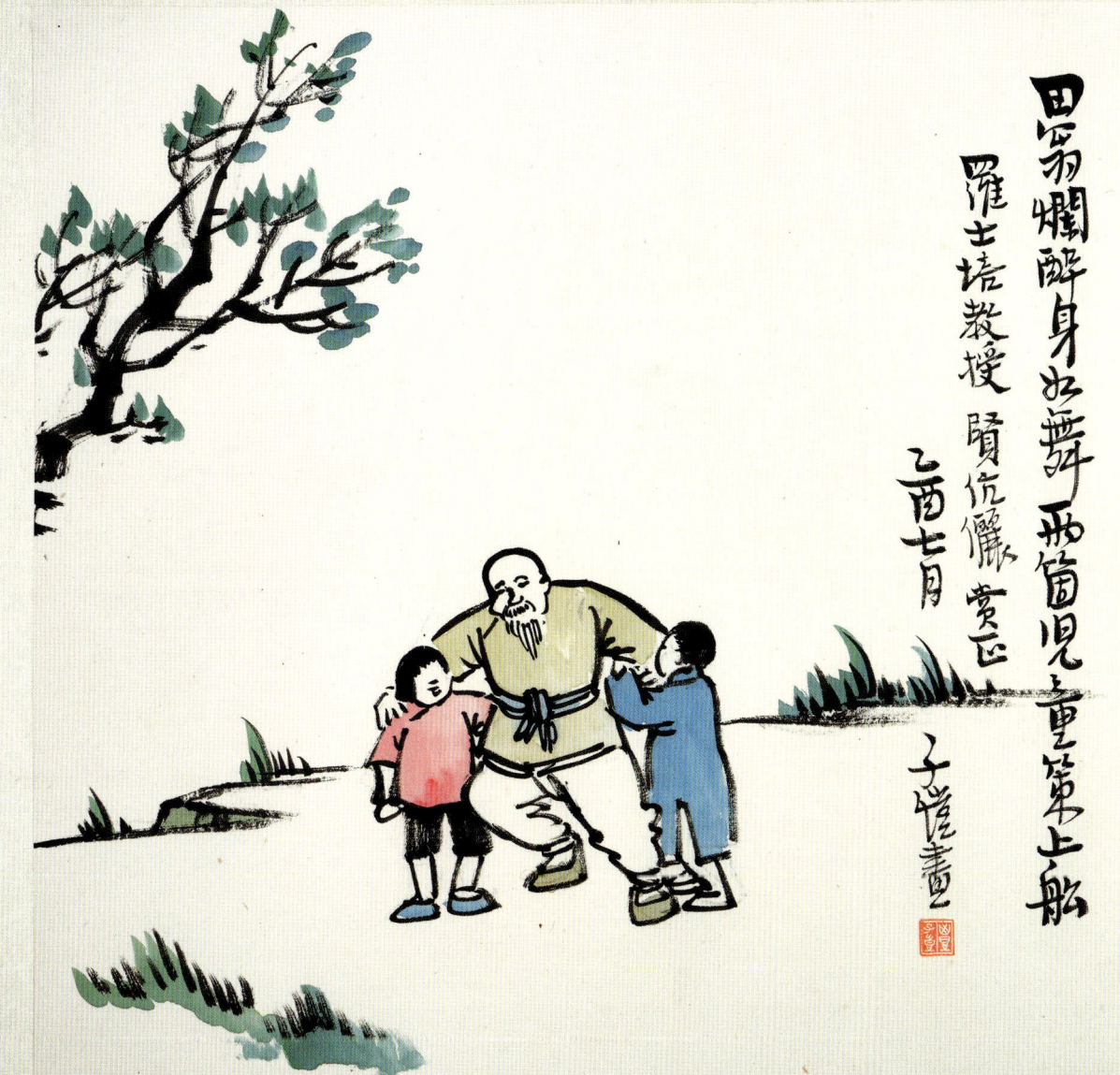

蜀翁爛醉身如舞
兩箇兒童策上船

羅士培教授
賢伉儷雅正
乙酉七月
子愷畫

CROSSING THE UNIVERSITY CAMPUS BY TRAIN (1940s)

24

'Railway Office' plate (coloured aquatint) from *Coloured views on the Liverpool and Manchester railway, with plates of the coaches, machines, &c., from drawings made on the spot by Mr. T.T. Bury. With descriptive particulars, serving as a guide to travellers on the railway* (London: R. Ackermann, 1831). 37 × 30 cm.

From the bequest of Sir Charles Sydney Jones, 1947.

In 1830 The Liverpool and Manchester Railway was opened as the first inter-city passenger and freight railway in the world. The railway allowed for goods to be transported between the port of Liverpool and factories in Manchester more quickly and efficiently. In Liverpool the steam locomotives terminated at Edge Hill, where the land flattened. To reach the city, the locomotives were removed and passenger trains were taken to Crown Street Station by ropes connected to steam engines and towed back using horses. The goods could reach the docks from Edge Hill through the Wapping Tunnel by freight trains.

It was soon realised that the Crown Street Station was located too far from the city centre to be practical, so in 1836 the Lime Street tunnel was bored under Liverpool to connect the railway to the city centre. Originally it was an enclosed twin track 1,811 m long, but in the 1880s it was decided to increase the capacity to four tracks. As more powerful steam locomotives were travelling all the way to Lime Street, the tunnel was also converted to a deep cutting to avoid steam build-up.

Coincidentally, at the same time the University acquired the site with some buildings near Ashton Street. This meant that the cutting would pass directly under what is now the University of Liverpool campus, with a major opening right in place of the University Square. As the university expanded, this made the conditions on campus insufferable. In 1929, in his letter to the LMS Railway Company, Hector Hetherington, Vice-Chancellor (1927–36) wrote: 'In some rooms, lectures have to be suspended while the trains thunder beneath: but that is tolerable. The dirt and sulphur, which are quite inevitable, are not tolerable if there is any possible means of escaping from them.' He asked that the possibility of covering parts of the cutting at any cost to eliminate the problem be considered.

However, the original proposal agreed on by the railway company was considered ineffective, as the smoke would simply come out in other places in larger quantities. Thirty years later, in 1960, this idea was revisited, as the smoke affected the appearance of the University buildings, while very high walls along the edge of the cutting broke the appearance of open areas and made the planning of a cohesive campus incredibly difficult. This time it was agreed that the University could fully cover the opening between Mount Pleasant and Bedford Street. The new plan meant the area was zoned out for University development and could be included in the redevelopment scheme. The University Square was planned by Blades & Partners as a paved pedestrian area with seating and vegetation to make it a part of the public realm accessible to both students and general public. A bus enclosure was also considered due to the development of the new Metropolitan Cathedral nearby. As the new area would be available to the general public, the Finance and General Purposes Committee agreed to contribute £5,000 to the University on behalf of the City Council towards the cost involved in covering the railway cutting.

An unexpected problem arose when the railway company demanded an annual rental of £500 for the newly enclosed area. The university deemed this unjustifiable, as the area would exist only after a £30,000 investment, while the rent of the nearby vacant land was much lower. It was proposed to keep rent at £50 per annum, but the company replied with an offer of £200 per annum. Due to the lack of further correspondence, it is unclear how this issue was resolved.

With steam-powered trains no longer used, it is now

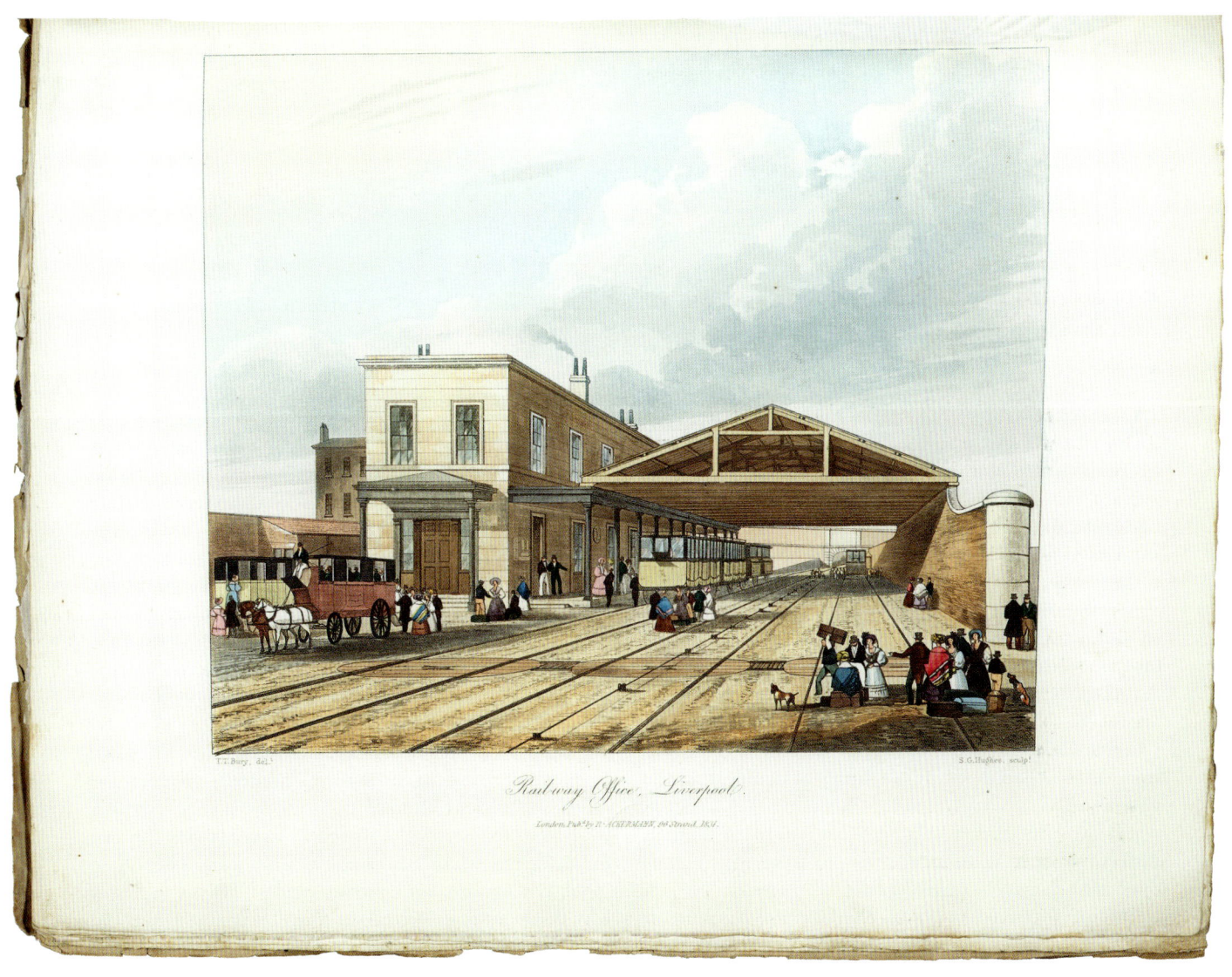

Railway Office, Liverpool.

hard to spot remaining railway cuttings on campus. You can still see them next to the Crown Place student accommodation and behind the Engineering Building and Brodie Tower in the North Campus. Although barely visible, the sound of passing trains gives the tunnel away.

The University cultural heritage collections hold many items that tell the story of the railway before and after its extension through campus. In addition to the Library's 1831 *Coloured Views* (bound with *Six Coloured Views*), with engravings by Henry Pyall (1795–1833) and S.G. Hughes from drawings by Thomas Talbot Bury (1809–77), there are separate prints by Bury in the Art Collections. The later railway cutting is shown in one of the watercolours by Allan Peel Tankard commissioned for a book celebrating the University's Golden Jubilee, which was reproduced as a University greetings card in the 1980s, a generation after the cutting and its smoke disappeared from view.

Ekaterina Mulyk

65

A SIXTEENTH-CENTURY MUSCLE MAN (1940s)

25

Twelfth muscle figure (book 2, page 244) and diagram of ligaments (book 2, page 255) in Andreas Vesalius, *De humani corporis fabrica libri septem* (Basle: Joannes Oporinus, August 1555). 884 pages with woodcut illustrations designed by Jan Stephan van Calcar. 41 × 28.5 cm.

Purchased for the University using funds provided by Mrs Stella Permewan in memory of William Muspratt Permewan, 1948. Previous owner's inscriptions include Olof Rudbeck (1660–1740), Uppsala professor of medicine.

Andreas Vesalius (1514–64) is routinely cited as the 'Father of Modern Anatomy'. Born in Brussels, he studied medicine in Paris and Louvain, where his passion for the structure and function of the human body prevailed. Following completion of his doctorate at the University of Padua, Vesalius was offered the chair of anatomy.

Vesalius championed the use of human cadavers to study anatomy, performing dissections for his students and, indeed, getting them to dissect for themselves. Although normalised now, at the time this was a novel approach that represented a radical break with the Church, which limited the study of anatomy to animals; thus Vesalius had to secure his supply of bodies from the gallows.

It was in Padua, through his study of human dissections, that Vesalius was able to write his magnus opus *De humani corporis fabrica libri septem*, which translates as 'Seven books on the fabric of the human body'. This magnificent work was a revelation when it was first published in 1543, as it fundamentally transformed how human anatomy was understood. The 1555 edition contains Vesalius' final revisions to the text and more than 200 woodcut illustrations. The most famous of these are the epic depictions of the musculo-skeletal system, which use full-length, posed subjects to accurately display the anatomy in a spectacular artistic style. The large illustration here shows a figure from which the skin, fat, and superficial muscles have been removed to demonstrate the deeper musculature in detail. Although Vesalius's *Fabrica* is well known for these

full-page woodcuts, they form only a small section in a book that represents the first ever detailed, exhaustive, illuminating, and, frankly, anatomically correct text that had ever been written. Vesalius was also keen to ensure the readers understood the descriptions by linking the text directly to the numerous diagrams, such as the smaller illustration shown. It is a demonstration of the working of the retinaculum around the ankle: a small band that ensures tendons do not bow when the muscle contracts. Such a demonstration is not far from what we do in classrooms today to encourage students to appreciate the 'living' functional anatomy.

Prior to the publication of this book, little work had been carried out in Europe on anatomy. Anatomists relied on ancient Roman texts, such as those written by Galen, for nearly 1,400 years. Vesalius was the one to challenge what was 'known' and was unafraid to speak out against his contemporaries. This is precisely why the work is so special, and why it is important that we hold and celebrate such a text. It is a testament to scientific thought, the fearlessness of questioning others' work, the subsequent considered investigation, and the clear dissemination of results. It is exactly these attitudes that we attempt to instil in our students, anatomists, and clinicians as they graduate from our degrees and become members of the wider scientific community. It is our hope that our alumni find inspiration in scientists such as Vesalius, and in *De humani corporis fabrica*, as they push scientific boundaries and make world-changing discoveries.

Alistair Bond

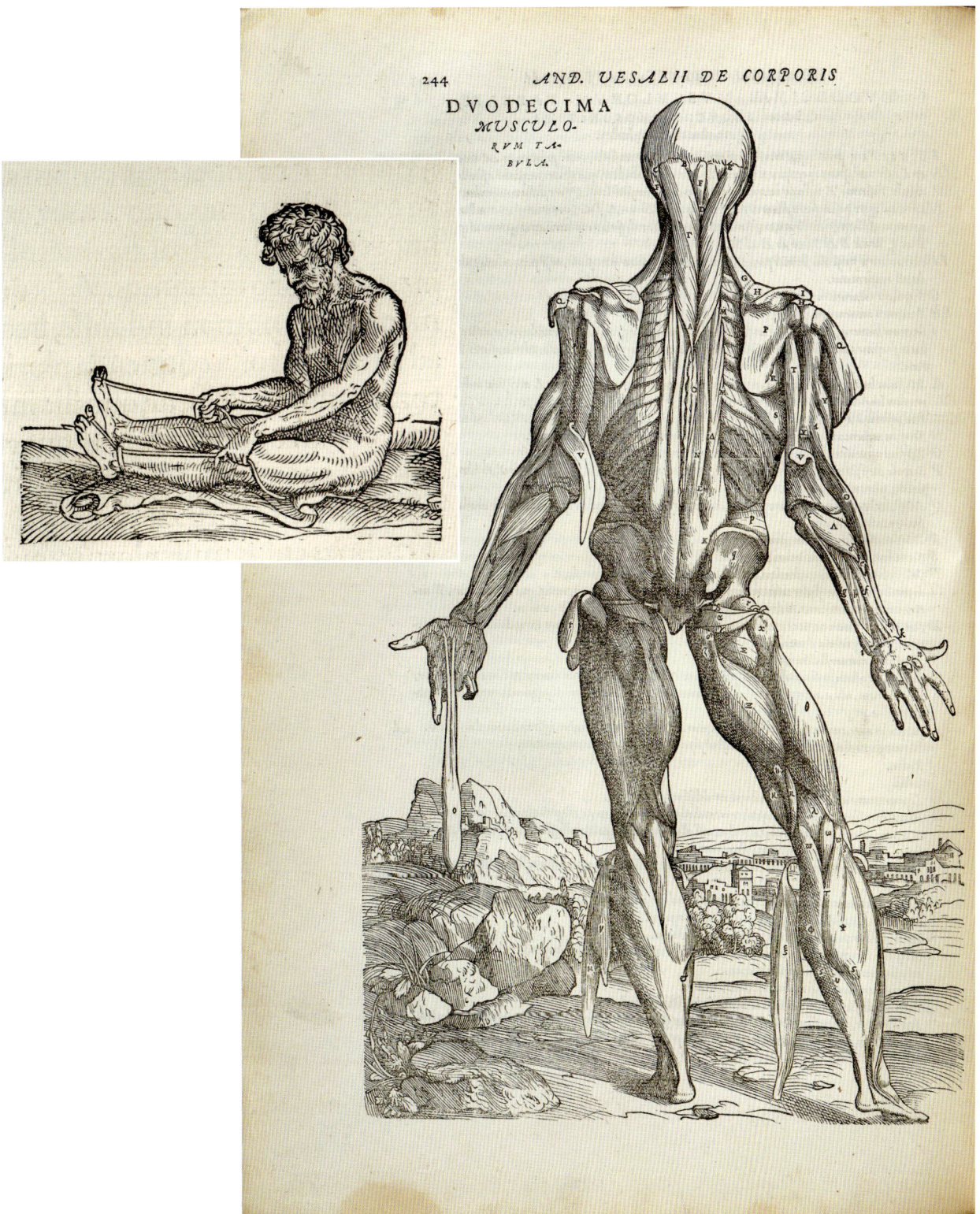

DVODECIMA
MUSCULO-
RVM TA-
BVLA.

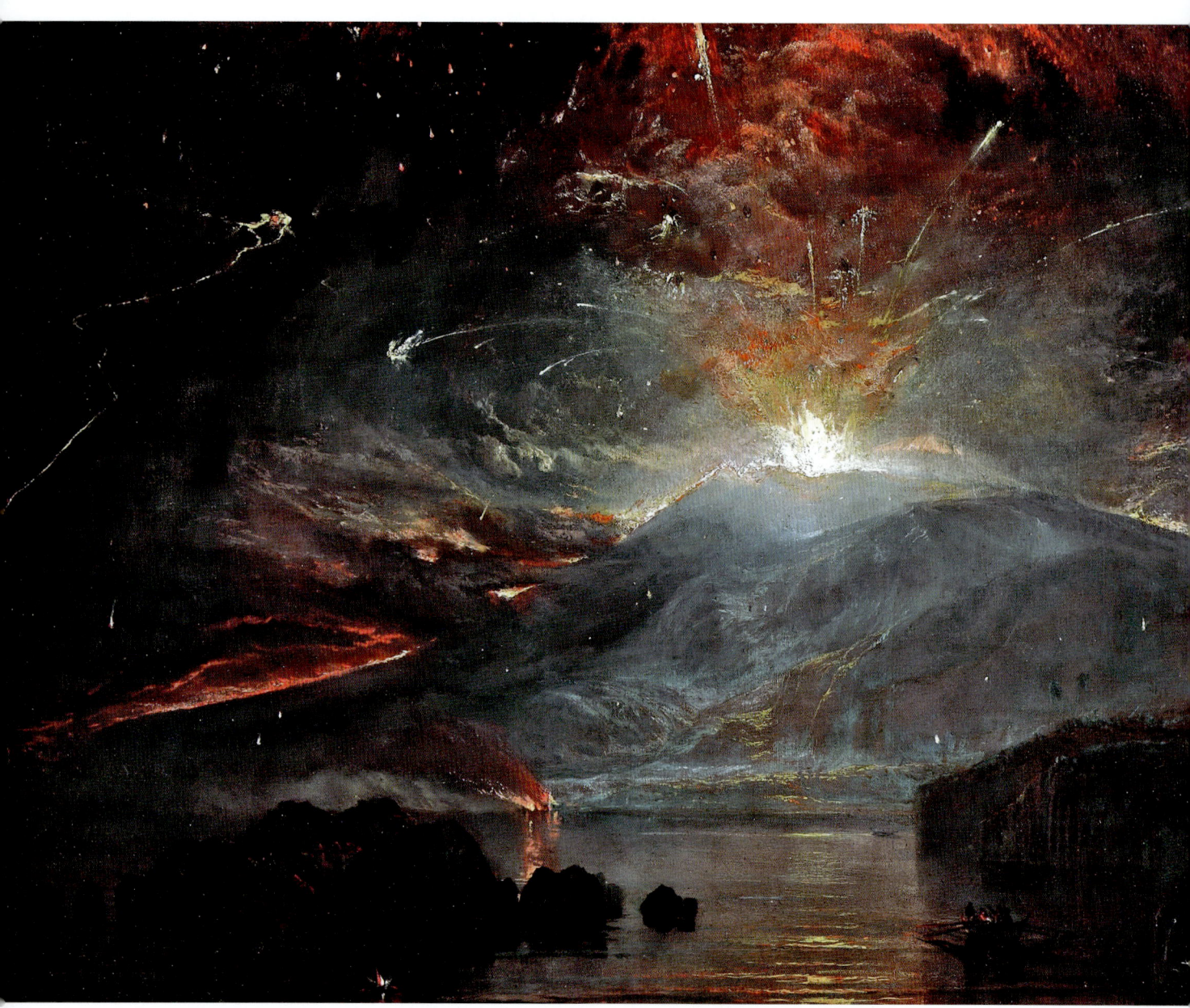

THE ERUPTION OF THE SOUFRIÈRE MOUNTAINS IN THE ISLAND OF ST VINCENT, 30 APRIL 1812 – A VOLCANOLOGIST'S PERSPECTIVE (1940s)

26

Oil on canvas by J.M.W. Turner, 1815. 79 × 105 cm.

Donated by Raymond Richards, 1948.

In 1815, at the time of Turner's painting, volcanology as a science was a very new discipline. Little was known about volcano monitoring or what kinds of hazard volcanoes such as La Soufrière, on the Caribbean Island of St Vincent, might be capable of producing, and therefore what the risk to the local population might be. The most recent eruption (1784) was effusive (lava-dome forming) and its impacts would have been restricted to the summit of the mountain; nobody alive had witnessed the previous explosive eruption (1718) and its far-reaching impacts.

La Soufrière is the most active subaerial volcano in the Eastern Caribbean and is part of the Lesser Antilles Volcanic Arc. Here a chain of volcanic islands has been created over the past 40 million years by the subduction of the Atlantic oceanic crust beneath the Caribbean Plate. Geologists today have found that the island of St Vincent records volcanism going back three million years.

News of the 1812 eruption, and particularly of the events of 30 April, did not reach the UK for a few weeks. This eruption had a rapid explosive sequence and has been classified by volcanologists today as VEI 4 (Volcanic Explosivity Index), meaning that more than 100 million cubic metres of pyroclastic deposits (volcanic debris produced by the fragmentation of lava or rock as a result of explosive volcanic activity) had erupted. The 1812 explosion excavated a crater 500 m wide and 60 m deep at the summit of the volcano, with devastating consequences for the north of the island and the people living and working there.

An unpublished paper 'Particulars of the eruption of the Souffriere mountain, in the island of Saint Vincent',

read before the Liverpool Literary and Philosophical Society in 1812 (LUL MS.53), describes the terrible events of that day. This narrative relates how, in the months preceding the eruption, more than 200 earthquakes were felt on the island, disquieting the local population but not to such an extent as to dissuade visits to the summit, which actually increased in frequency even up to the day before the eruption started. Those visitors described a 'conical hill' (lava dome) from which a 'thin, white smoke was constantly emitted, occasionally tinged with a slight, bluish flame', sitting within the great amphitheatre of the crater. The smoke and flame are indicative that this lava dome was active and growing, with hot and viscous lava slowly extruding from a vent within the crater.

The explosive eruption began with a 'vast column of thick, black, ropey smoke', a volcanic plume that carried ash downwind and soon showered down 'sand' (small volcanic rock fragments) onto the north of the island. Activity escalated over subsequent days, reaching a climax on 30 April, when the volcano produced several rapid, hot pyroclastic density currents that wreaked devastation in the surrounding towns and plantations. As sulphur gases from the eruption spread through the atmosphere 'the clouds reflected a bright copper colour'. This is the night depicted in Turner's painting.

Turner is likely to have read about the eruption of La Soufrière in the weeks following the eruption, as news spread rapidly through contemporary eyewitness accounts published in newspapers across the UK, including the *Liverpool Mercury* (whose report closely resembles the Liverpool Literary and Philosophical Society paper). Around this time he came across a sketch of the eruption by Hugh Perry Keane, Esq., a barrister, sugar-plantation owner, and enslaver, who was on the island at the time and who kept several diaries. Turner used this sketch as inspiration for his piece, first revealed at the Royal Academy exhibition in 1815 and now displayed at the Victoria Gallery and Museum in Liverpool.

Turner's painting captures both the beauty of a volcanic eruption and the excitement and terror it instils as its deadly force begins to unfold. A thick, dark volcanic ash plume fills the sky, glowing red, orange and yellow near the volcano summit. Dense rocky blocks are shown being thrown from the volcano, and glowing fragments are scattered in the air. The summit is also glowing, as hot, solidified lava rocks tumble down the volcano flanks. Fires rage all around, being created as the hot rocks rained down on the land in 'showers of cinders' and as the energetic flows were 'scaling every obstacle … carrying rock and wood' and setting anything flammable on fire. At least 34 enslaved people lost their lives during these days and in the devastating floods (lahars) of the following months.

Owing to the limited information we have about the 1812 eruption, Turner's painting represents an important additional source of evidence for the eruptive history of the volcano. The story of this eruption and how it unfolded provides important contextual information used by monitoring teams today at La Soufrière. The volcanic processes of the 1812 eruption have some similarities to the most recent eruption, which occurred in 2020–21 and forced the evacuation of around 16,000 people from the north of the island. Fortunately, no lives were lost in that eruption and this is testament to the world-leading advances in volcano monitoring, effective communication, and volcanic crisis management that have been made in this region over the past 30 years.

Janine L. Kavanagh

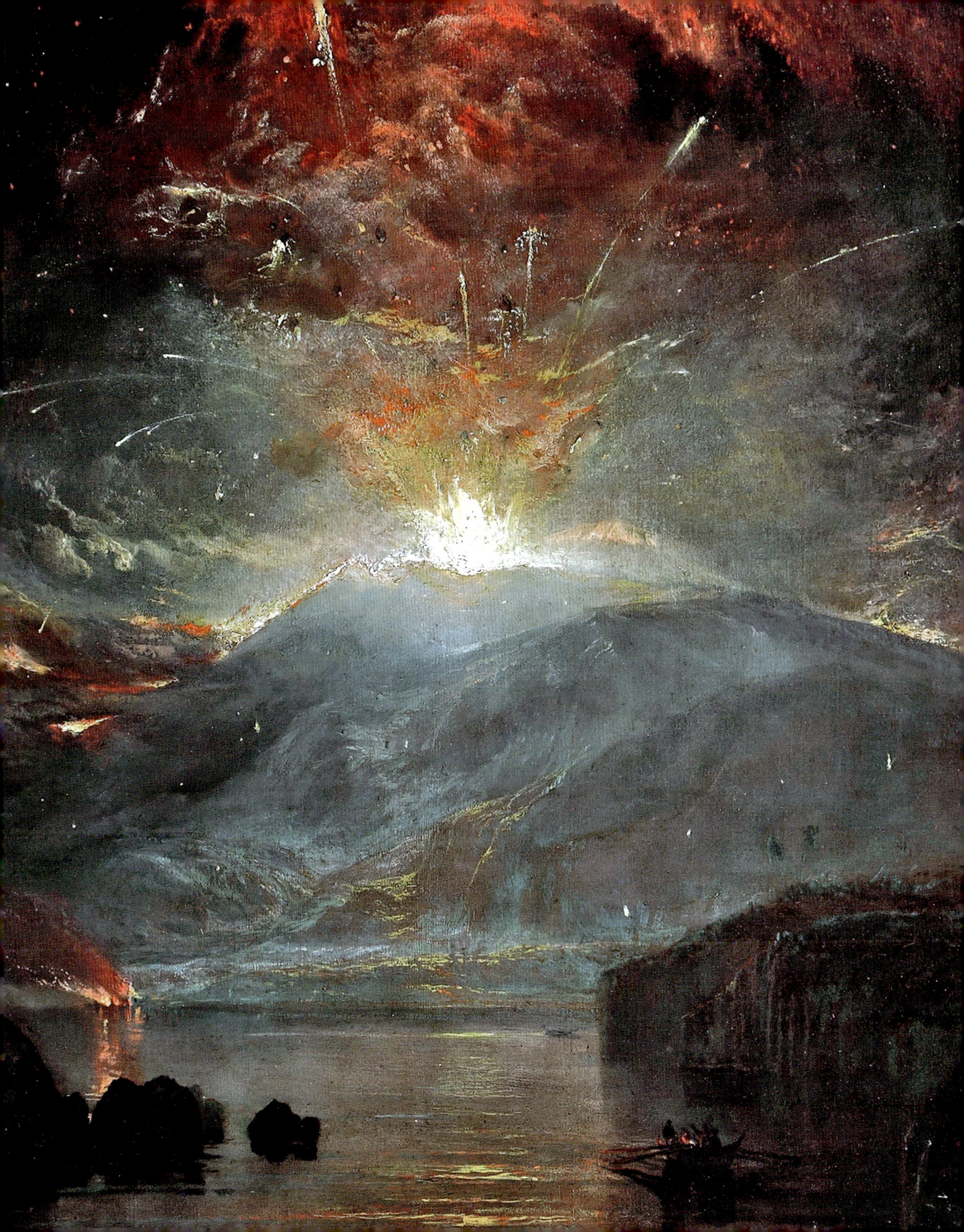

Seven centuries of singing (1950s)

27

Folio 5r from Dominican antiphoner MS.F.4.13, on parchment with historiated and decorated initials. Italy (Pisa). Early fourteenth and early fifteenth century; i + 66 + i leaves. 32.5 × 23.5 cm.

Presented to the University of Liverpool by the conductor Sir Adrian Boult in 1950.

'O beautiful crown!' sang the Dominican friars of medieval Pisa, using the book now MS.F.4.13 to perform an elaborate ceremony in honour of their most prized relic. The manuscript is a remarkable survival, speaking to both widespread and highly local musical culture. The most lavishly decorated section, originally a separate booklet, contains the feast of the Crown of Thorns (folios 5r–46v), a set of Christian rituals connected to the narrative of Good Friday. Like most antiphoners (bound collections of short chants sung as part of a Christian liturgical service), MS.F.4.13 contains no prayers or readings, but it conveys everything that is musically necessary. It is possible to sing directly from it today, as indeed have some of the students from the Department of Music.

The manuscript was owned by the church of Santa Maria del Pontenovo, renamed in 1332 as Santa Maria della Spina (St Mary of the Thorn) when the friars acquired a single thorn believed to have originated at Christ's Crucifixion. Ownership of this miraculous relic led to the creation of a local version of the Crown of Thorns liturgy, drawing on Parisian and Dominican traditions, of which MS.F.4.13 remains a unique source. The liturgical ritual in MS.F.4.13 was designed to draw pilgrims to the thorn and to strengthen faith. Commemorations at Pisa rivalled those of the royal Sainte-Chapelle in Paris, which owned a full crown that had been given to King Louis IX. The thorn of Pisa would have been displayed in a prominent reliquary and carried in processions around the city on special occasions.

As can be seen in the main image (folio 5r), the page was illuminated by an artist associated with the school of Francesco Traini (active 1321–65). The historiated (story-telling) initial that dominates the written space shows Christ being mocked, while Mary and Joseph pray for mercy at their Son's feet. Some crowd members have contorted facial expressions or wear distinctive hats (see, for example, the red hat in the top right), and one blows an animal horn; these were common ways for Christian artists to visually identify Jews. The image is part of the stereotyping that Jewish communities endured. Users of the manuscript today are visually reminded that some of the Christian liturgy's most beautiful and celebratory music was part of a discourse that included deep-seated antisemitism.

Additions to the manuscript from the fifteenth century indicate that it passed to a community of Benedictine nuns along the river. They included chants honouring St Matthew, to whom their convent was dedicated. Other additions link imaginatively with the Crown of Thorns liturgy itself. One verse of the *Salve regina* (Hail, Queen of Heaven) includes melodic decorations on the word 'thorn', deviating from the standard melody and drawing the listener's attention to the importance of the relic (folio 4v): 'Funde preces tuo nato, crucifixo vulnerato, et pro nobis flagellato, *spinis* puncto felle potato' (Offer our prayers to your Son who for us was crucified and wounded, beaten, pierced by thorns, and made to drink gall).

Inscriptions by later owners track this manuscript's journey from Italy to Liverpool: it was bought in Pisa in 1837 by naturalist Walter Calverley Trevelyan (1797–1879) for his wife Pauline Trevelyan (1816–66), an art patron and a close friend of John Ruskin; at the 1895 Sotheby's sale of the library of London printer C.W. Reynell (1798–1892) it was sold to Henry Young, bookseller in Liverpool; and thence to Cedric Boult, whose son Adrian, conductor and Liverpool honorary graduate, gave it to the University, where its musical settings can once again be heard.

Lisa Colton

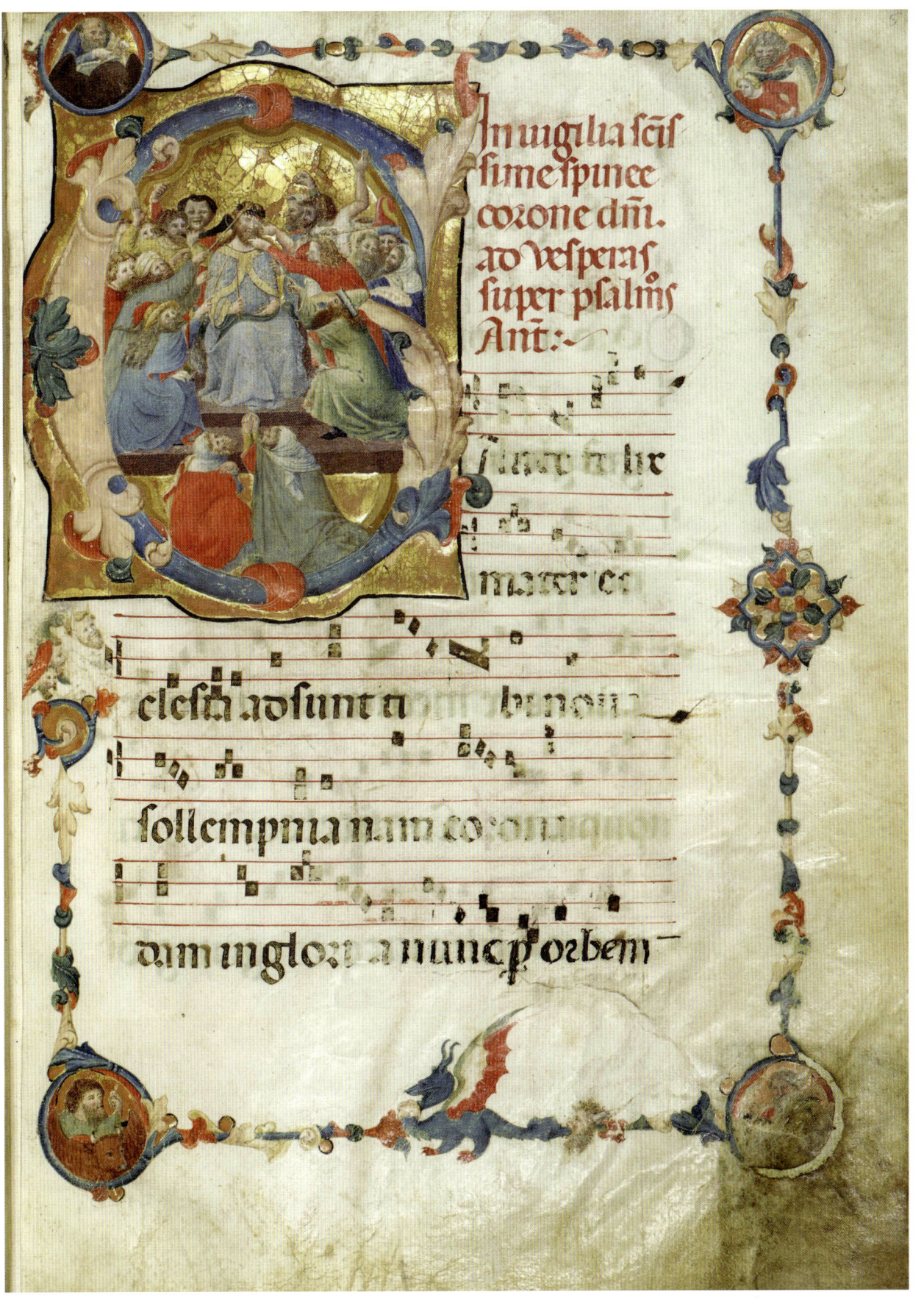

In uigilia sctī
sum̄e spinee
corone dm̄.
ad uesperas
super psalm̄s
Ant:-

sī uicp̄ tu lic

matri ci

cleseī aosunt a   bme nou

sollempnia nam coron

am ingloria nuncp̄ orbem

Celebrating Purim in Liverpool (1950s)

28

Book of Esther (1845); parchment scroll containing the Book of Esther in Hebrew, in blue silk wrapper. Written in Liverpool by Ellis Samuel Yates (1805–49), paternal grandfather of Dora Esther Yates. 26 × 351 cm.

Book of Esther (about 1860); parchment scroll with ivory handles and cylinder carved by Assur Keyser (1844–1922), uncle of Dora Yates. Written in London by Moses Keyser (1810–72), maternal grandfather of Dora Yates. 14 × 401 cm.

Both scrolls presented by Dora Esther Yates (1879–1974) in 1955.

The Book of Esther, known in Hebrew as the *Megillah*, is a scroll of profound religious and cultural importance within Jewish tradition. The story of Esther is the heart of the festival of Purim, a celebration of deliverance and survival. The two Book of Esther scrolls housed in the University of Liverpool's Special Collections, donated by the prominent Liverpool-born scholar Dora Esther Yates, serve not only as ritual objects but as a testament to the enduring resilience of the Jewish people.

The Book of Esther recounts an episode during the Jewish exile in Persia in which the exiles are saved from a plot of annihilation orchestrated by the Persian official Haman. Esther's courage, selflessness, and beauty see her rise to become the Persian queen and, guided by the wisdom of her faithful cousin Mordecai, she foils their enemies and overturns the plot. Esther's actions, notably her intercession with her husband, King Ahasuerus, without initially revealing her Jewish identity, encompass themes of survival through adaptation and the careful negotiation of identity in hostile environments, all deeply resonant with Jewish history.

Significantly, the Book of Esther is the only biblical text in which the name of God is never explicitly mentioned. This absence invites a range of interpretations, with many scholars suggesting that the text emphasises human agency in ensuring the survival of the Jewish people. In this way, the story captures the sense of both divine providence and human responsibility, concepts central to Jewish theological reflection, particularly during times of persecution.

The Yates Purim scrolls are unique in their design while still following the traditional format of Purim scrolls. Handwritten on parchment and wound onto wooden spools, this classic scroll structure has been maintained over centuries, the combination of material and form playing an essential role in their ritual significance. When read aloud during the Purim festival, the scroll serves as a direct link to the collective memory of Jewish survival and triumph, with listeners actively participating through the use of graggers (noise-making devices) to drown out the name of Haman, symbolically muting the oppressor. This lively practice reflects the joyous and celebratory nature of Purim, a holiday that transforms what could have been a moment of mourning into a festival of unbridled joy.

Yet Purim is not merely a story of survival; it is also a time for reflection on the fragility of power and the possibility of reversal. The 'hidden' nature of God's presence in Esther echoes through centuries of Jewish thought, suggesting that, even in the darkest times, deliverance can come from unexpected quarters. This message of hope and reversal makes the Book of Esther particularly beloved within Jewish communities worldwide.

The scrolls donated by Dora Esther Yates have additional significance in the context of the University of Liverpool's collections. Yates, herself a scholar deeply committed to the preservation of Jewish heritage, saw the importance of ensuring that these sacred texts were available for both study and celebration. Thus, the scrolls' inclusion within the University's Special Collections speaks not only to the richness of Jewish cultural and religious life but also to the role of community figures such as Yates in preserving and sharing these traditions with wider audiences.

Şizen Yiacoup

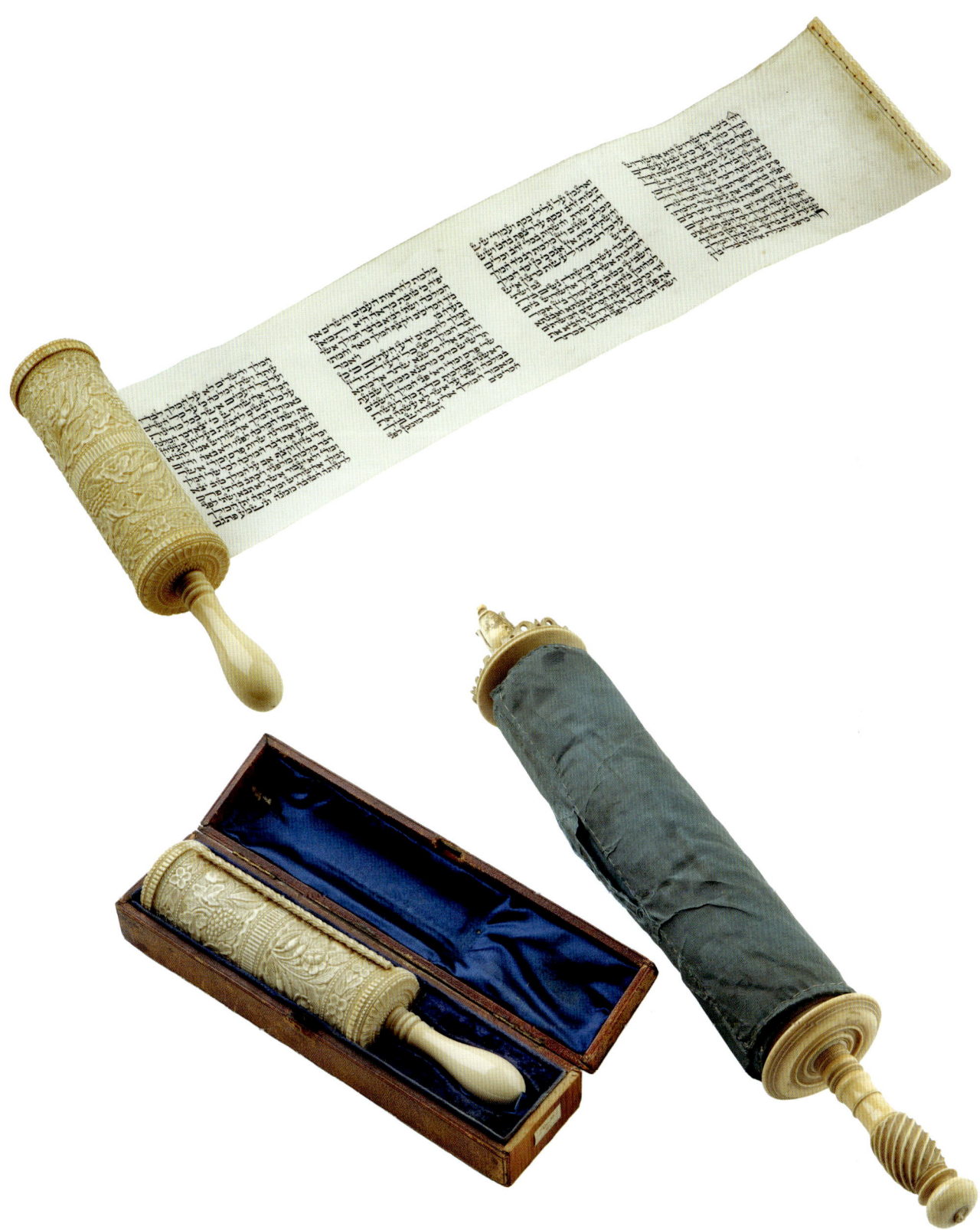

An Authentic Account of an Embassy from the King of Great Britain to the Emperor of China (1950s)

29

Plate showing the Great Wall of China from George Staunton, *An Authentic Account of an Embassy* (1797); two volumes of text with illustrations and portraits, 30 cm; one volume of 44 plates, including maps, 60 × 45 cm.

Text volumes donated by Liverpool Free Public Library; volume of plates donated by Sir John Hobhouse (1893–1961), 1957.

Sir George Staunton's *An Authentic Account of an Embassy from the King of Great Britain to the Emperor of China* is a foundational text in the history of Anglo-Chinese relations. Staunton (1737–1801) was secretary to the Macartney Embassy of 1792–94, and in 1797 he published the official account of the mission, drawing on his personal experience and the papers of leading figures who were involved. His book was the first informed account of imperial China on the threshold of the nineteenth century, and its descriptions, and accompanying images of Chinese life and culture, made a profound impact in Britain and Western Europe. By the mid-eighteenth century the style known as 'chinoiserie' had become a widespread aesthetic mode, deriving from the extensive import of Chinese porcelain and fabrics that began in the seventeenth century. But Staunton's book represented in unprecedented detail the reality of China under the Qing Dynasty and stimulated a new level of interest in its history, politics, and culture.

In 1792 the home secretary Henry Dundas appointed George Macartney to serve as Great Britain's first ambassador to imperial China. Trade with China was increasingly important, but laboured under significant disadvantages due to the so-called 'canton system', which severely restricted the terms of trade. The Macartney Embassy aimed to initiate direct diplomatic relations with the ruling Qing emperor Qianlong, with a view to negotiating more favourable trading terms between two nations of equal standing. The Embassy sailed from Southampton in September 1792 on a mission that was to take more than two years. Three ships carried more than 100 people, including diplomats, civil servants, scientists, doctors, musicians, and two artists to make a pictorial record, accompanied by a further 400 or so sailors and marines. There were also a large number of gifts to be presented to the emperor, representing the most advanced productions of British technology. The journey to China took nine months, and Staunton's *Account* contains much fascinating detail of the stopping places during the voyage, including the Canaries, the Cape Verde Islands, Rio de Janeiro, Tristan da Cunha, Amsterdam Island, and a series of coastal areas of Java and modern-day Vietnam.

The Embassy's reception in China has been characterised as 'the collision of two civilisations'. Britain was in the grip of the accelerating Industrial Revolution, which was enabling the country to build a huge colonial enterprise and to reach a scale and power of manufacturing and military capability new in human history. China, on the other hand, had remained for centuries under self-imposed isolation from the world, and believed itself to be the unchallengeable supreme nation on earth.

The Embassy ended in complete failure. Qianlong and his court regarded the British as emissaries of an essentially barbarian race, and once it became clear that Macartney would not agree to perform the 'kowtow', because he wished to affirm and demonstrate the equal global status of the emperor and the British king George III, the entire British force was dismissed and sent back southwards from Beijing to Hangzhou along the 1,000 miles of the Grand Canal – the marvel of ancient Chinese engineering already at that time more than 2,000 years old – to begin their homeward journey. The episode led to further attempts at diplomatic contact,

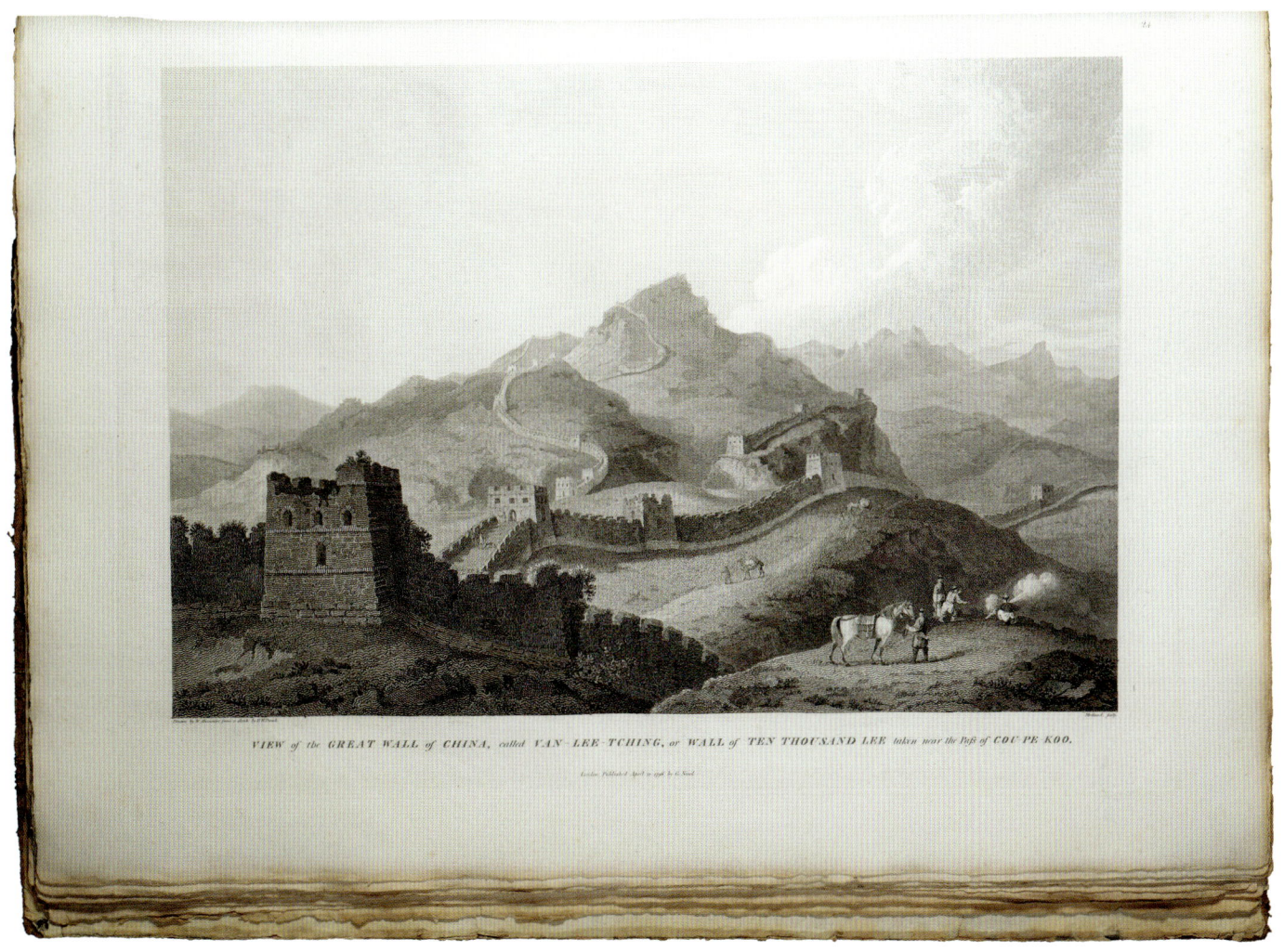

VIEW of the *GREAT WALL of CHINA*, called *VAN-LEE-TCHING*, or *WALL of TEN THOUSAND LEE* taken near the Pass of *COU PE KOO*.

London, Published April 11. 1796. by G. Nicol.

and when these too failed to satisfy British ambitions the deteriorating dialogue ended by the mid-nineteenth century in the 'Opium Wars', in which British naval power and military technology exposed the fundamental weakness of the Chinese empire. This catastrophic 'clash of civilisations' has profoundly influenced the Chinese self-image, and its attitude to the West, ever since.

Macartney's homeward journey took the mission through the 'Soochow' of Staunton's account, which is the beautiful ancient city of Suzhou. Today that city is the home of the Chinese University 'XJTLU', created and part-owned by the University of Liverpool in partnership with Xian Jiaotong University. It is a venture which, in its conspicuous success, has demonstrated how at least some of the damage done by nineteenth-century British imperialism in Qing China can be healed by constructive dialogue and the sharing of means to achieve mutual goals. And it allows the University of Liverpool to take its proud place in the difficult history of Sino-British relations over the past 250 years.

Kelvin Everest

CABLE AND WIRELESS
LIMITED.

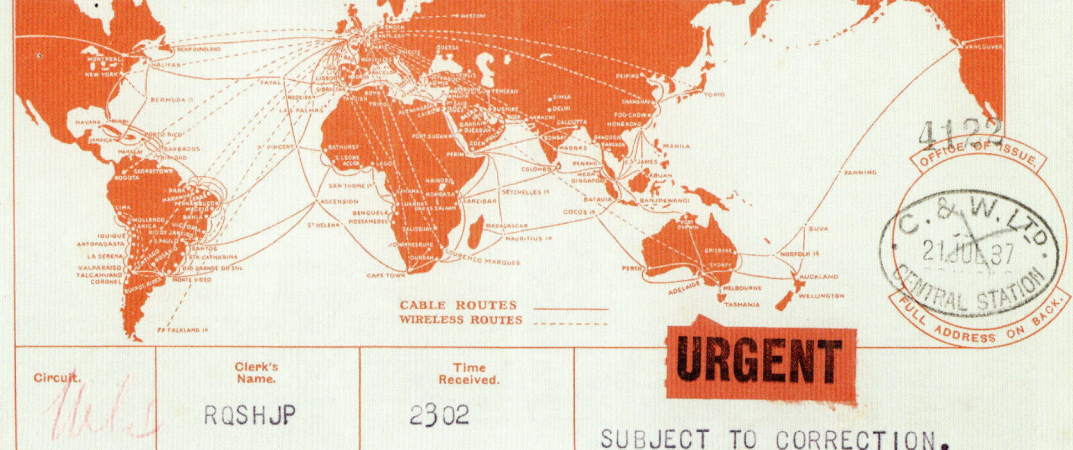

CABLE ROUTES _____
WIRELESS ROUTES - - - - -

4122

OFFICE OF ISSUE.

C. & W. LTD.
21 JUL 37
CENTRAL STATION
FULL ADDRESS ON BACK.

URGENT

Circuit.	Clerk's Name.	Time Received.
	RQSHJP	2302

SUBJECT TO CORRECTION.
45 WORDS +

BPA74 D SANTANDER 44 21 1100 H/SPANISH 2210 ETAT

VIA BARNA SPANISH = URGENT = RATHBONE 50 ROMNEY

ST LONDON SW1 =

BRITISH STANGROVE TONNAGE TWOHUNDRED LEFT

RIBADESELLA THREE TUESDAY MORNING FOR SANTANDER

FOR REFUGES SHOULD HAVE ARRIVED MIDDAY STOP NO

FURTHER NEWS FEARED SHE MAY BE CAPTURED STOP BOT

FITTED WIRELESS STOP URGENT YOU INQUIRE ADMIRALTY

FOR NEWS = PURSE +

Rescuing refugees from the Spanish Civil War, 1937 (1950s)

30

Telegram from Commander H. Pursey to Eleanor Rathbone. Cable & Wireless Ltd
printed paper telegram. 22 × 21.5 cm.

Donated by the Rathbone family, 1950s.

Eleanor Rathbone (1872–1946) was a British politician and social reformer known for her dedication to humanitarian causes. She was the first woman elected to Liverpool City Council, serving as an Independent councillor for Granby ward between 1909 and 1934, and was elected as an Independent MP for the Combined Universities in 1929, serving until 1945. Her archive, held at the University of Liverpool, reveals her passionate personal and political commitment to providing refuge for those fleeing persecution, which earned her the nickname 'MP for refugees'.

Rathbone was the first female MP to speak out against Hitler's regime. In a statement to the House of Commons on 13 April 1933 she spoke of the uncontrolled power of the Nazi party, 'inflicting cruelties and crushing disabilities on large numbers of law-abiding peaceful citizens, whose only offence is that they belong to a particular race or religion or profess certain political beliefs' (Rathbone Papers XIV.3.9). As fascism continued to take hold in Europe during the 1930s, taking action to rescue its victims was for Rathbone the practical complement to her outspoken opposition to policies of appeasement.

At the outbreak of the Spanish Civil War in 1936 Rathbone joined the National Joint Committee for Spanish Relief, a cross-party group coordinating aid to Spain, which managed to persuade the government to accept the children desperately trying to flee. In 1937 Rathbone and her fellow MP, Kitty Murray, organised the rescue of 4,000 children from the Basque combat zone.

This telegram, dated July 1937, records a moment in the campaign to bring people fleeing Franco's forces from the Spanish coast to safety in Britain. Many of the thousands of refugees were concentrated in Santander. The steamer *Stangrove*, named in the telegram, was one of a number of private vessels contracted to carry refugees on a hazardous journey that involved running blockades operated first by the Allies and then by the Spanish Nationalists. On 26 October 1937, in words that resonate in 2025, Rathbone reported to the House of Commons 'the scenes which these merchant captains have described – Gijon in flames, people rushing to the sea and people struggling in the water where small boats had capsized owing to the storm and other people clinging to rafts'.

For Rathbone, the refugee issue was a matter of justice and human dignity. Britain, as a democratic state and global leader, she argued, had a responsibility to act compassionately in the face of the growing refugee crisis. Rathbone's speeches and letters to government officials reveal her frustration with the British government's immigration policies. While Britain did accept some refugees, the process was bureaucratic, slow, and restrictive. In 1938 she established the Parliamentary Committee on Refugees as a vehicle for her campaigns.

Rathbone deployed the lessons learned in the Spanish Civil War in her work helping Jews and socialists to flee occupied Czechoslovakia, founding the National Committee for Rescue from Nazi Terror and supporting refugees in Britain during the course of the war.

Eleanor Rathbone's legacy as 'MP for refugees' is an important part of her broader social reform work. Whether it was her pioneering work in social welfare, the advancement of women's rights, or British immigration policy, she used her political platform to speak for the voiceless and advocate for some of the most vulnerable in society. It was, she believed, the moral duty of government to defend social justice, equality, and human rights.

Elizabeth Williams and Eve Rosenhaft

GREETINGS SINCERE

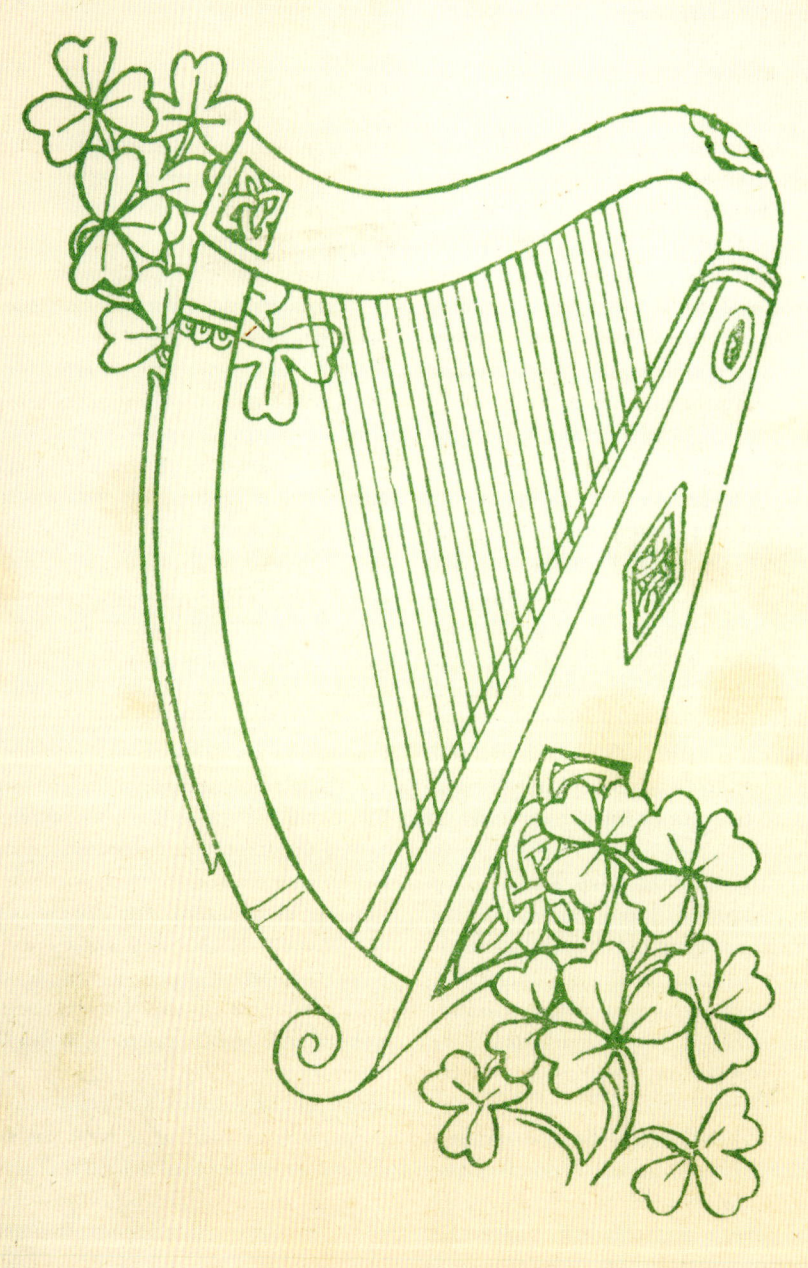

St Patrick's Day card (1960s)

31

Greetings card designed to be sent from Ireland to Irish emigrants, with enclosed pressed shamrock, from the Power/O'Neill papers. 12.7 × 8 cm.

Part of Power family correspondence donated by Michael O'Neill, son of Kathleen O'Neill (née Power, 1905–83), to the Mac Lua Library, Institute of Irish Studies. Transferred to Special Collections and Archives in 2022.

This greetings card comes from the personal collections of the Power/O'Neill family within the MacLua Library Archive. This archive was transferred from the Institute of Irish Studies to Special Collections and Archives and includes a range of materials, from pamphlets associated with paramilitary groups during the times of the 'Troubles' to early records of the British Association of Irish Studies, and even a complete run of the *Irish Post* (1970–2008), the newspaper whose founding editor, Breandán MacLua, the library is named for.

The Power/O'Neill family papers are an excellent representative collection of a family who emigrated from Ireland to Liverpool in the 1920s, with the O'Neills establishing a successful tobacco and convenience store in central Liverpool at 46 St James Street. An interesting detail about this card is the inclusion of dried shamrock, which often signified luck and good fortune in Irish tradition. Along with this, the sentiment of 'Greetings Sincere' is quite unique and gives an indication of the date of the card, as this is a phrase that has fallen out of use within approximately the last 40–50 years. Most of these correspondences are dated from the 1920s to the 1950s, allowing us to date this card to around this period.

Kathleen O'Neill, the matriarch of the family and the person who kept a lot of these letters and greeting cards, moved to Liverpool once she got married: the collection contains some correspondence from the period just before her marriage, through the 1920s, and all the way to the late 1940s. The collection of correspondence and business records donated by this family shows the rich history of their links to both Ireland and Liverpool, as well as giving an insight into personal experiences and opinions surrounding the historical events of this period.

A steady stream of Irish migrants had begun to arrive in Liverpool from the early nineteenth century onwards, with that stream turning into a torrent during the years of the Great Hunger (1845–52). In that period well over a million Irish passed through Liverpool, many on their way to what they hoped would be better lives in America, but many made their homes along the banks of the Mersey. So plentiful were the Irish that the city's Scotland Road constituency even returned an Irish Home Rule MP in the general election of 1885. And Irish migrants to Liverpool came not just from the Catholic community: many Protestant Irish also journeyed across the Irish Sea and, as with Glasgow and Edinburgh further north, sectarian battle lines were drawn via membership of organisations such as the Loyal Orange Lodges or the Ancient Order of Hibernians. By the time the Powers and O'Neills arrived in the 1920s, there was an established Irish community in Liverpool, ranging across faith and classes – a situation that persists right up to the present, with traces of Irish history and culture scattered across the city.

Sophie Smith and Frank Shovlin

The Harp and the Shamrock are the Emblems of Ireland, Worn with pride for our Patron so true; When we proudly display them on his feast in the homeland We'll be thinking and praying for all friends like you.

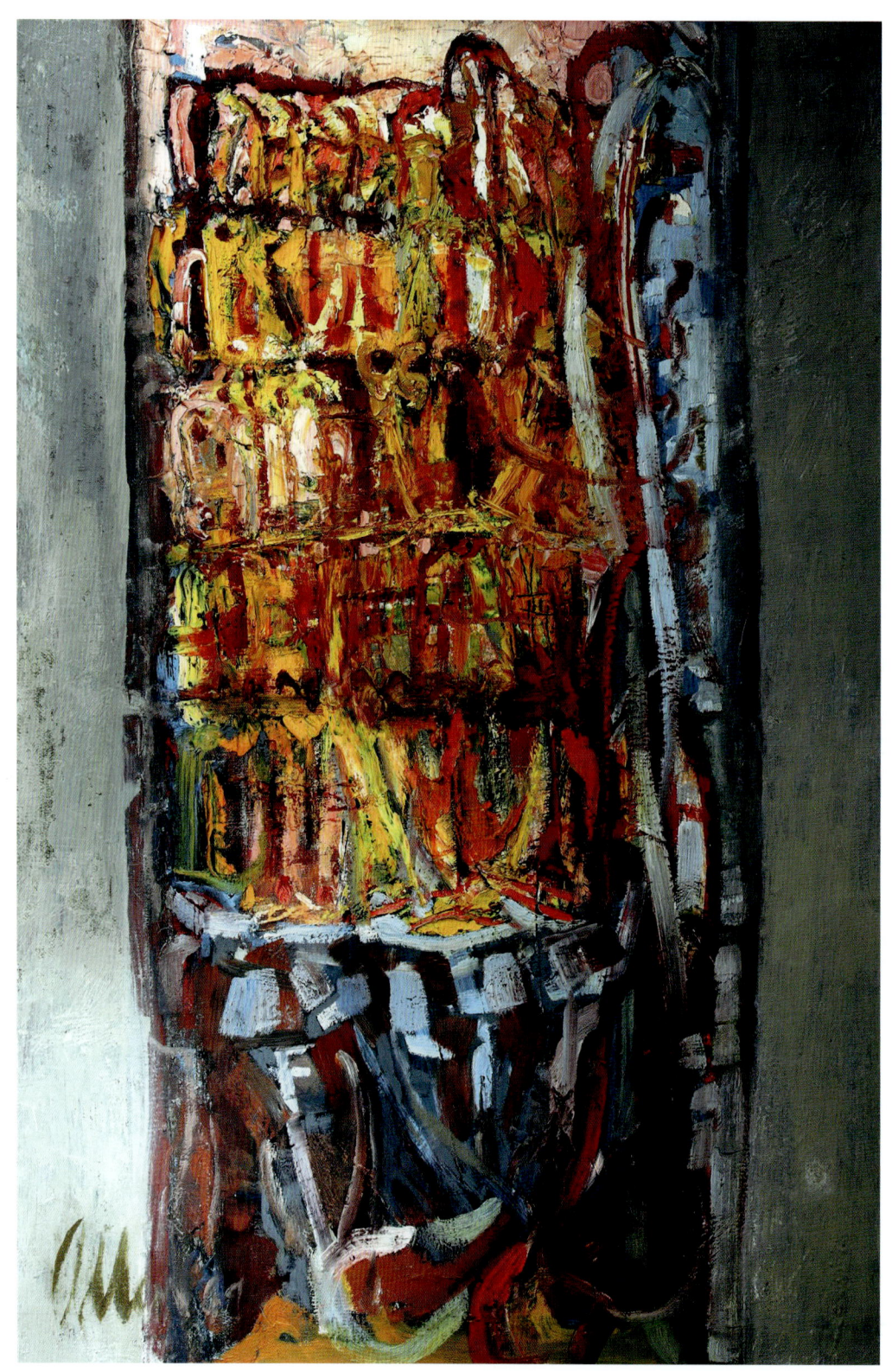

Computer updates (1960s)

32

LEO Computer Storage Unit, 1964. Oil on canvas by Kathleen Saywell Allen (1906–83). 151 × 100 cm.

Purchased, 1965.

During the Second World War the artist, designer, and teacher Kathleen Saywell Allen (1906–83), who spent many years in Bloomsbury's Mecklenburgh Square, was seconded one day a week to record war industries and the effects of bombing in the City of London. A bomb dropped on her own studio in the London Blitz and destroyed all her paintings. Following the war, Allen joined the Society of Industrial Artists (now the Chartered Society of Designers). This painting shows the wiring of LEO (Lyons Electronic Office), the first computer used for commercial business applications. By the time the University purchased Allen's painting, it already had a pioneering computer produced by the same organisation, the English Electric Company.

Following the English Electric Company's acquisition of the Marconi Company (in 1946) and LEO (in 1954), the English Electric LEO Company was keen to widen its presence in consumer electronics, adding to the original focus on armaments and aviation from its origins in 1918. The DEUCE (Digital Electronic Universal Computing Engine) was one of the outcomes: a production standard version of the Pilot ACE (Automatic Computing Engine, itself a simplification of Alan Turing's ACE).

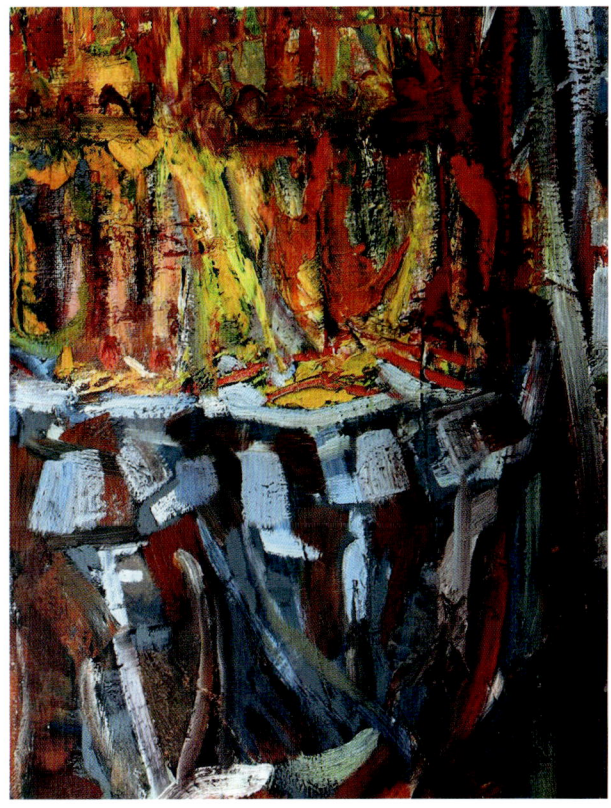

In 1959 the University purchased a DEUCE to be shared between sub-departments of the School of Mathematics. Photographs taken by the Liverpool firm Carbonora Ltd show Dr Andrew Young discussing the installation with English Electric Company staff.

The heavy use of this facility would have two consequences: its replacement by a much more powerful machine (the KDF9, also produced by English Electric) and the formation of an independent Computer Lab, separate from the Numerical Analysis Department, in 1964. The Computer Lab was renamed Computing Services in 1992 (now IT Services).

In 1966 Statistics and Numerical Analysis was combined into the department of Computational and Statistical Sciences (CSS), under its first head of department Andrew Young (1919–92), later the first Professor of Mathematics at the recently instituted New University of Ulster.

In 1982, after further restructuring, CSS was divided into the Department of Statistics and Computational Mathematics (SCM) and the Department of Computer Science. Several members of CSS (including Ann Maybrey) together with some Computer Lab staff, joined Computer Science under the first head of department Professor Michael Shave. Pioneer names in this new department live on in prizes awarded to this day, including the Andrew Young prize for excellent undergraduate performance and Ann Maybrey prizes for excellent MSc performance and project work.

The Department of Computer Science is now an internationally leading centre, recognised for its work in AI and Theoretical Computer Science, particularly Algorithmics, Computational Complexity, and Computational Game Theory.

Paul Dunne

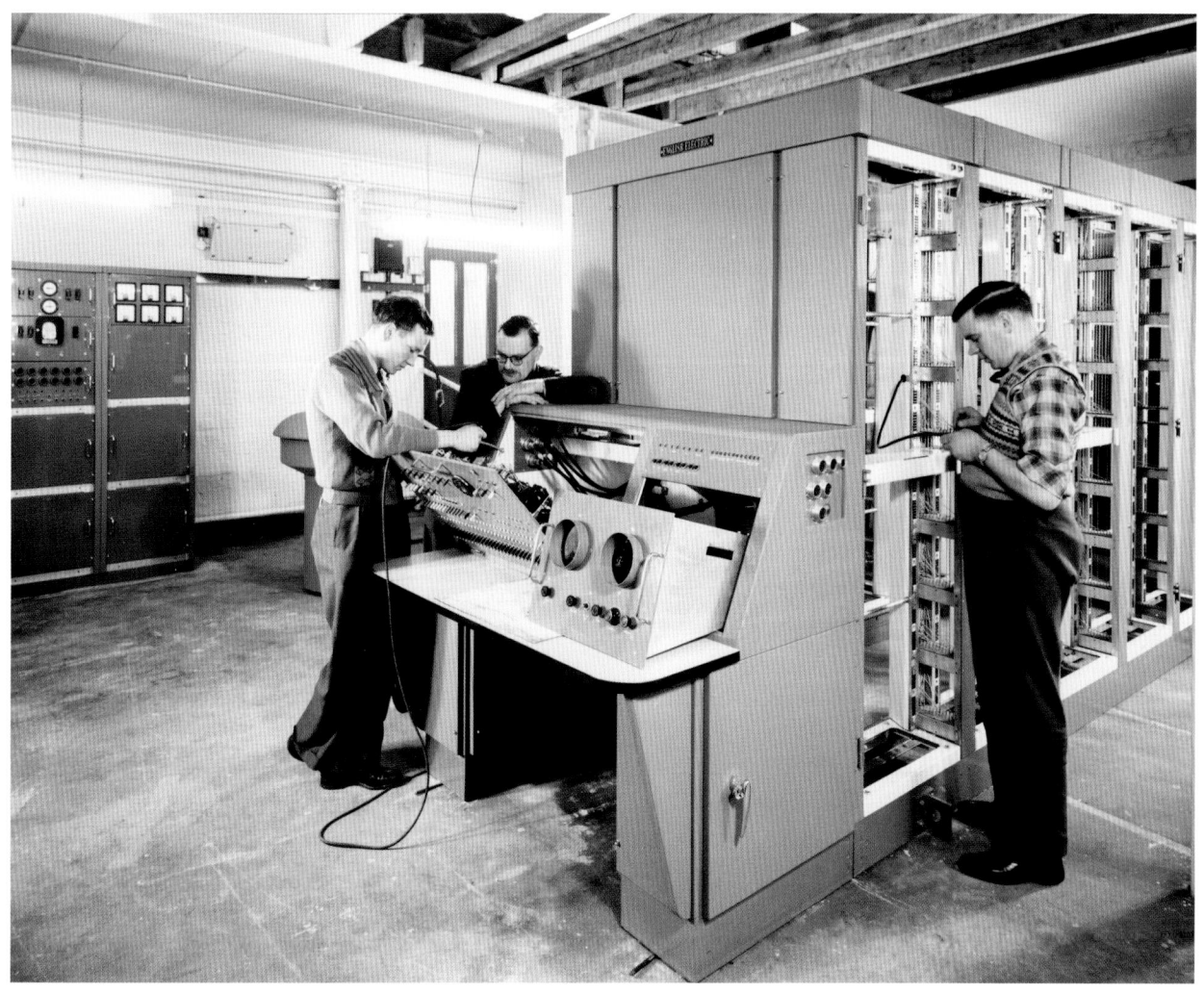

Computer Laboratory's English Electric Deuce Computer, 1959. Black and white captioned photograph by Carbonora Ltd, Liverpool.

WORLDBUILDING (1970s)

33

Olaf Stapledon's holograph manuscript of timelines for *Last and First Men*, 1930s. Ink on paper. 63 × 27 cm.

Deposited (later gifted) with the Olaf Stapledon collection, 1970.

Stapledon's timelines are perhaps one of the most beautiful ways of presenting worldbuilding in the science fiction canon. That said, Stapledon's works are not in many ways 'science fiction', being written before the term was coined, but are rather intellectual exercises in imagining the future of humanity written in fictional form. Olaf Stapledon (1886–1950) was a philosopher at the University of Liverpool in the early twentieth century, and among his philosophical interests was the moral advancement of humanity. Much of his work and thinking took place 'between the wars' in the 1920s and 1930s, in which Stapledon sought to understand how conflict and upheaval might give rise to a better world. *Last and First Men* was his first attempt to use fiction to present these possibilities to a more general readership, later followed by *Star Maker* (1937), which had an even broader ambition. Both works were widely regarded by better-known peers such as Virginia Woolf and Bertrand Russell as important contributions to thinking about human experience, as well as seeding the imaginations

of writers such as Arthur C. Clarke (1917–2008), Naomi Mitchison (1897–1999), and Brian Aldiss (1925–2017).

To give an example of the scale of Stapledon's imagination, the scope of *Last and First Men*'s vision is extreme; over several million years and 18 different versions of humanity (from us, today, through various evolutions) he considers what will become of humanity after political upheavals, wars, environmental cataclysms, and technological advancements and regressions. What his timelines reveal is a snapshot view of this soaring intellectual ambition, distilled into a striking image that looks something like a mathematical diagram, with multi-coloured lines and densely packed information.

The trick to understanding Stapledon's timelines is to see that each vertical line represents a different length of time, with the middle of the line always being his present, the top being the past and the bottom being the future. The leftmost lines represent the smallest length of time (400 years into the past and into the future on one timeline, 2,000 years into the past and into the future on the other).

So in just one 'line' Stapledon can add information on 800 years or 4,000 years of human development. He notes scientific developments such as 'Relativity' (meaning Einstein's Theory of General Relativity) or individuals such as 'Newton' and 'Jesus Christ' historically, but then also projects forwards into the future, adding notes to 'Decline of Science' or 'End of Oil Fuel'.

This is impressive enough, but Stapledon's true insight – and what reveals the extent of his long-term thinking – is to situate this next to another vertical line with a longer timespan. All the historical and futuristic events on one timeline fit into a small section of the timeline to its right (indicated by the diagonal lines). And he does this not just once but repeatedly, until in the rightmost lines humanity is situated in the middle of 400,000,000,000 and 16,000,000,000 years of the universe. Suddenly, the human scale of events (wars, historical eras, and significant individuals) disappears into the broader history of the cosmos, with the formation of stars, including our Sun, and nebulae the most significant events.

This is an 'inhuman' view in some ways, reducing the importance of human events against a backdrop of the universe, but that is why Stapledon presents the shorter and the longer sweeps of time – we can see both the human and the universal in one clear image, all through the trick of using multiple timelines, and we can flick back and forth between them. There is a beauty in the way the timelines enable us to do this, and they are to all intents and purposes a work of art, forcing the audience to think about the gap between what is presented and what is not, and how they situate themselves in relation to the ideas the image contains. It might appear to be a type of scientific diagram, distilling an author's astounding imagination onto the page, but the timelines remain one of the most thought-provoking ways of showing the scale of this in science fiction history, and reveal Stapledon's expansive vision of where we fit in the universe.

Will Slocombe

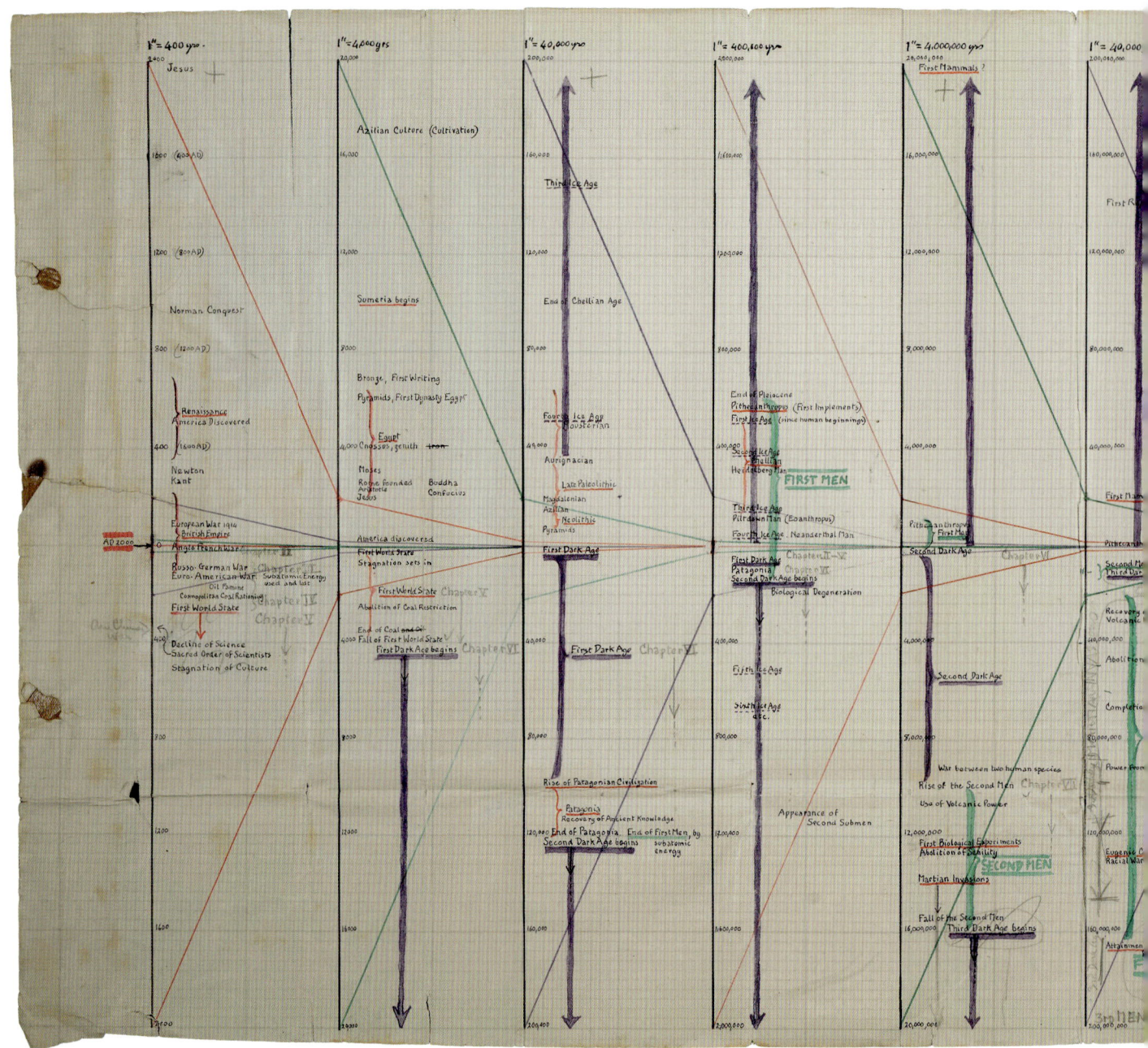

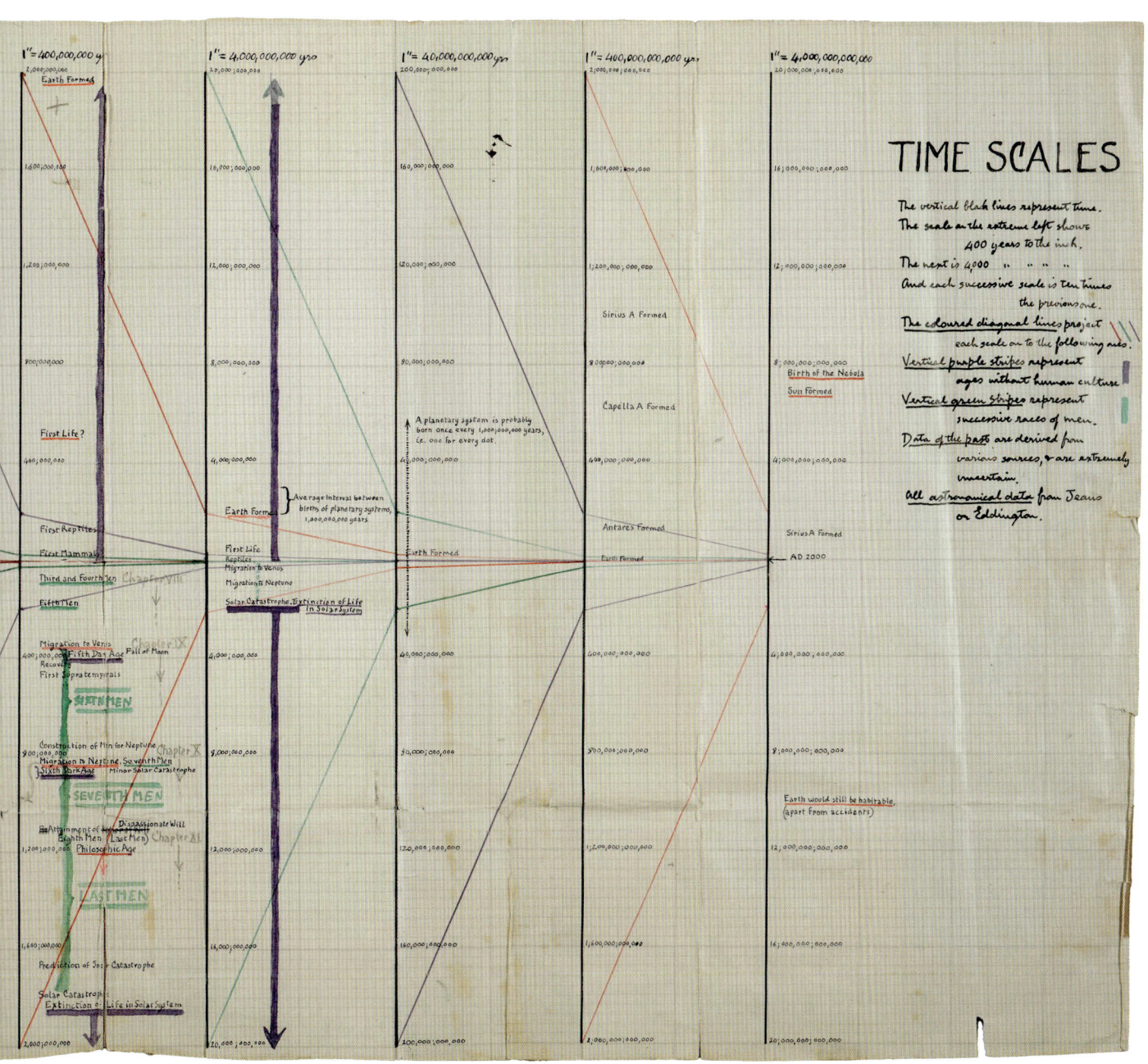

Do try this at home (1970s)

34

The Boy's Playbook of Science, by John Henry Pepper, illustrated by H.G. Hine; new edition (London: George Routledge and Sons, between 1865 and 1879). 448 pages, four plates; publisher's binding of green cloth stamped in gilt and black. 19 × 12.5 cm.

Acquired for the Library of the School of Education.

Chemistry is a branch of science that deals with the properties of matter and its changes. It is part of our everyday lives, and chemists make a difference by studying and modifying materials. Chemists research atomic and molecular structures and their changes and use their knowledge to create new materials. They observe, test and, generate models to make sense of the universe.

Experimentation plays an important part in learning science. Hands-on experiments in chemistry labs enhance students' understanding of the relevant theories, develop their critical thinking, and improve their practical abilities. Practical courses in chemistry are a vital part of the curriculum as a means of making sense of the universe. Therefore, helping students build confidence and competence in the lab is one of most the important aspects of chemistry education.

The Boy's Playbook of Science is an illustrated book that explains the various manipulations and arrangements of chemical apparatus required to perform scientific experiments successfully and offers a set of experiments for young pupils to explore scientific concepts, including chemistry. The book, first published in 1860, was written by John Henry Pepper (1821–1900), a chemist and illusionist with a great interest in education. He lectured at the Royal Polytechnic Institution in London and incorporated experiments, illusions, and magic lanterns into his popular science lectures. In *The Boy's Playbook* he details experiments in such a way that any young person may conduct them at home or in the classroom, organising them systematically, simply, and engagingly in an effort to inspire young schoolchildren to learn chemistry. Pepper's approach has been used and improved over time to teach practical skills in this modern world. A profound example is the Royal Society of Chemistry's engaging collection of popular science books that put chemistry into the context of daily life.

Entertaining and accessible, they offer summaries on a wide range of chemical science subjects.

The *Boy's Playbook of Science* is a classic work of popular science that has inspired generations of young scientists. However, it reveals the historical context of science education. Although the experiments are designed to be fun and accessible, accompanied by clear instructions and illustrations to explain each step, they are offered only to young boys. Pepper's male audience highlights a common belief of the Victorian era that women and men were fundamentally different. Male scientists pushed women out and marginalised them. They believed that 'feminine creatures' were incapable of science work, and there was a gendered assumption about who should learn science. While Pepper's gendered assumptions reflect the limitations of his time, the work represents the history of science education and serves as a valuable resource to teaching chemistry. Several initiatives and resources to support the teaching of practical courses, such as videos and simulations, have been built upon Pepper's approach to enhancing students' confidence and competence in chemistry labs.

Notably, discussions around gender in science education have shifted significantly in today's landscape. There are collective efforts to close the gender gap in science. The Royal Society of Chemistry highlights the importance of diversity to our mission to advance the chemical sciences. The University of Liverpool is committed to actively tackling barriers to gender equality. Several networks and groups at the University promote and celebrate gender equality. LivWiSE (Liverpool Women in Science & Engineering), a joint initiative by the Faculty of Science and Engineering at the University of Liverpool, celebrates, supports, and promotes women in science. The Department of Chemistry offers exciting opportunities for students at all levels to delve into the fascinating world of chemistry. The Department,

internationally known for its research, covers a broad scientific spectrum and operates in five flexible research groups: chemical models; chemistry world of health; energy and interfaces; materials chemistry; and organic synthesis and catalysis.

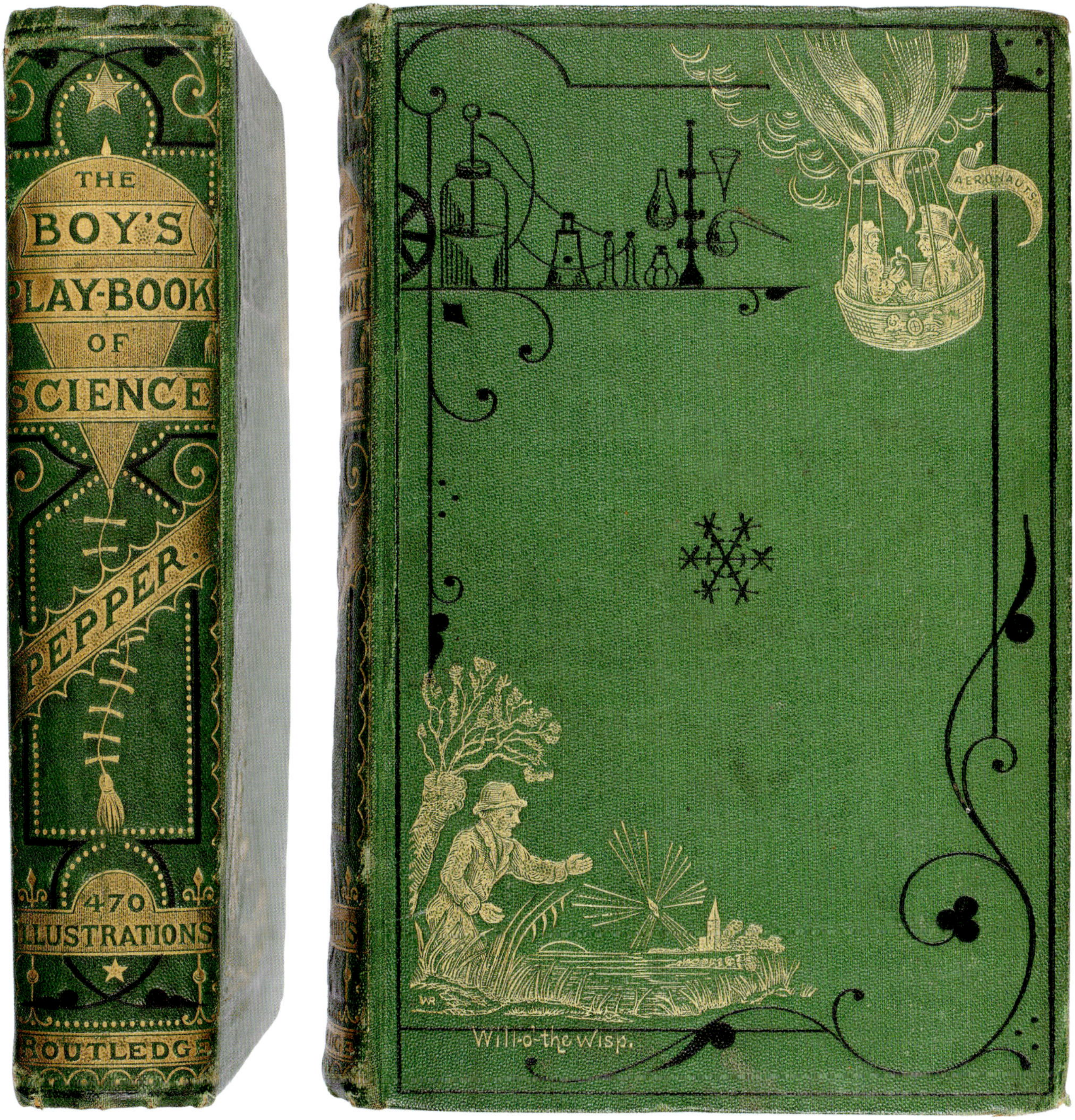

Gita Sedghi

How to not grow up (1970s?)

35

Peter Pan Keepsake. Printed pamphlet (Chatto and Windus, 1907), edited by Daniel O'Connor (1880–1951). Foreword by W.T. Stead (1849–1912). 44 pages, illustrations, portraits, music. 29 × 22.5 cm.

Acquired for the Library of the School of Education, 1970s?

Since 1928 Peter Pan has had a home in Liverpool's Sefton Park. In that year the park staged 'The Pageant of Peter Pan', accompanied by the unveiling of Sir George Frampton's statue. The pageant featured a model pirate ship on the park's lake and a cameo performance by the then Lord Mayor, Margaret Beavan (1877–1931). The occasion was marked by a telegram sent from J.M. Barrie (1860–1937) in London to 'Peter Pan, Sefton Park', telling Peter to 'behave today if only for the time' and instructing him not to grow up 'when they remove your swathing sheet'.

The Special Collections of the Sydney Jones Library is home to a fascinating memento of *Peter Pan, or The Boy Who Wouldn't Grow Up*. The *Peter Pan Keepsake* is a souvenir programme from the 1907 Christmas performances at London's Duke of York's Theatre. The colourful cover is taken from Charles Buchel's posters for the first 1904 production and features Peter flying with a night-gowned Wendy through a dark, starry sky; not over London or even Neverland, but a rural English village complete with church spire and invitingly lit cottage windows, perhaps suggesting the focuses on 'home' and national identity that underpin the fantasy and adventure of the play and the later novel, *Peter and Wendy* (1911). The *Keepsake*'s aesthetic appeal is unmistakable, but the programme is also of significance in terms of theatre archives, the development of the character of Peter Pan in literature and in the popular imagination, and social history.

W.T. Stead's introduction establishes that the *Keepsake*'s purpose is to encourage others to see the play so that it may 'make a thousand kiddies happy', but he also comments on the production's rejuvenating effects for adult audience members: 'twice a day, six days a week' it 'makes old boys grow young again'. This suggestion, and Stead's claim that watching the play transports him from 'grey-bearded grandfather' to feeling as though he had 'never grown up', emphasises the place of Barrie's Peter Pan, 'the boy who wouldn't grow up', in the Edwardian narrative or 'cult' of childhood. It also highlights the ongoing debate about the intended audience for Barrie's works as a part of this wider discourse: Stead's introduction frames the production as very much intended for children, but records show that the audience for the first performances in 1904 were predominantly adults.

The significant content of the *Keepsake* is 'The Story of Peter Pan', a prose retelling of 'Mr Barrie's Fantasy' by Daniel O'Connor. He later published this work as *The Peter Pan Picture Book* (1907), authorised by Barrie and complete with illustrations by Alice B. Woodward (1862–1951). Our collections include an edition of this and other items, such as editions of *Peter Pan in Kensington Gardens* and *Peter and Wendy*, illustrated by Arthur Rackham (1867–1939) and Mabel Lucie Atwell (1879–1964), which show the mutable nature of the Peter Pan narrative.

In the programme O'Connor's story is accompanied by photographs from the performances themselves, providing evidence of the elaborate sets and costuming – including that of Arthur Lupino, who played Nana – and extracts from John Crook's musical score. There are studio portraits of the adult actors who played Peter and Wendy, including Nina Boucicault, who first played the part of Peter in 1904 aged 37, a reminder of the 'old grown young' theme. The images also highlight the early establishment of the iconography of Peter Pan – his tunic and tights, his hat and pan-pipes.

The commercial value of this 'branding' is also evident in the *Keepsake*; it is filled with fascinating advertisements that give socio-historical insights into middle-class Edwardian life and the commercialisation of childhood that accompanied the cult. Some of the advertisements are for Pan-related merchandise: a

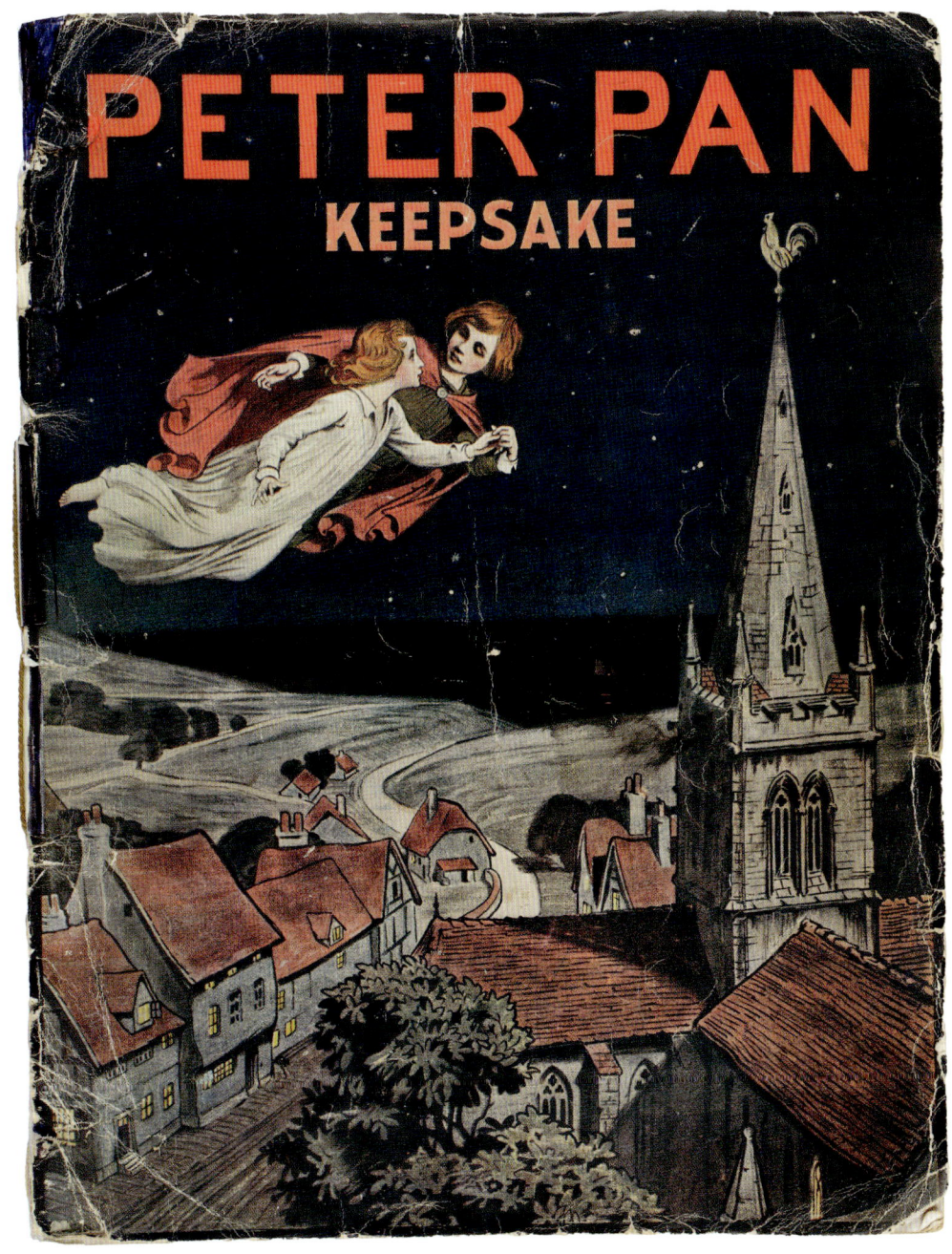

'reconstructed miniature' of the play, with 'over 120 coloured figures' (price 12s. 6d.), a box of 'Peter Pan Crackers' (price 3s. 6d,) or, for the very fortunate, an actual 'Peter Pan Nursery', designed for your home by Story and Trigg. Some products merely take advantage of the play's tropes: Wright's soap – 'The Nursery Soap'; Viyella nightdresses; and children's footwear marketed with the slogan 'if every child had a mother'. In this way, the *Keepsake* offers insights into not only a specific theatrical performance but also wider literary, theatrical, and social narratives intertwined with the story of the boy who refused to grow up.

Esme Miskimmin

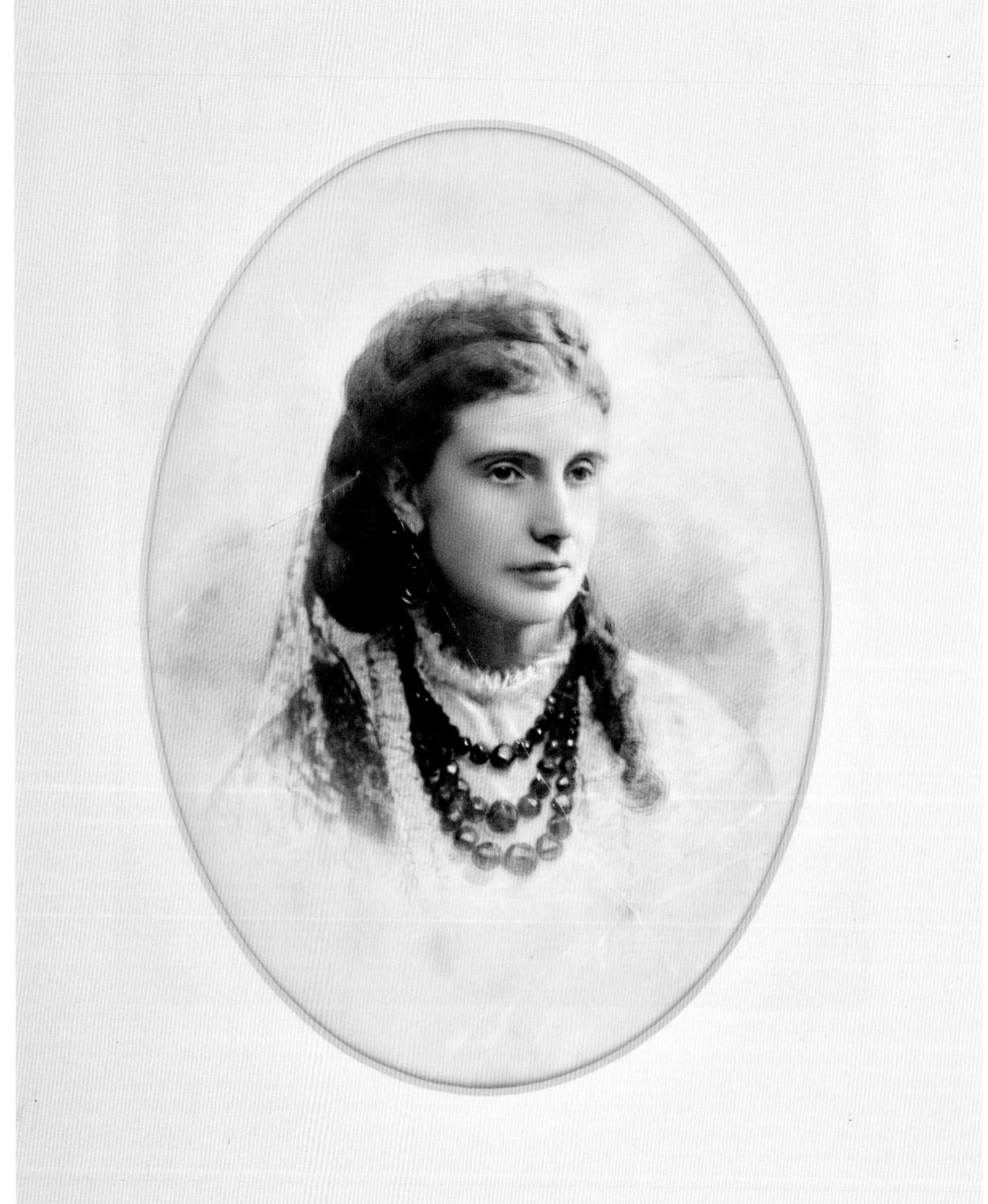

JOSEPHINE BUTLER IN LIVERPOOL (1970S)

36

Portrait of Josephine Butler. Opalotype (photograph printed on opaque, translucent white glass), from carte-de-visite by Robinson & Thompson, Liverpool, *c.*1869–70; head and shoulders. In original frame: 20 × 14 cm.

Transferred from Josephine Butler Memorial House, c.1975.

The hard outlines of Josephine's jet jewellery, presumably worn in mourning for her young daughter Evangeline (Eva, 1859–64), stand out against the soft focus of the opalotype photograph. Eva's death in an accident in 1864, two years before Josephine Butler and her husband, the Revd George Butler (1819–90), moved to Liverpool on his appointment as headmaster of Liverpool College, was a source of the lifelong grief that Josephine confided to her son during her last illness. But, accepting Eva's death as part of a divine plan and already aware of the impact of poverty on women's lives, she grasped the opportunity to learn from the suffering of others by agreeing to visit the female inmates in Brownlow Hill workhouse. There she helped to pick oakum (unravelling hemp fibres mixed with tar) and listened to the women's accounts of experiences markedly different from those of her privileged Northumbrian childhood and comfortable middle-class life. Risking criticism and the danger of infection, she opened her home to women from the oakum sheds, engaging some as servants and providing nursing care for others, later opening a Home of Rest to provide women with work and rehabilitation. She is perhaps best known for her campaign against the injustices of the 1864 Contagious Diseases Acts. Under this legislation, operating primarily in naval ports and military towns, the arrest, forcible genital examination, and temporary incarceration of women suspected of prostitution was used to try to control venereal disease. No man was arrested or examined. Repeal was achieved in 1886 through the work of the Ladies National Association for the Repeal of the Contagious Diseases Acts, of which Josephine was a prominent member. She also fought hard for the sexual protection of women and girls and against legalised prostitution in Britain, Europe, and British India. Convinced that women and men were entitled to equal respect and opportunity, Josephine actively supported the movements for female suffrage and the advancement of women through education. She served as president of the North of England Council for Promoting the Higher Education of Women from 1867 to 1871, a post that complemented her husband's later active involvement in the foundation of the University of Liverpool, and she was an active member of the Married Women's Property Committee.

The opalotype photograph is printed on opaque, translucent white glass, using a technique patented in Liverpool in 1857. It is part of an important national collection held at the University in which photographs and portraits, together with personal papers, campaigning literature, correspondence, and biographies of members of her family and notable Christians, including St Agnes and St Catherine of Siena, all demonstrate Josephine's wide interests and busy pen. The collections include those of Josephine Butler Memorial House, deposited on its closure in the mid-1970s, when its training for Anglican welfare workers was fully incorporated into that for social workers at the University of Liverpool, where the department, one of the first in the country, had been established in 1905.

Pat Starkey

FRANK BOWLING'S *BIG BIRD* (1970S)

37

Big Bird, 1964. Oil and velvet on canvas by Frank Bowling. 179 × 200 cm.

Gift from the Contemporary Art Society, 1975.

Richard Sheridan Patrick Michael Aloysius Franklin Bowling was born in Bartica, British Guiana (now Guyana) in 1934. Bowling arrived in England at just 19 to a country beset with coronation fever. After completing his National Service with the RAF, Bowling studied at Chelsea School of Art and then won a scholarship to study at the Royal College of Art in London.

Big Bird is a large oil diptych painting in two sections, and features an energetic, yet contorted, swan. The swan is depicted flying upwards on the left panel and descending on the right in a medley of colour blocks, grid-like, reminiscent to some degree of Dutch artist Piet Mondrian, on whom Bowling wrote a thesis. The painting incorporates colours such as blood red, lush green, and amber, and the textures can be felt, giving the impression of deserts, lunar landscapes, and tectonics typical of many of Bowling's pictures.

The painting was gifted to the University of Liverpool in 1975 by the Contemporary Art Society, and for many years it has been displayed in the Central Teaching Hub on campus. On several occasions it has quite literally flown its nest and been part of exhibitions, such as Bowling's 2019 retrospective at Tate Britain, showcasing his 60 years of exploration and experimentation with 'staining, pouring, and layering, adopting a variety of materials and objects'. His large, ambitious paintings are known for their distinctive textured surfaces and colourful, luminous quality (Tate 2019).

During the retrospective, *Big Bird* was displayed in the same gallery as his works *Swan I* and *Swan II* (both 1964). Swans were a recurrent theme for Bowling in the early 1960s, as he often saw them on his walks near the Thames. They symbolised different aspects of his complicated life. A successful artist sometimes struggling with the stresses of domestic life, Bowling saw himself as a bohemian artist with a serene exterior, hiding inner struggles.

In 1966 *Big Bird* was submitted to the First World Festival of Negro Arts in Dakar, Senegal, where it won the grand prize for painting. However, Bowling had reservations about being categorised as a Black painter rather than simply a painter, wanting never to be constrained by what people expected a Black artist to be or to paint. He was elected to the Royal Academy in 2005, becoming the first Black artist to have this honour, and was knighted in 2020.

Big Bird's connection to Liverpool is significant. British Guiana, sometimes referred to as 'Booker's Guiana', has strong links to the Booker family, particularly brothers Josias, George, William, and Richard, merchants from Liverpool, who had a major influence on the economic life of the country from the early nineteenth century until its independence in 1966. This influence included the ownership of sugar plantations and the use of scores of enslaved individuals to work on them. After the 1833 Slavery Abolition Act members of the Booker family received compensation for 52 emancipated individuals (UCL 2024). Although Booker Bros. & Co. no longer exists, *Big Bird* does, and it is available for generations of students to admire.

Richard Benjamin

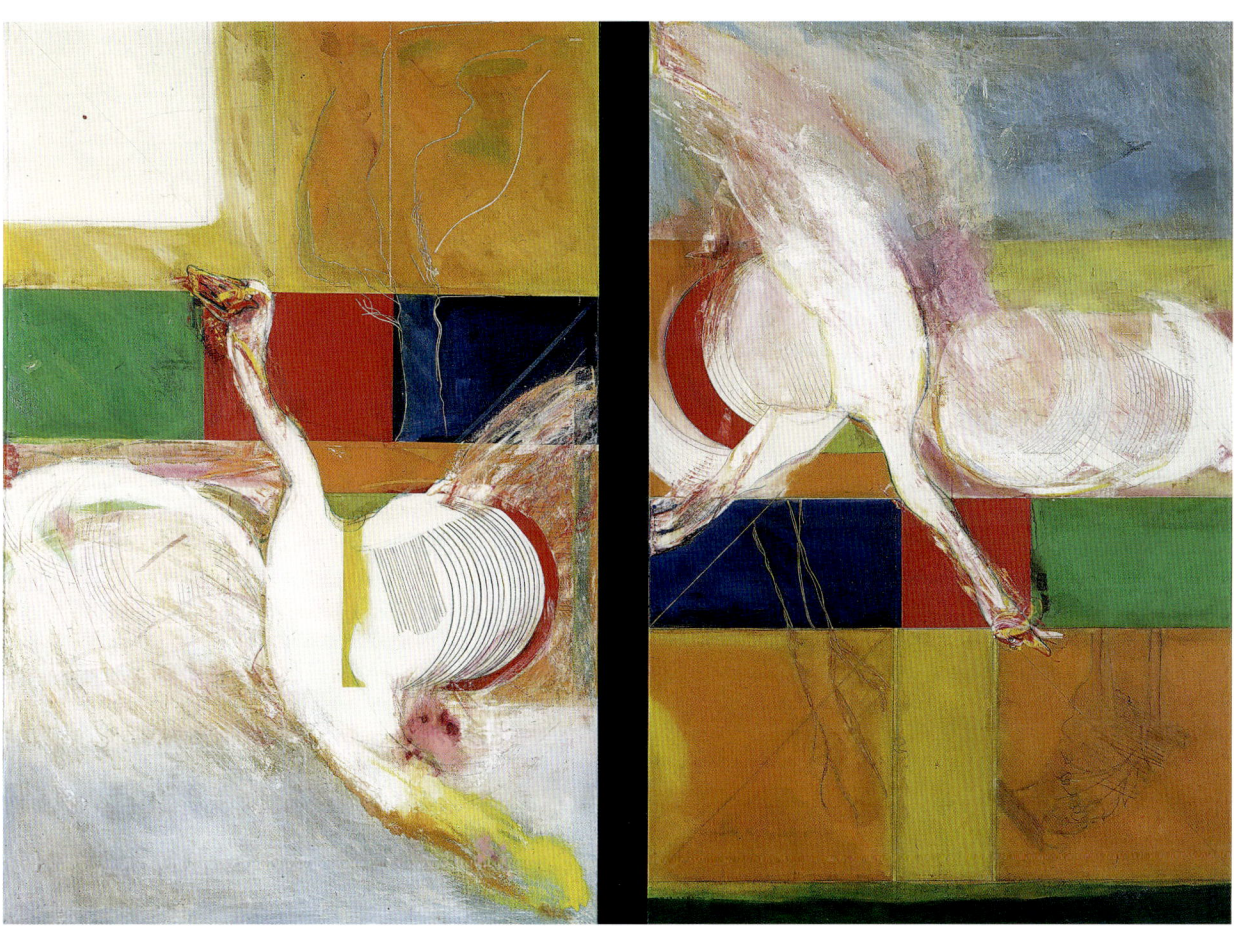

ADRIAN HENRI, ARTIST, POET, MUSICIAN (1980s)

38

'Love Is … ', 1965. Manuscript draft by Adrian Henri, ink on paper. 33 × 20.5 cm.

Purchased from Adrian Henri, 1983.

Love Heart, 1967. Painting by Adrian Henri, acrylic on paper. 18 × 14 cm.

Purchased from Adrian Henri Estate, 2007.

Adrian Henri (1932–2000) was an artist, poet, and musician whose eclectic interests and interdisciplinary art practice placed him at the centre of distinctively local yet internationally connected counter-cultures.

Born in Birkenhead, Henri trained as a painter at King's College, Newcastle, under Victor Pasmore (1908–98) and Richard Hamilton (1922–2011). He moved to Liverpool in 1956, later teaching at the Art College (1964–68). His early Pop Art sensibility is displayed in urban imagery, collages, and assemblages. He exhibited alongside David Hockney (1937–), Peter Blake (1932–) and Pauline Boty (1938–66), and his first one-man show was held at London's ICA in 1968, yet his affinities lay with European and US Neo-Dada artists rather than with the Royal College of Art brand of Pop.

Henri was also a pioneer of Happenings, setting up the first UK 'Events' in 1962. These performances were collaborative: a combination of live painting, poetry, music, and light show, involving the audience in a new type of participative experience at once radical and entertaining. Staged in Liverpool in the basement of Hope Hall (on the site of the Everyman theatre) or at the Cavern Club on Mathew Street, Henri's Happenings explored modernity or satirised politicians, racism, and the nuclear threat. His book on *Environments and Happenings* (1974) was a landmark publication.

Although he always thought of himself predominantly as an artist, Henri came to prominence as a writer alongside Roger McGough (1937–) and Brian Patten (1946–) in the best-selling poetry anthology *The Mersey Sound* (Penguin, 1967). Capturing the mood of the 1960s, the 'Liverpool Poets' wrote of young love, pop idols, atomic bombs, and sci-fi superheroes. Their readings made poetry a part of youth culture and fostered a Live Poetry scene in the UK.

LOVE IS ....

Love is feeling cold in the back of vans
Love is a fanclub with only two fans
Love is walking holding paintstained hands
Love is

Love is fish and chips on winter nights
Love is blankets full of strange delights
Love is when you don't put out the light
Love is

Love is the presents in Christmas shops
Love is when you're feeling Top of the Pops
Love is what happens when the music stops
Love is

Love is white panties lying all forlorn
Love is a pink nightdress still slightly warm
Love is when you have to leave at dawn
Love is

Love is you and love is me
Love is a prison and love is free
Love's what's there when you're away from me
Love is ....

Adrian Henri
Nov. 1965

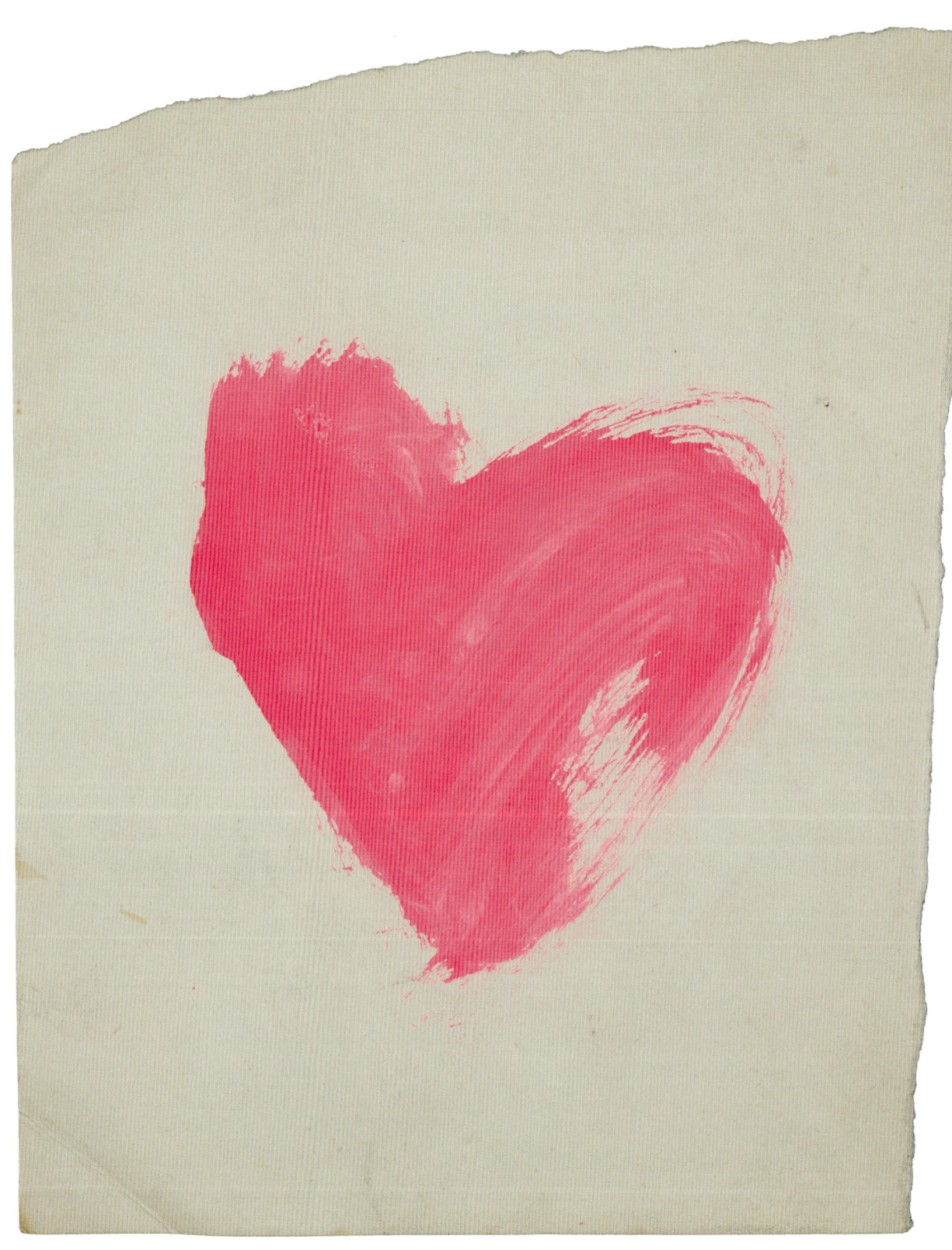

Performance was at the heart of Henri's practice, as a visual artist and as a poet. From 1968 he fronted the eccentric poetry-and-rock group *Liverpool Scene*, signed by RCA. Their debut album was produced by John Peel (1939–2004), who dubbed Henri 'one of the great non-singers of our time'. In 1969 the band performed at the Isle of Wight Festival, supported Led Zeppelin, and toured the USA.

Painting, poetry, and music came together again in *Love Nights*, three events held at the Everyman theatre in May–June 1967, with various artists contributing love poems, songs, and images.

Henri's love poems chart chance encounters, everyday enchantments, false starts, and reluctant separations. Often, intimacy is infused with references to popular culture and politics, as in 'Without You':

Without you green apples wouldn't taste greener,
Without you Clark Kent would forget how to become Superman,
Without you indifferent colonels would shrug their shoulders and press the button.

In a 1968 essay Henri explained:

I'd like to think that if you read through a dozen or so of my poems, which are mostly love poems, you'd be able to say what my views on most political or social or artistic questions were. I'd rather do it this way than write an overtly political poem or a straight love poem. [...] What fascinates me about art is the process of metamorphosis. This is why I find the new twentieth century tradition of collage/assemblage so exciting. One thing I think is interesting about working today is a sort of awareness about how much personal content can go into a work of art and not violate its universal validity.

Personal in content yet universal in scope, 'Love Is ... ' is deliberately accessible. Its images are immediate, and the structure and rhythm, based on repetition, eschew traditional scansion to adopt Pop idioms. Henri performed this poem to music at *Love Nights*. He also painted pink hearts that were distributed to the audience during the event – an apposite prelude to the Summer of Love.

Catherine Marcangeli

Taking tea with a dragon (1980s)

39

Dragon bowl, about 1760. Porcelain, attributed to Richard Chaffers.
6.6 × (diameter) 15.5 cm.

Purchased with the support of the V&A Purchase Grant Fund, 1986.

During the early eighteenth century Liverpool grew rapidly in size and importance. In 1700 it was a small port with just over 5,000 inhabitants. By 1750 its population had expanded to more than 18,000, and by the end of the century it had risen to nearly 78,000. This rapid growth was driven by an increase in the port's coastal trade in coal and salt, and particularly by the transatlantic trade in enslaved African people to the West Indies and North America. Growth in trade was actively encouraged by an entrepreneurial town corporation that oversaw the opening of Britain's first wet dock as early as 1715, and by the continual development of the dock system thereafter.

The merchant class that sprang up in the booming port and growing town were eager to display their rising social status and refined tastes through their personal and household possessions. Ritualised social customs, including tea drinking, marked out the emerging mercantile elite. Chinese porcelain, especially in the form of tea wares, was highly prized but prohibitively expensive, as it was imported only by the East India Company, who held the monopoly.

In the first half of the eighteenth century knowledge of the method by which Chinese hard-paste porcelain was made had not yet reached England, nor had the raw materials required been discovered. But from the 1750s onwards two forms of the less durable soft-paste porcelain were developed, both used in the making of tea wares in Liverpool. One, known later as phosphatic porcelain, included burnt animal bones (bone-ash) in the clay mixture, producing a strong white translucent ceramic body. The other, known as steatitic porcelain, included soaprock, a mineral mined on the Lizard peninsula in Cornwall, which increased the ware's resistance to thermal shock when in contact with boiling water.

This bowl, now admired for its decorative, aesthetic qualities, was originally a utilitarian object. It was made as a slop bowl, part of a tea service, for tipping the dregs of cold tea into before more hot tea was poured into a cup. Its interior design of a dragon chasing a burning pearl, surrounded by stylised clouds and with its tail flipped over the edge and extended around the exterior, is typical of such bowls.

In Chinese art the dragon has imperial associations while the pearl signifies wisdom. The dragon is generally shown, as here, with four claws, while five-clawed dragons were reserved for objects used only by the emperor. English dragon bowls were influenced by Chinese hard-paste porcelain versions, which had been made for centuries in Jingdezhen, in Jiangxi province, the centre of the Chinese ceramics industry.

This bowl has been attributed to the pottery of Richard Chaffers (1722–65), situated on Liverpool's Shaw's Brow, now William Brown Street. From 1746, in partnership with Philip Christian, Chaffers manufactured tin-glazed earthenware, otherwise known as delftware, at these premises. But in 1755 he and Christian entered into an agreement with Robert Podmore, formerly a potter at the Worcester Porcelain Company, to begin making porcelain. Podmore brought with him knowledge of Worcester's secret recipe for making soaprock porcelain, crucial to the success of Chaffers' business. The Worcester pottery had begun using soaprock, sourced in Cornwall, in 1752 when they took over the Bristol Porcelain Company, the first English pottery to use soaprock in the manufacture of soft-paste porcelain.

Chaffers was keen to let his customers know about the resilient qualities of his porcelain. In the first advertisement for it, published in *Williamson's Liverpool Advertiser* in December 1756, he stressed that 'All the Ware is proved with boyling Water before it's expos'd to Sale.'

When Richard Chaffers died in 1765, his widow Ann Chaffers and his partner Philip Christian continued making porcelain at the Shaw's Brow pottery until 1770, when Christian bought Ann's share of the business. The name Chaffers may have disappeared with time, but his pots, like this beautiful bowl, are his long-lasting legacy.

Pauline Rushton

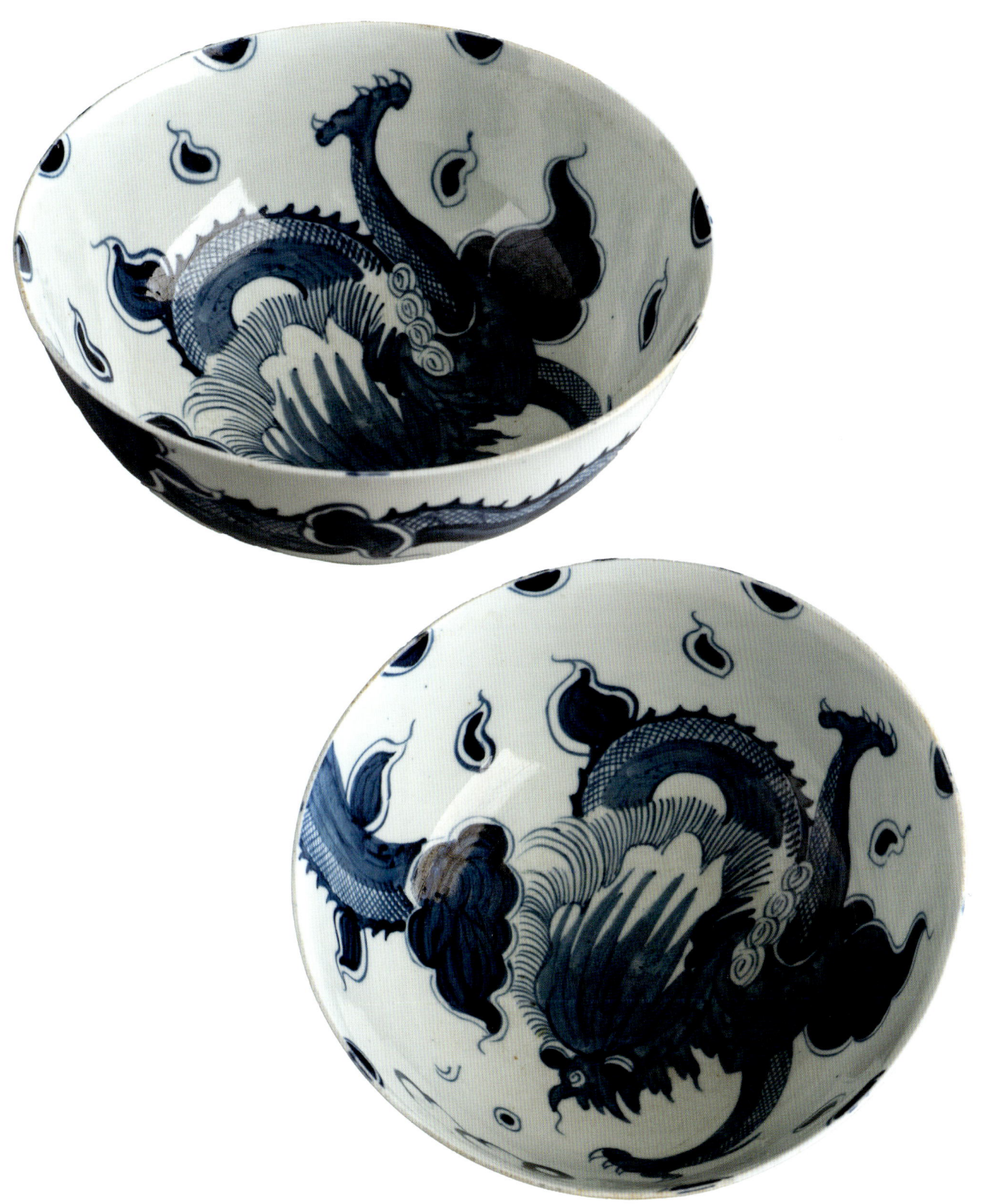

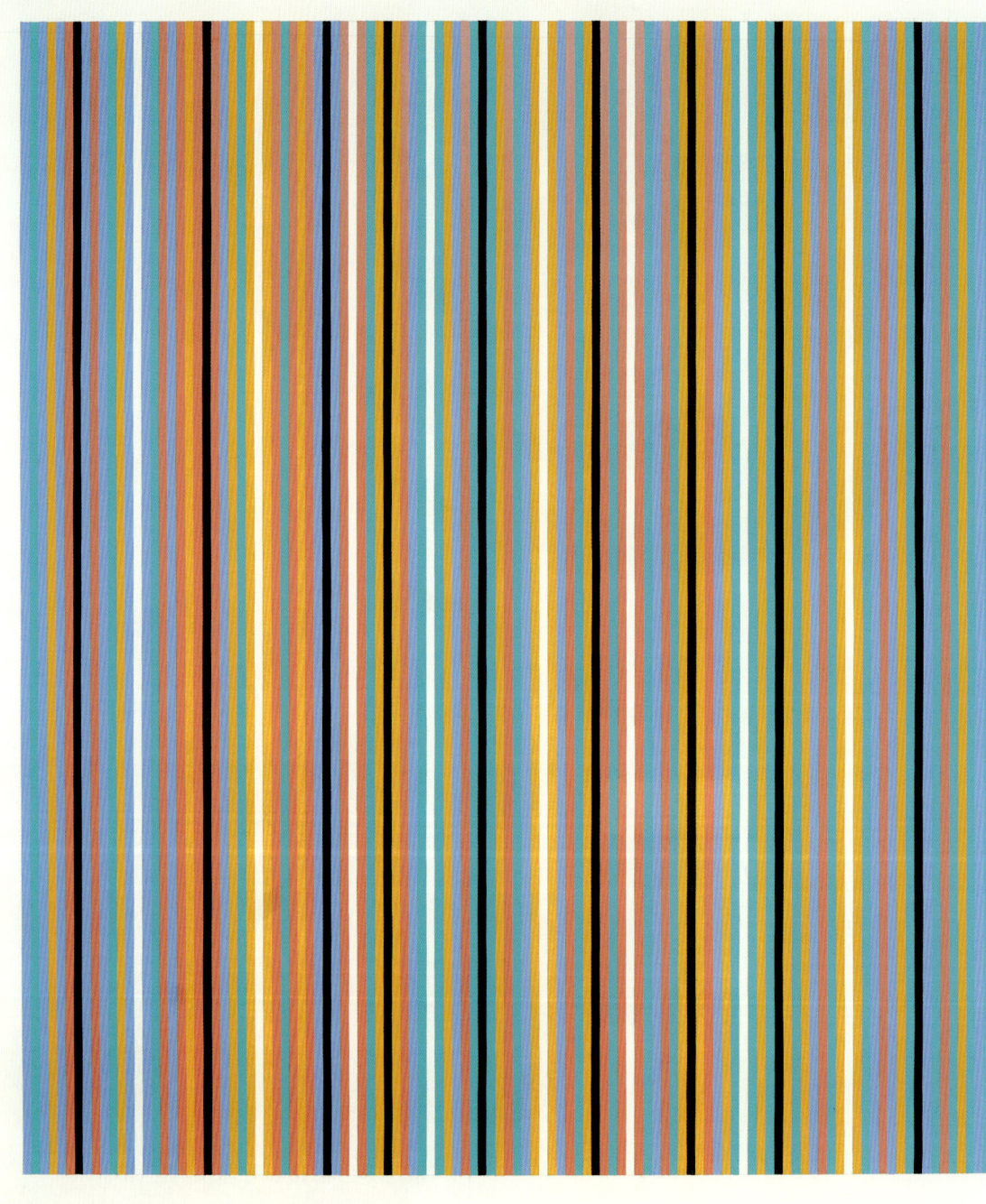

BRIDGET RILEY IN EGYPT AND LIVERPOOL (1980s)

40

Study for 'Ra', 1980. Gouache & pencil on paper by Bridget Riley. Signed and dated bottom right: Bridget Riley 1980. Inscribed bottom left: Final Study for Ra/Free organisation./Four colours, black and white./Light passages interspersed with blue'd sequences. 114 × 83.6 cm.

Presented by the Contemporary Art Society, 1982.

Bridget Louise Riley CH CBE (b. 24 April 1931) is an English painter known for her optical art paintings. She graduated from the Royal College of Art in 1952 and developed her Op Art style of work in the early 1960s, which established her as one of the UK's most famous female artists. Riley's early Op Art works and better-known pieces were abstract patterns created in black and white that typically give the viewer the impression of movement or flashing and vibrating patterns. The complexity of visual processing requires almost 50% of our brain, and the precise alternating and contrasting patterns and lines employed in Riley's art exploit the brain's attempt at resolving and understanding movement and depth in images received by the eye. Riley herself has said 'My work has developed on the basis of empirical analyses and syntheses, and I have always believed that perception is the medium through which states of being are directly experienced.'

As Riley's work began to explore the use of colours within her templates of shapes and forms, a trip to Egypt gave inspiration for the work shown here. The fixed palette observed in the pyramid and tomb paintings, used for up to 3,000 years, led Riley to observe that 'the precise shades of these colours had evolved under a brilliant North African light and consequently they seemed to embody the light and even reflect it back from the walls.'

Riley's large mural *Blue Intervals* was installed at the Royal Liverpool University Hospital in 1983. The mural was commissioned specifically for the hospital as part of an effort to incorporate significant artworks into public spaces within the building. This initiative also included several artists from the north-west of England tasked to enrich the hospital environment, blending different styles and artistic approaches to create a varied and stimulating visual experience for patients, staff, and visitors alike. As someone who has fallen under all three categories within the hospital (1993–2018), I can personally regard this as a success and a welcome juxtaposition to the imposing monolithic grey exterior of the hospital. Alas, while her artwork was not a temporary exhibition, but a lasting installation appreciated for years, the closure of the hospital means that the scale of the artwork is now lost. However, the decoration was dismantled and a version was installed at Chinati foundation, Marfa, in Texas in 2017–19 and Riley's 'Five studies for the Royal Liverpool Hospital' of 1981, in gouache and pencil, were purchased for the University with support from the V&A Purchase Grant Fund and the Contemporary Art Society in 1983. As Riley's work will continue to inspire wonder in future generations to come, it is a source of pride that her work was shared and appreciated by so many who were passing through the otherwise stale clinical environment of the Royal Liverpool University Hospital.

Carl Sheridan

LARKS IN THE PARK (1980S)

Pre-publication page for *Merseysound* fanzine no. 18, 1981, collage of print on paper. 29.5 × 21.5 cm.

Donated by Roger Hill, 1980s–1990s.

This page from a fanzine captures two aspects of Merseyside's thriving 1980s alternative music culture. The fanzine is *Merseysound*, which was produced from 1979 to 1982 and eventually sold across the north-west of England and beyond (including London). A fanzine was a publication somewhere between a magazine and a newsletter and was distinguished by its DIY ethos and its minimal production budget, supplemented by a lot of voluntary contributions and enthusiasm. If you contributed it was because you were a fan and virtually all of the fanzines of the late 1970s and early 1980s were dedicated to music – punk, post-punk, and new wave. I had been a punk fan since my arrival in Merseyside in 1978, but I had never thought to edit a fanzine until I was invited to help launch *Merseysound*. I was working on an education project in Liverpool at the time and one of my students introduced me to his brother, who was on an employment scheme and planning to put out a fanzine in the local area – his name was Ronnie Flood. Ronnie saw this enterprise as a way to launch himself on the route to fame and fortune beyond the steep slopes of Everton. Alas for Ronnie, and most fanziners, there was no money to be made in low-level publishing, but we set out hopefully.

Merseysound came and went well before desktop publishing. A dedicated team of volunteers brought together acres of typed text, scalpels, Pritt stick, Letraset, and photographic prints to create pages that returned from the printers as respectable looking fanzines. This issue was no. 18, produced in the summer of 1981. Most of its 1,000 copies were sold for the sum of 20p at clubs, gigs, shops, and the more enlightened arts venues. By this time there were a number of fanzines in circulation in Merseyside, but *Merseysound* had a reputation as the 'fanzine of record' during these years and each issue took progressively more time and investment to produce. By now we had even branched out into tapezines – cassette-magazines. Also in *Merseysound* no. 18 were articles on local bands The Wild Swans and The Last Chant, features on Nico and reggae, and reviews of new records. The fanzine movement did much to expand and develop the music scene, not least by listing gigs. Issue no. 1 listed twelve gigs at two venues and by no. 18, partly due to a better rapport with promoters, we could report 108 gigs at seven venues.

One of the live music events we featured was Larks in the Park, here reviewed by Steve Nelson. Staged on the bandstand of Sefton Park over a number of August Bank Holidays, with six bands a day over three days, Larks was another enterprise kept afloat by voluntary contributions and minimal funding, and I played my part as a DJ and a member of the organising team. Bucket collections at the gig covered PA costs and other practicalities, the bandstand came courtesy of the city council, the free programme was paid for by advertising and the rest was for the love of it all, but these were heady days for Mersey music. Bands had success in their sights and *Merseysound* and Larks were worth giving their time to for free to gain attention.

And then history moved on. The 1981 Toxteth Riots were just (literally) round the corner. Soon a more diverse social and musical community took over the park duties, with the Earthbeat Festival and eventually a proper budget. Just before its 26th and final iteration I handed over *Merseysound* to Steve, as I had been head-hunted to present the alternative music programme on BBC Radio Merseyside. Just as Ronnie had discovered a couple of years before that there was no money to be made in fanzine production, so we soon concluded by 1982 that there was money to be lost and reluctantly shut up shop. But by then the local alternative music scene had an unstoppable momentum. Frankie Goes To Hollywood – who had played Larks – were on their way. It had all been an overture to something even bigger, but what an overture!

Roger Hill

Larks in the Park

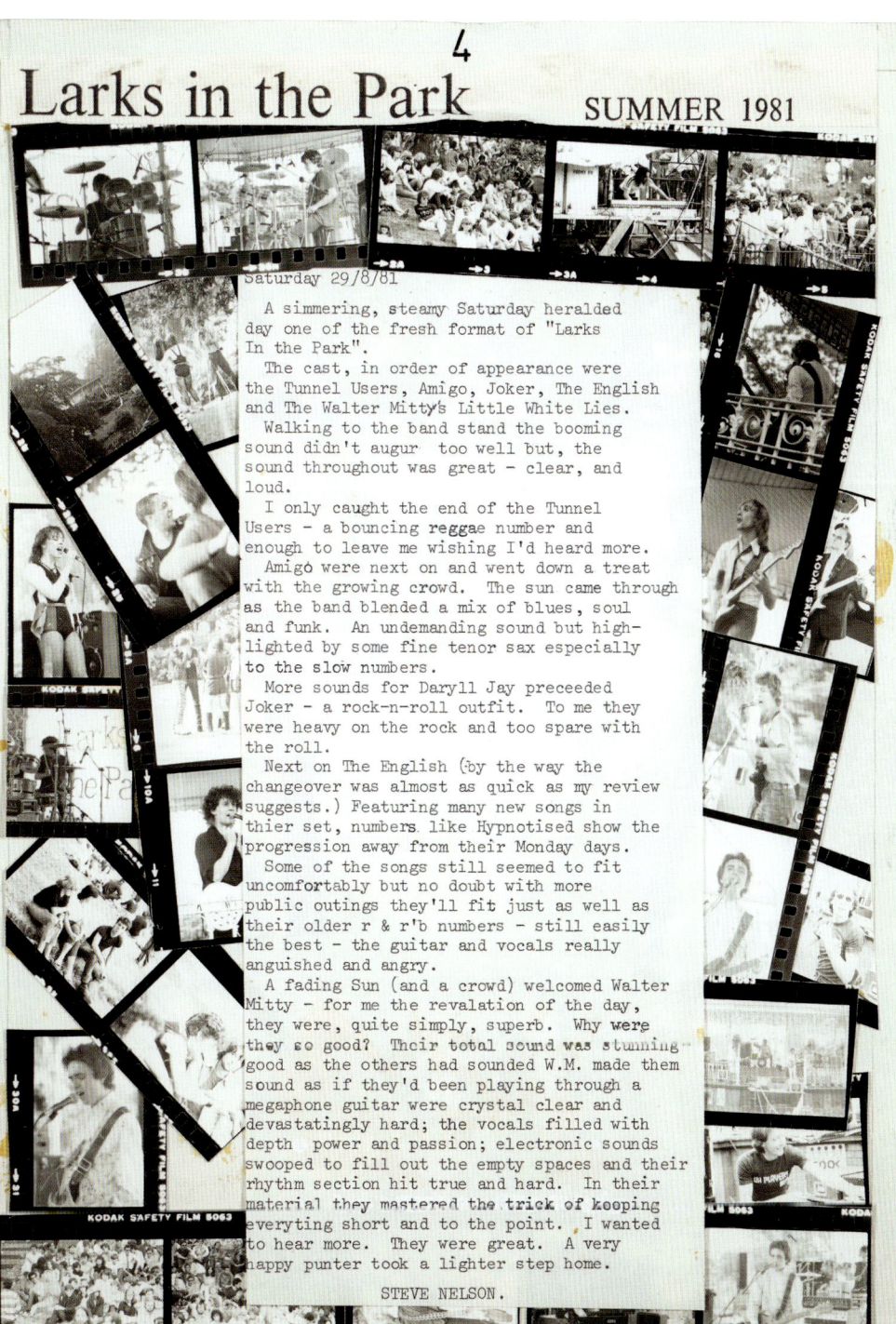

Saturday 29/8/81

A simmering, steamy Saturday heralded day one of the fresh format of "Larks In the Park".

The cast, in order of appearance were the Tunnel Users, Amigo, Joker, The English and The Walter Mitty's Little White Lies.

Walking to the band stand the booming sound didn't augur too well but, the sound throughout was great – clear, and loud.

I only caught the end of the Tunnel Users – a bouncing reggae number and enough to leave me wishing I'd heard more.

Amigo were next on and went down a treat with the growing crowd. The sun came through as the band blended a mix of blues, soul and funk. An undemanding sound but highlighted by some fine tenor sax especially to the slow numbers.

More sounds for Daryll Jay preceeded Joker – a rock-n-roll outfit. To me they were heavy on the rock and too spare with the roll.

Next on The English (by the way the changeover was almost as quick as my review suggests.) Featuring many new songs in thier set, numbers like Hypnotised show the progression away from their Monday days.

Some of the songs still seemed to fit uncomfortably but no doubt with more public outings they'll fit just as well as their older r & r'b numbers – still easily the best – the guitar and vocals really anguished and angry.

A fading Sun (and a crowd) welcomed Walter Mitty – for me the revalation of the day, they were, quite simply, superb. Why were they so good? Their total sound was stunning good as the others had sounded W.M. made them sound as if they'd been playing through a megaphone guitar were crystal clear and devastatingly hard; the vocals filled with depth power and passion; electronic sounds swooped to fill out the empty spaces and their rhythm section hit true and hard. In their material they mastered the trick of keeping everyting short and to the point. I wanted to hear more. They were great. A very happy punter took a lighter step home.

STEVE NELSON.

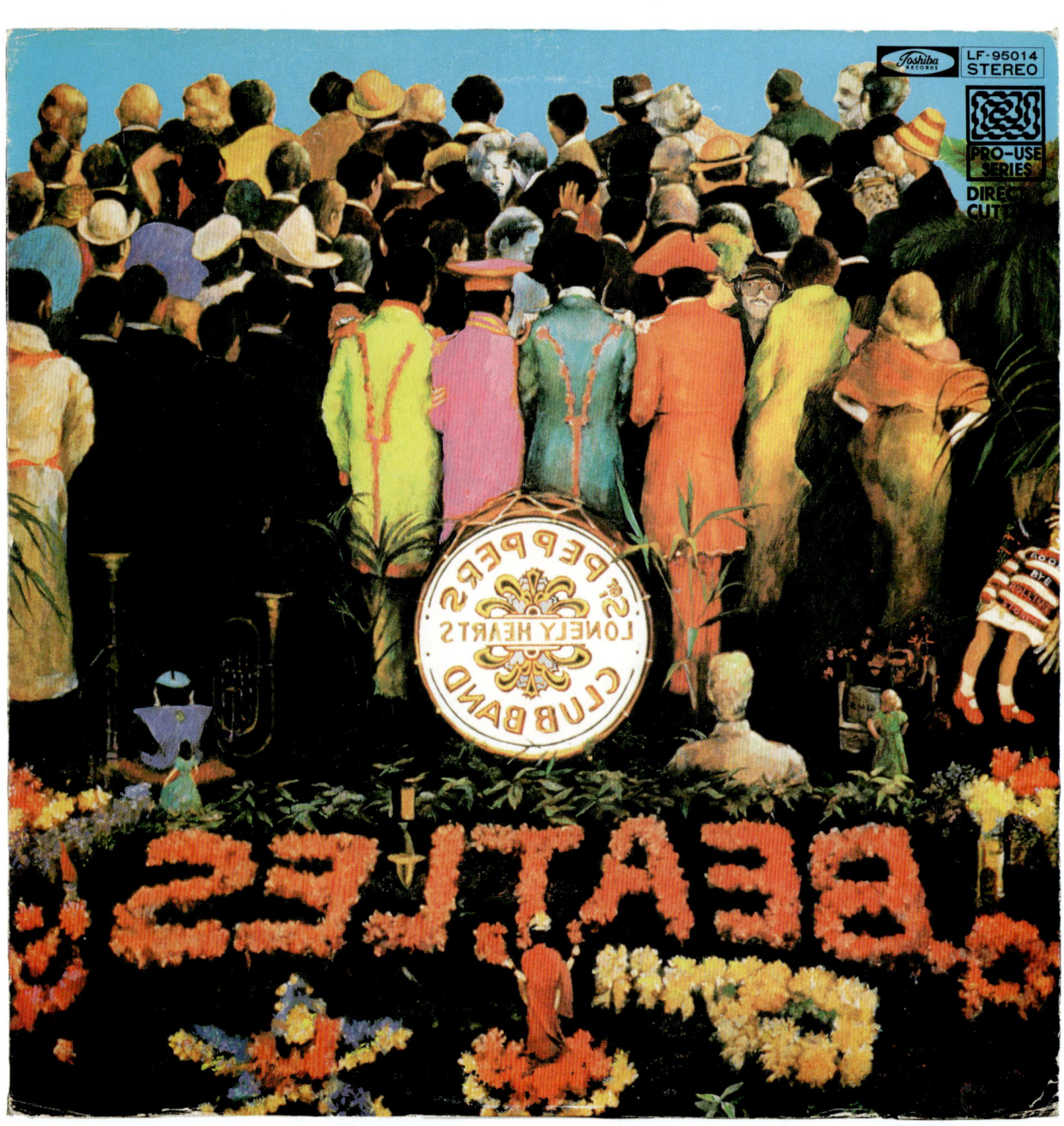

THE BEATLES, REVERSED (1980S)

Parody album cover for *Sgt Pepper's Lonely Hearts Club Band*, 1977. Vinyl LP by Jun Fukamachi (1946–2010) and card record cover with illustration by Fumio Tamabuchi, Toshiba Records, 1977. LF-95014. 31.3 × 31.3 cm.

Collected by the Institute of Popular Music.

Album cover parodies of The Beatles' records have existed for almost as long as The Beatles themselves. One of the earliest was *We're Just In It For The Money* (1969) by Frank Zappa's band The Mothers of Invention, which featured a parody of the cover of The Beatles' 1968 release *Sgt Pepper's Lonely Hearts Club Band* in a not-so-subtle critique of The Beatles' perceived commercialisation of youth culture.

Since then, by some counts more than 2,000 different albums with Beatles album cover parodies have been made, many with little musical similarity to anything Beatles. In addition to *Sgt Pepper's*, 1963's *With The Beatles* and 1969's *Abbey Road* have also been the source of much cover design inspiration, having been parodied by artists such as ABBA, the Red Hot Chili Peppers, Kanye West, and Sesame Street; in fact, there are at least 25 examples with album covers that parody The Beatles within the University's Institute of Popular Music Archive alone. One particular highlight is Japanese pianist Jun Fukamachi's *Sgt Pepper's Lonely Hearts Club Band* (1977), notable both for its quirky cover visuals, provided by artist Fumio Tamabuchi, and for its pioneering jazz fusion sound.

Fukamachi's *Lonely Hearts Club Band* occupies an interesting musical space between cover work and original creation. The melodies of six songs from the original album are recreated on piano, synth, and percussion without vocals but with a decidedly jazzier texture to the harmonics, caused in part by the synth notes blurring slightly out of tune. The album was recorded direct-to-disc, meaning that each side is one live take performed solo by Fukamachi. Despite performing alone, Fukamachi was able to evoke the sounds of multiple performers by switching fluidly between a variety of sounds and textures on his synth and by simultaneously playing a bass pedal and tambourine.

Fukamachi's very first album, *Piano Solo Best of Beatles*, for Polydor in 1972, was also a Beatles cover album. But Fukamachi's oeuvre extends far beyond just The Beatles; he is arguably better known for his vibrant and energetic solo work in albums such as *On The Move* (Alfa, 1978) and *Quark* (Alfa, 1980), which formed cornerstones of the emerging funk-infused genre of Japanese jazz fusion. He also performed with other giants of the genre, including Masayoshi Takanaka and the band Casiopoeia, as well as internationally recognised artists such as Steve Gadd and The Brecker Brothers.

Perhaps most notoriously, though, his work as a composer for high-profile private events led him to create a record for fashion brand Nicole's 1986 Spring and Summer Collection event subtitled *Instrumental Images*. For years this record went without an official release and fewer than 1,000 pressings, and was available only on vinyl to staff and guests of the event. Fukamachi had been regularly asked to create music for fashion events, but this particular production caught the attention of Andy Warhol and actress Candice Bergen, who were in attendance. Due to both its obscurity and acclaim from the few people who heard it, the record became a prize for collectors. This atmospheric and pensive album, inspired by Erik Satie's *Gymnopédies*, was eventually reprinted in 2017, seven years after Fukamachi died in 2010.

Val Capewell

Felicia Dorothea Hemans medal for lyrical poetry, 1899 (1890s and 1990s)

Signed sketches of designs by Elkington & Co. Ltd., 25 Church St, Liverpool, sent with quotation for making bronze medals, 7 January 1899. 11.2 × 9.5–8.5 cm.

University Archive, 1899.

Bronze proofs of obverse and reverse of medal (mounted in wooden plaque), 1900. By Charles John Allen (1862–1956). Diameter 12.5 cm.

Presented by Martin and Geoffrey Gibbs, grandsons of Charles J. Allen, in 1990.

Felicia Hemans was born in Liverpool in 1793 and lived there until she was seven, before moving to North Wales. Nothing short of a prodigy, her first book of poems, *Poems by Felicia Dorothea Browne*, was published in 1808 when she was fourteen years old. Married at 18 and then separated from her soldier husband, who left her and her five sons to fend for themselves, Hemans published nineteen books of poems and was often included in lists of the now more well-remembered Romantic poets such as Wordsworth and Keats. Her work, on which she depended for her income, is notable for the range of its exploration with genre, moving across the lyrical, narrative, dramatic, and elegaic.

Hemans died in 1835, but her presence endured into the twentieth century through the anthologisation of her poem 'Casabianca' (first published in 1826), which is so bedded into the cultural imaginary that it has been referenced and parodied by authors as diverse as Arthur Ransome in the second of the Swallows and Amazons series, and Spike Milligan. 'Casabianca', which begins 'The boy stood on the burning deck' – words probably memorised by generations of schoolchildren across the English-speaking world of the Victorian empire – is a ballad that refers to the death of a French sea captain and his son during the Battle of the Nile in 1798. The poem tells the story of the young boy who promises to stay on the burning ship until his father tells him otherwise. Unaware that his father has died, the boy cries out over and over to ask if he can move yet. Ostensibly a poem

that reinforces the importance of filial duty, fidelity to promises, and a Victorian pedagogy of obedience, the poem nevertheless subtly undercuts and destabilises such merits through the pathos and needlessness of the boy's death. The poem was memorably rewritten by the great twentieth-century American poet Elizabeth Bishop (1911–79) in 1946, playfully but painfully exploring the loneliness, complex inner life, and losses of a child reciting the poem under duress.

The University's archive holdings of Hemans offer an intriguing insight into her complex character and include several handwritten letters and autograph copies of poems. Among the holdings are a set of letters from 1899 discussing the setting up of a memorial fund and exploring designs by Elkington and Co. of Church Street for a commemorative bronze medal to be awarded to the winners of the University's Felicia Hemans Prize for lyrical poetry. The prize, renamed the Felicia Hemans Poetry Prize, and now worth £30, is still awarded every year for a poem written by a member of the University or beyond. The image on the commemorative coin was to be based on an existing bust of Hemans, photographs of which are also in the collections. The medal, however, was apparently never completed, though another design, by Liverpool sculptor Charles John Allen (1862–1956), received the commission. The proposed design, and the final bronze coin, are shown together here.

Deryn Rees-Jones

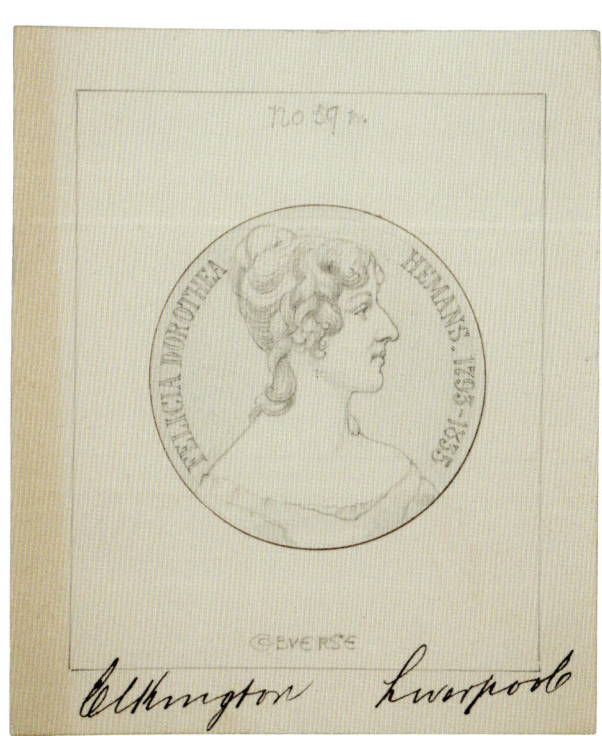

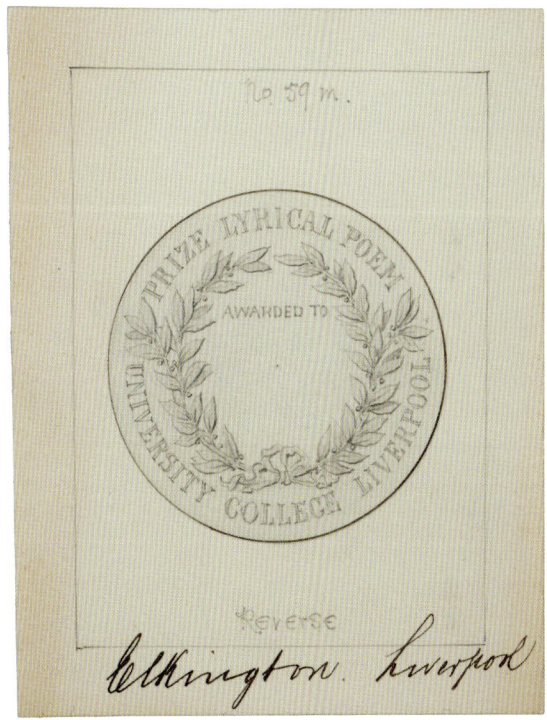

Inscribed obverse: 'FELICIA DOROTHEA HEMANS 1793–1835' Inscribed reverse: 'PRIZE LYRICAL POEM. UNIVERSITY COLLEGE LIVERPOOL.'

Signed obverse above right shoulder: 'C J Allen 1900'. Inscribed obverse: 'FELICIA DOROTHEA HEMANS 1793–1835'. Inscribed reverse at left: 'PRIZE LYRICAL POEM'. Inscribed reverse at right: 'UNIVERSITY OF LIVERPOOL'.

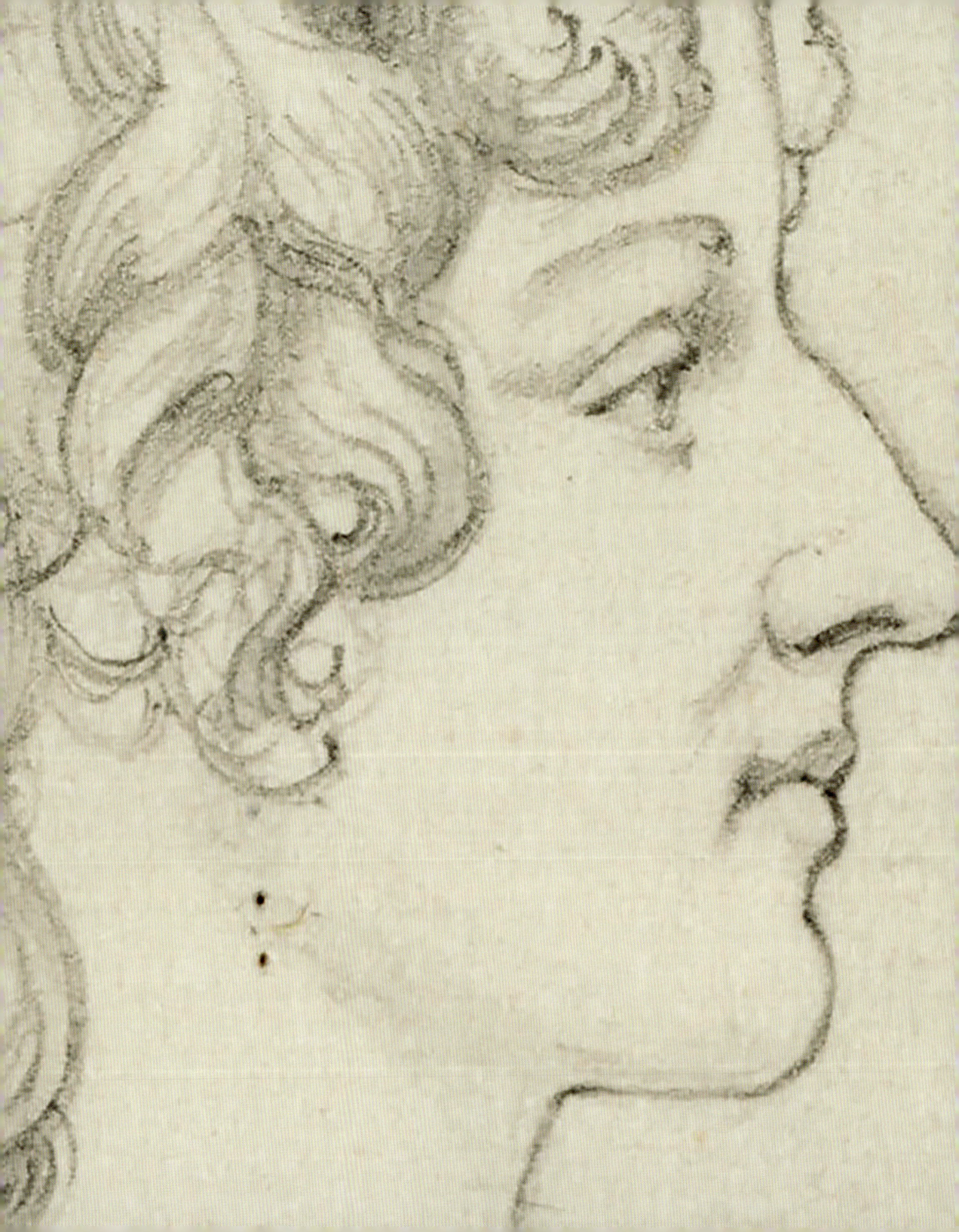

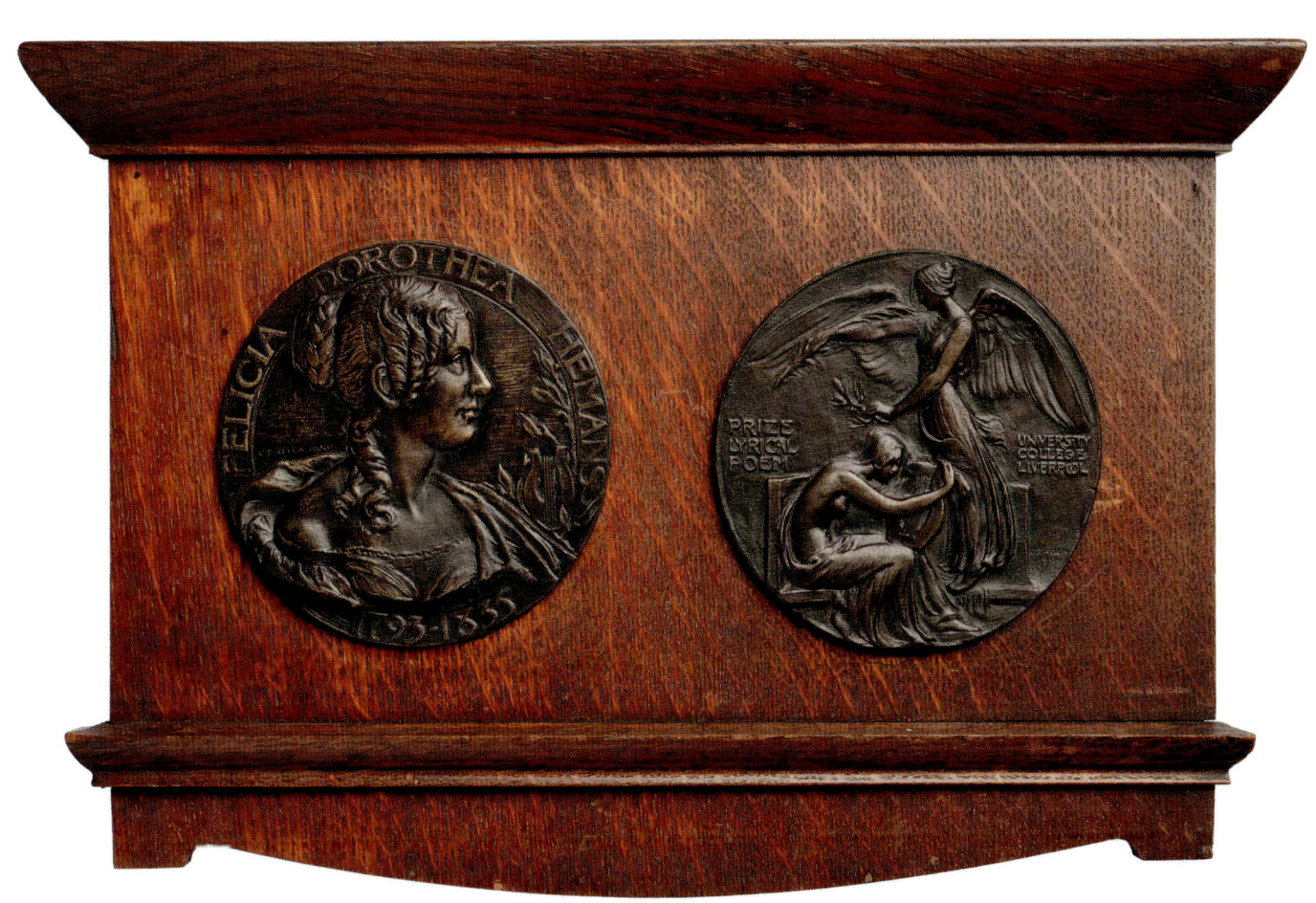

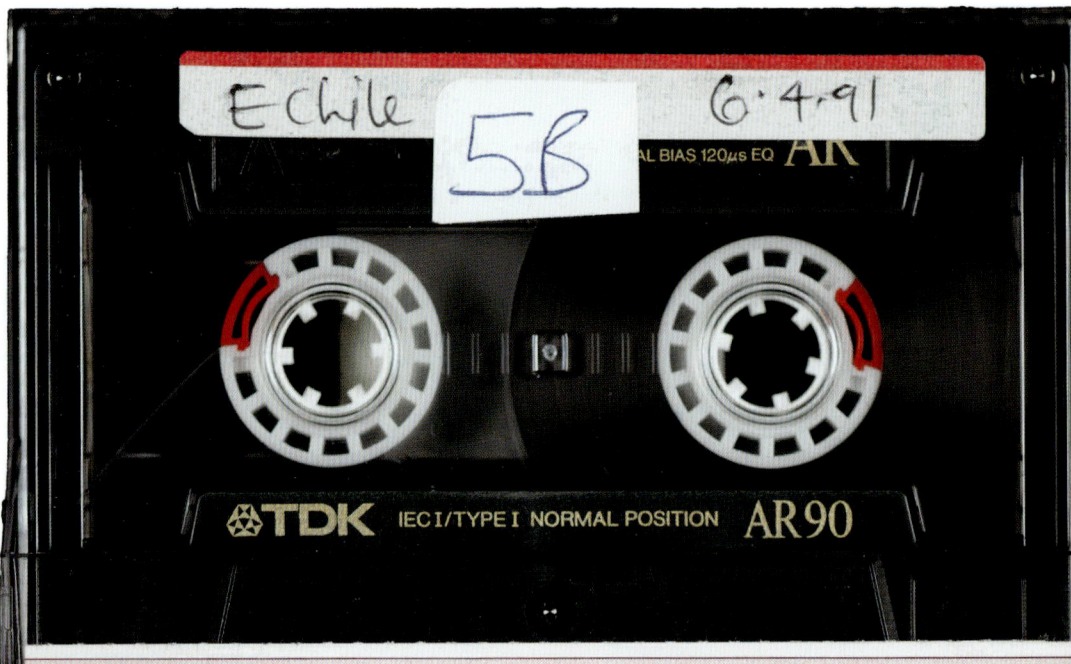

AL BIAS 120µs EQ   AR

◈TDK   IEC I/TYPE I NORMAL POSITION   AR90

A	DATE/TIME NOISE REDUCTION ☐ON ☐OFF	B	DATE/TIME NOISE REDUCTION ☐ON ☐OFF

6 April 1991

Concert-cum-mass-meeting in ESTADIO CHILE
(Santiago) to "purify" the Stadium and
commemorate those who died or were held there
in September 1973 — event largely centres on
the figure of Víctor Jara. [Recorded by Jan
Fairley.]

Institute of Popular Music Archive, Robert Pring-Mill and Jan Fairley Collections (1990s)

44

Audio cassette in plastic case with card insert, 1990s. Robert Pring-Mill's copy of Jan Fairley's recording of Canto Libre: Jornadas de Purificacion el Estadio Chile, 5–6 April 1991, with his typescript notes. 11 × 7 × 1.5 cm.

Given to the IPM, 1996.

Colour photograph of artwork created in tribute to Victor Jara at Canto Libre: Jornadas de Purificacion el Estadio Chile, 5–6 April 1991. 15 × 10 cm.

Jan Fairley collection given to the IPM, 2012.

The *Estadio Chile* (Chile Stadium) was the venue for the *Primer festival internacional de la canción popular* (First international festival of popular song) in Santiago, Chile, in June 1973. During the 1960s folk revival of the *Nueva Cancion* (New Song) movement Chilean musicians such as Violeta Parra (1917–67), Inti-Illimani, and Victor Jara (1932–73) had drawn on tradition to create a new popular music with a message of social change. Many musicians had supported the election of the socialist government of Salvador Allende (1908–73) in 1970. Inspired by chants heard at political rallies, Quilapayún debuted their new song 'El Pueblo Unido Jamás Será Vencido' ('The People United Will Never Be Defeated') at the festival.

Less than three months later, on 11 September 1973, a coup overthrew the Allende government and the *Estadio Chile* was used as a detention centre for hundreds of political prisoners, among them Victor Jara. Jara was shot and killed in the stadium. Jara's songs of change, alongside those of other *Nueva Cancion* musicians, became anthems in the pro-democracy struggle. Under the Pinochet dictatorship, *Nueva Cancion* music was banned and its performers killed or exiled. Yet in exile it continued to develop and find new audiences

around the world, raising awareness. Performers such as Quilapayún, Inti-Illimani, and Patricio Manns (1937–2021) continued to make music, often contributing to campaigns for Chilean Solidarity.

The dictatorship ended in 1990. A year later an event was held in the *Estadio Chile*, organised by the Jara family. The 'Canto Libre: Jornadas de Purificacion el Estadio Chile' ('Free Song: Days of Purification of the Estadio Chile') event brought together hundreds of musicians, artists, and actors to commemorate those detained and killed in the stadium and to reclaim the place as a site of memory. Chilean performers such as Inti-Illimani returned from exile and the international support garnered in exile drew names including Peter Gabriel, Michelle Pfeiffer, and Richard Gere.

The event was recorded by musicologist and Latin American popular music academic Jan Fairley (1949–2012). Born and brought up on the Wirral, Fairley lived in Chile from 1971 until the coup of 1973 forced her to leave. Studying for an MPhil in Latin American studies at Oxford University put her in touch with Robert Pring-Mill (1924–2005), a Hispanist at Oxford who shared a keen interest in popular song of struggle and hope. This cassette is Pring-Mill's copy of Fairley's recording, with his typescript notes describing the contents as 'a concert-cum-mass-meeting … to "purify" the stadium'. It is one of many cassettes, records, books, and documents in Pring-Mill's collection of Latin American popular song, held in the University's Institute of Popular Music archive. Fairley often lectured at the University of Liverpool and had a close connection with its Institute of Popular Music. The photograph is from her collection and shows one of the artworks created at the 'Canto Libre' event as a tribute to Victor Jara. Fairley's original sound recordings of this and other performances are an important record of Chilean popular song. The Pontificia Universidad Católica de Chile cares for part of her archive, while part is cared for at the University of Liverpool alongside the Pring-Mill collection and other material relating to politically oriented popular music.

Louise Bruton

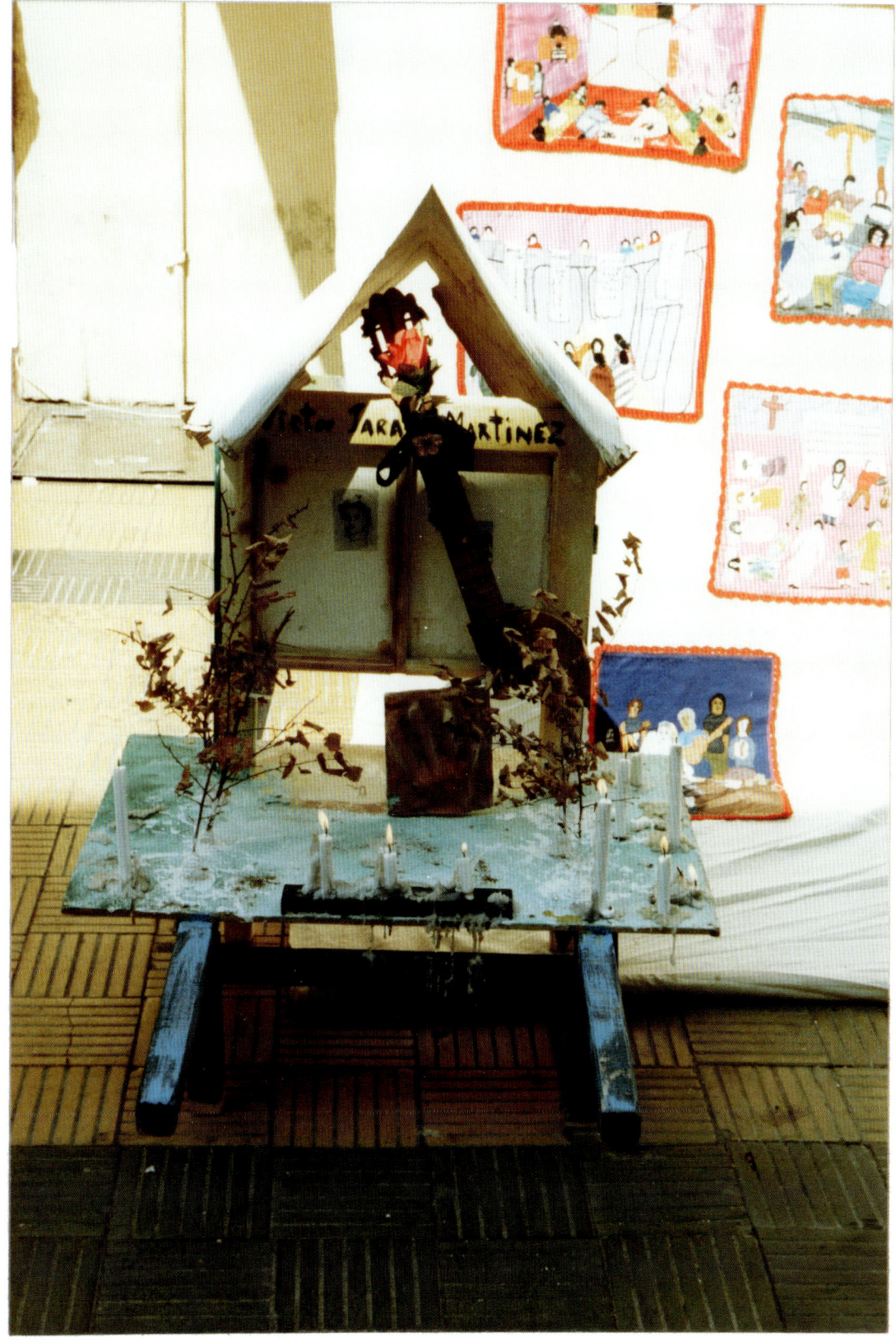

Oliver Lodge and syntonised telegraphy (2000s)

45

Radio-Craft: for the Professional-Serviceman-Radiotrician, Vol. 1 no. 6, December 1929, edited by Hugo Gernsback. Pp. 241–88. Includes 'Men who made radio: Sir Oliver Lodge' (p. 247) and cover portrait of Lodge by Walter Edward Blythe (1887–1966). 29 × 21.5 cm.

Donated by Mike Houlden, 2007.

Oliver Lodge (1851–1940) was appointed the first Professor of Physics at University College Liverpool in 1881. He was born in Stoke on Trent, the pottery district, where his father ran a successful business dealing in china clay. Initially, on leaving school at 14, the young Lodge joined his father, but his interest in science soon led him to enrol and take his degree in physics from London University. He followed this, in 1877, with a DSc while working as a research assistant at University College. Lodge's talents as a lecturer were recognised in his post as physics lecturer at Bedford College, then a women-only institution, and he was invited to give public lectures and demonstrations on such topics as Edison's phonograph and Alexander Graham Bell's recently invented telephone.

In Liverpool Lodge set up his laboratory in a converted lunatic asylum with inspiration coming from Germany, where scientists such as Heinrich Hertz (1857–94) were heavily engaged in investigating electrical phenomena. It was Hertz who, in 1888, performed one of the great experiments in physics when he provided incontrovertible proof that electromagnetic waves, having the well-known properties of reflection and refraction typical of light, could be generated and detected. His demonstration of these effects in the laboratory confirmed James Clerk Maxwell's monumental mathematical theory of 1862 that such high-frequency waves, which would forever after be called radio waves, existed and could be detected. Lodge concentrated all his efforts on investigating these Hertzian waves, as they became known. To Lodge such waves were a scientific curiosity having no obvious practical application. However, that perception was to change – with dramatic effect.

In August 1894, at a scientific meeting in Oxford, Lodge demonstrated signalling by wireless. The occasion was a meeting of the British Association attended by many distinguished scientists who soon realised the importance of what they had seen. Every time the key on the spark transmitter was pressed by Lodge's assistant in a building 60 yards away, a spot of light swung across a screen in the lecture theatre. The receiver was a Lodge invention containing a device known as a coherer connected to a light-spot galvanometer that oscillated in accordance with the transmitted signals and so represented the Morse code letters being sent. This was the first transmission of information by radio, as it would subsequently become known.

Lodge pursued his experiments vigorously once he realised that his apparatus could be used for signalling over much greater distances than the 60 yards demonstrated in Oxford, including from the tower of the new Victoria Building to the tower of Lewis's store in the centre of Liverpool. Perhaps his most significant contribution to the radio art was his invention of the means by which radio signals could be constrained to a narrow band of frequencies and so enable many simultaneous transmissions to take place without causing mutual interference between them. Lodge had discovered this effect some years before when experimenting with oscillating electrical waves travelling along two parallel wires. Under carefully controlled conditions he discovered that it was possible to cause a marked enhancement of the propagating waves that was akin to the plucking of the string of a musical instrument. He called this effect 'syntony', a far more euphonious term than the utilitarian word 'tuning'. In 1897 he patented this concept as 'Improvements in Syntonised Telegraphy' and to this day that patent is recognised as the basis for all methods of selective tuning used in radio, television, and radar.

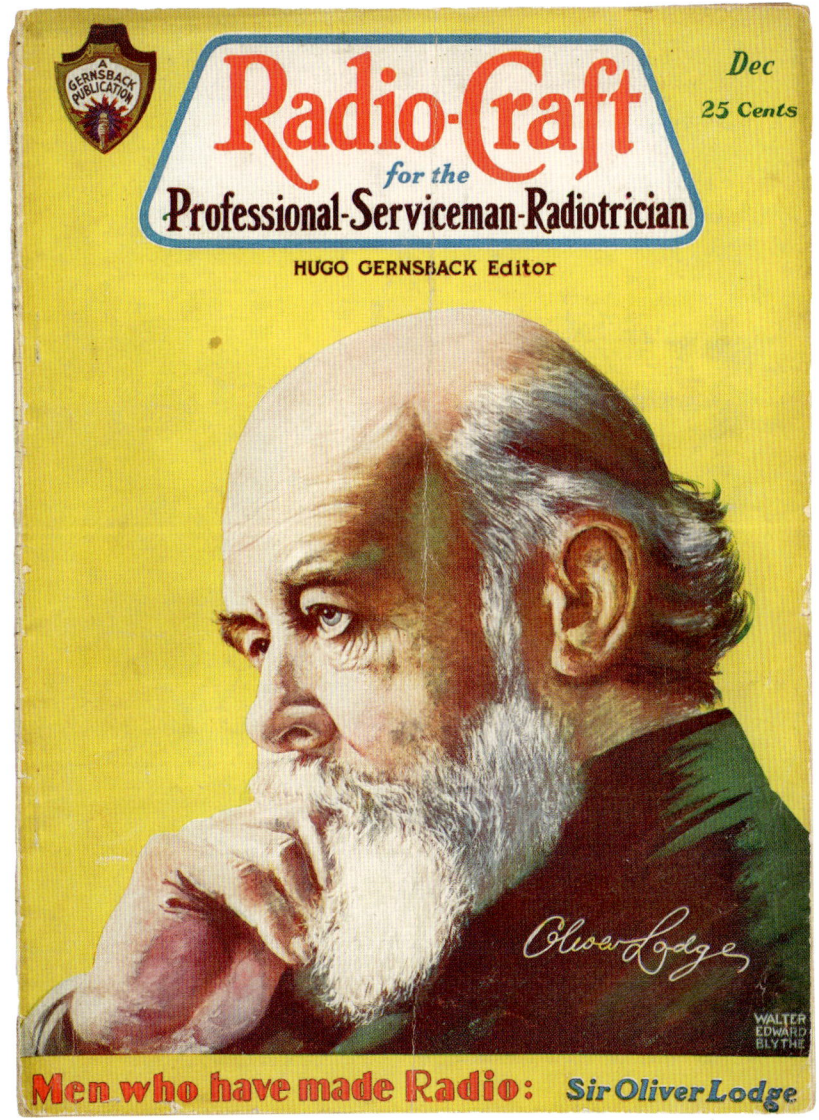

A GERNSBACK PUBLICATION

Radio-Craft

for the

Professional-Serviceman-Radiotrician

Dec
25 Cents

HUGO GERNSBACK Editor

WALTER EDWARD BLYTHE

Men who have made Radio: *Sir Oliver Lodge*

Oliver Lodge was a polymath. Not only did he foresee the part that electricity would play in the daily lives of those about him but, on a scientific level, he speculated that the sun might radiate radio waves and he even attempted to detect them, though thwarted by the insensitivity of the equipment then available. This was undoubtedly the first attempt at what is now called radio astronomy, which took another 38 years to come to fruition. Not only was Lodge a brilliant experimental physicist but he was a highly accomplished lecturer whose public discourses to the Liverpool Physical Society attracted large audiences.

In 1900 he became the first principal of the newly founded University of Birmingham and in 1902 he was knighted for his services to science. Lodge is strikingly commemorated as the bronze figure of Education on the Queen Victoria Monument (1902–06) in the centre of Liverpool, described as the magnum opus of sculptor C.J. Allen (1862–1956).

The Oliver Lodge papers held at the University of Liverpool include 30 of his research notebooks dating from 1870 to 1913, which contain notes on experiments, diagrams and charts, and lecture notes.

Brian Austin

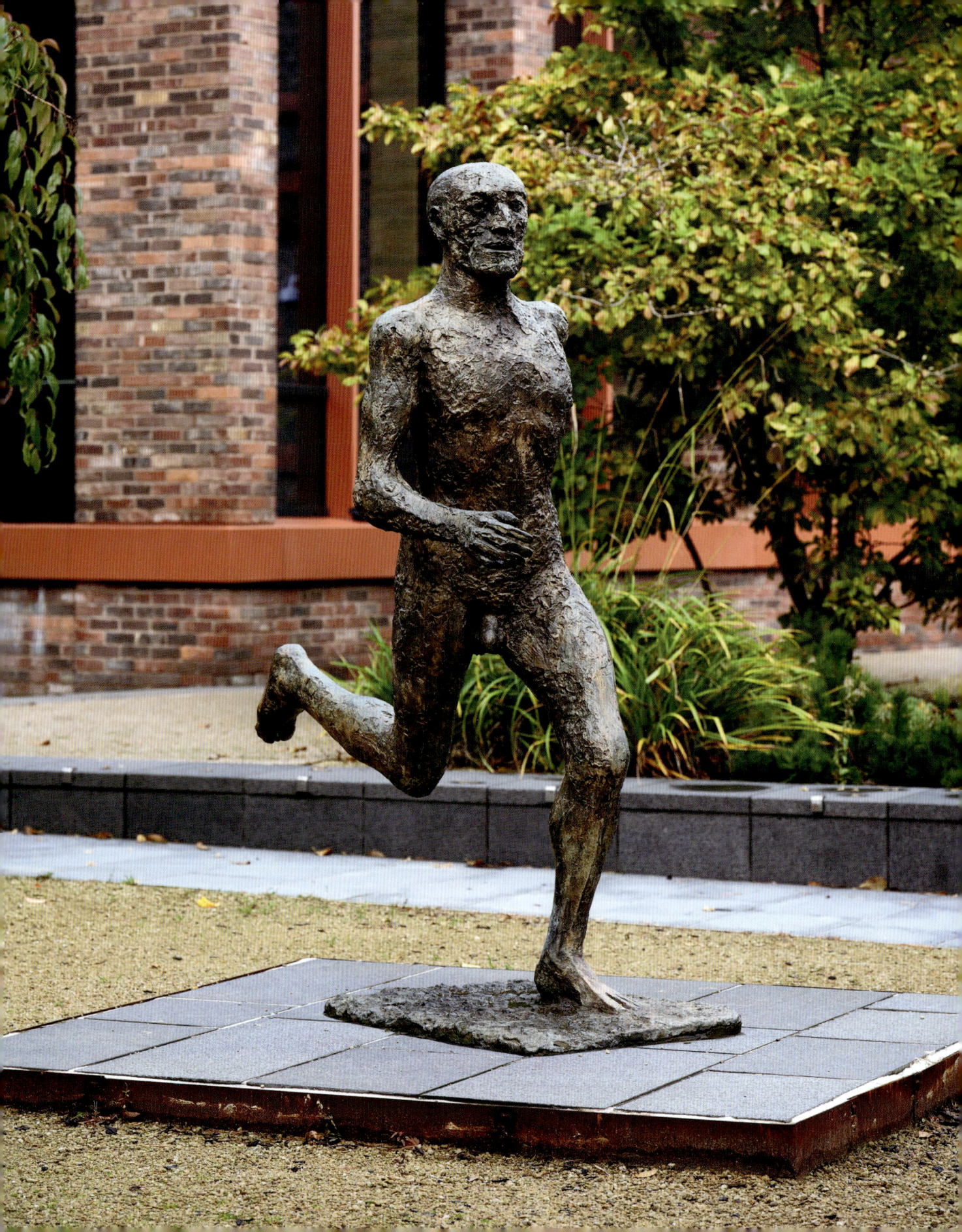

Running man (2010s)

Front Runner. Bronze sculpture by Elisabeth Frink, 1987. 195 × 71 × 137 cm.

Donated by Eric and Jean Cass through the Contemporary Art Society, 2010.

46

With sturdy stride and pumping arms, *Front Runner* gazes forward to a new destination. For the artist, Elisabeth Frink (1930–93), the figure represented an escape from political oppression and a race towards freedom. She was a passionate advocate for human rights and her very first commission for a public sculpture, which was awarded shortly after she graduated from art college in 1953, was entitled *The Unknown Political Prisoner.*

Throughout her career Frink's art focused mainly on animals, especially horses, and the male figure. When asked by an interviewer why she used the male rather than female figure in her work, Frink responded that she preferred the way they look. It wasn't that she didn't like women, she said, but she didn't find female bodies satisfying to sculpt. She went on to explain that she found men's heads and bodies a better vehicle for expressing a mood such as strength or sadness. The rough surface of her sculptures was created by chiselling into the plaster model before casting in bronze. The resulting pitted texture lends a vulnerability to the figures.

Frink was raised in Suffolk in a military family and the Second World War broke out when she was nine; her childhood experiences had a lifelong influence on her art and social conscience. The family home was near an airfield and Frink witnessed bombers returning in flames or crashing on landing; on one occasion, she had to hide from an attack by a German fighter plane. At the age of fifteen she saw news images of the traumatic scenes at Belsen concentration camp. Even as a teenager

Frink's artwork was dark in tone, featuring injured animals and falling men.

Frink studied at the Guildford and Chelsea Schools of Art and became part of a group of British sculptors known as the 'Geometry of Fear' school. Their work was characterised by alien-looking figures, conjuring up a dystopian, blasted world that expressed the societal anxieties of the post-war years. However, Frink's works from the late 1960s onwards matured into a more robust, Expressionist style. Her male figures tended to be slightly larger than life-size and were posed standing, walking, running, and, very occasionally, sitting in contemplation.

Frink is considered one of the leading sculptors of the twentieth century and her work is in major collections globally. Her contribution to British art was recognised by election to the Royal Academy in 1977 and, among other honours, she was awarded a damehood in 1982.

As well as *Front Runner*, The University of Liverpool is fortunate to have another Frink bronze – one of her *Goggle Head* series from the 1960s – in its collection, as well as lithographic prints. Perhaps Frink's best-known sculpture in Liverpool is *The Welcoming Christ* (sometimes referred to as *Risen Christ*), which is installed on the façade of the Anglican Cathedral. It was unveiled on Easter Sunday in 1993 and is the artist's very last completed work; she died seven days later.

Front Runner was generously donated to the University of Liverpool by Eric and Jean Cass in 2010 in association with the Contemporary Art Society.

Amanda Draper

REPLICATING DNA (2010s)

47

Form A. 240-grade brushed steel sculpture by Susan Forsyth, 2017.
1000 × 120 × 200 cm (overlap of plates 15 cm).

Commissioned by the University of Liverpool for the Apex plaza housing the Biosciences facilities, 2017.

I was shown Rosalind Franklin's X-ray photograph and, Whooo! that was a helix, and a month later we had the structure. (James Watson)

Science and everyday life cannot and should not be separated. Science, for me, gives a partial explanation of life. In so far as it goes, it is based on fact, experience and experiment. (Rosalind Franklin, in a letter to her father, summer 1940)

The Irish-born artist Susan Forsyth has described her sculpture *Form A* as '[a]n abstracted representation of a strand of DNA replicating itself' and commented:

My work is always specific to its setting. I studied some bioscience in my undergraduate years and the two slender, counter-posing planes have been inspired by the ground-breaking research taking place at the University. The scale of the sculpture is designed to respond to the lines of the building almost to the millimetre.

It was not Forsyth's first site-specific work with the University; her participatory exhibition 'Art Sheds', responding to the history and collections of the Victoria Gallery & Museum, was designed as part of the 2014 Liverpool Biennial and featured as one of the *Liverpool Echo*'s top picks.

Form A is located on the plaza between the William Henry Duncan Building and the Ronald Ross Building on West Derby Street. It is best viewed from the pavement: looking up at the sculpture, ideally with a blue sky and a few clouds to set if off, it complements and literally reflects the surfaces of the buildings in a careful consideration of the negative space, light, shadow, surface finishes, and colour of the backdrop. It is easy to envisage the setting as the outer cell wall, with the DNA at the centre. DNA as a crystalline structure can be graphically or physically represented; however, as a biochemical entity it functions as part of a larger collection of mechanisms, the cell. Its biological function is the storage of knowledge, variation, change, and the hope for the next generation. *Form A* – an inspiration for research and new ideas.

Form A was installed on the Apex plaza to mark the completion of an ambitious redevelopment project on North Campus, with the two state-of-art buildings housing hundreds of scientists working at the cutting edge of health and life sciences research. The sculpture is designed for resilience (including against pigeons, seagulls, graffiti, and skateboarders). It continues the University's long tradition of commissioning public artwork as part of the development of the campus.

John Jenkins

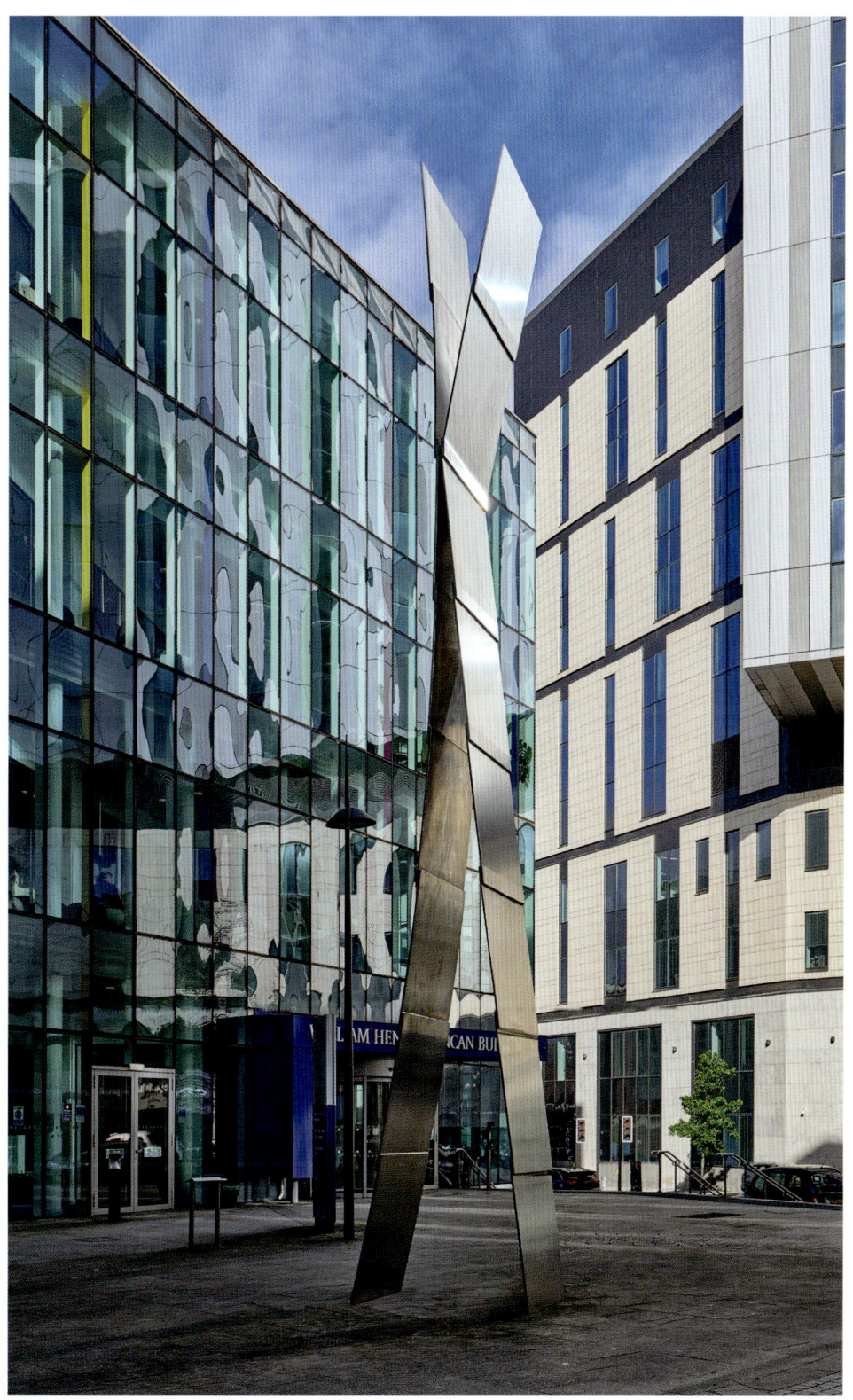

'Getting there is half the fun' – Cunard, its marketing, and its passengers (2010s)

48

Cunard publicity brochure, 1952. 15 × 10 cm.

Donated by John Langley, 2019.

In early July 1840 Cunard's *Britannia* slipped its moorings in Liverpool and set sail for Halifax, Nova Scotia. Although not the first steam-powered ship to cross the Atlantic, this voyage led to the first scheduled trans-Atlantic service. Samuel Cunard (1787–1865) made safety his priority. Not every line had the same view, others being prepared to take greater risks for faster crossings. 'Your ship is loaded,' Cunard told his captains: 'Take her, speed is nothing … safety is all that is required.'

The ships were safe, but they were not the most comfortable. Charles Dickens complained his bunk had 'a mattress … like a surgical plaster spread on an inaccessible shelf'. As technology changed ships became bigger, faster, and more luxurious, and new competitors entered the market. In the last quarter of the nineteenth century Cunard began the construction of so-called express liners. Persuading potential customers on board became a question of understanding the right mix of speed, reliability, interior design, and service, underpinned by an attention to safety that would meet any individual's particular needs and aspirations.

All these elements can be found in Cunard's advertisements and other marketing communications. These sought to balance the new and exciting with the safe and familiar. First Class passengers travelled in surroundings akin to the grand hotels and houses of their lives ashore. They would be comfortable with both surroundings and their fellow travellers. Elegantly dressed passengers aboard ships such as the *Franconia* (launched in the 1920s) are depicted relaxing in the smoking room (men), sitting at an elegant writing table (women), or together in the dining room – the distinctions being a reflection of the social mores of the time. For the emerging middle class of the 1920s and 1930s, now able to spend money on things beyond their immediate needs (including the shipping lines' new Tourist Third Class), there were opportunities epitomised by an article entitled 'The New Holiday':

> There was once a man whose greatest wish was to travel. But because he was just an ordinary fellow … the realisation … was exceedingly remote. Indeed [all he could do] was [to] read from cover to cover … guidebooks and travel folders. Until one night as he put down … the 'Glories of Greece' the [next] thing he read was a notice [that] a new class of travel made it possible to cross the Atlantic and back for the remarkable sum of £35.

Until the outbreak of the Second World War, travelling abroad was overwhelmingly by ship. The development of air travel in the 1950s and 1960s changed that forever. Now passengers could choose their mode of transport, could choose how long they spent travelling to their destination, could choose whether to risk the winter storms of the North Atlantic or to fly above the ocean where, according to American Overseas Airlines, 'the upper air … is as quiet and serene as at any time'.

As part of an answer to the challenge, Cunard presented the voyage as an integral part of the holiday. 'At first, perhaps, you thought of … your crossing merely as a means of transport … but now you've joyfully discovered it's … a holiday you wish would never end' – 'Getting there [became] half the fun!' Brochures highlighted the delights of shipboard life. 'Nothing quite compares with those sparkly, carefree days … the bright conviviality … the luxurious comfort … the marvellous food.' The brochure expands on the holiday theme. 'No holiday can equal the joys of an ocean voyage' with its 'healthful relaxation', 'frivolity', 'superb food', and 'perfect comfort'. Although there is a focus on First

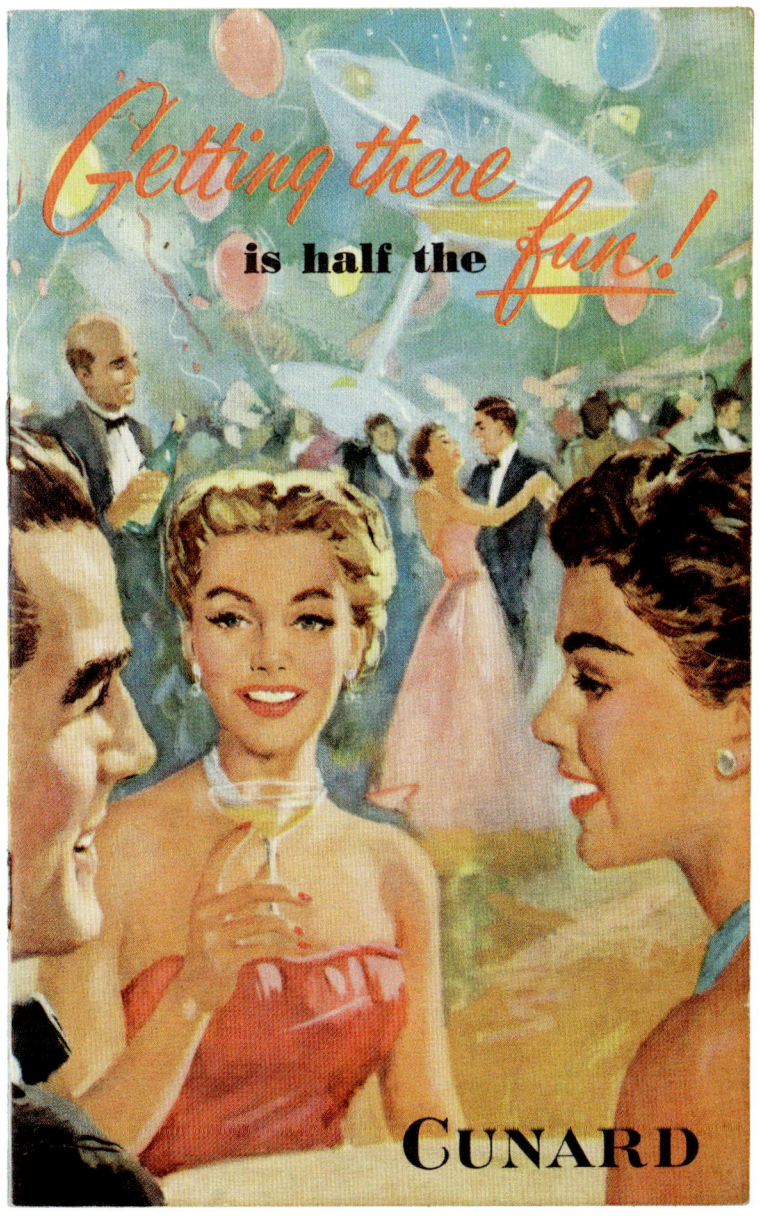

Class, Cunard is at pains to point out the quality of Tourist Class accommodation, highlighting 'hot and cold running water [and] touch control ventilation'. For the businessman, Cunard tried to portray the time at sea as something positive, suggesting 'you'll arrive … so much fresher … in fine fettle for the busy days ahead'.

Just as Cunard's first ship set sail from Liverpool, so its newest ship, *Queen Anne*, celebrated its naming ceremony in 2024 in sight of the Cunard Building.

The Cunard Archive gave the company unique access to designs from fabrics to furniture and decorations: Lee Powell, Vice President of Brand and Product at Cunard, said: 'Cunard is world-renowned for inventing the golden era of ocean travel. While we cherish our heritage, we also use it as inspiration for forward-looking ideas when we plan for the future.' Cunard's marketing aptly describes the new ship as 'modern, yet timeless'.

Graham Gladden

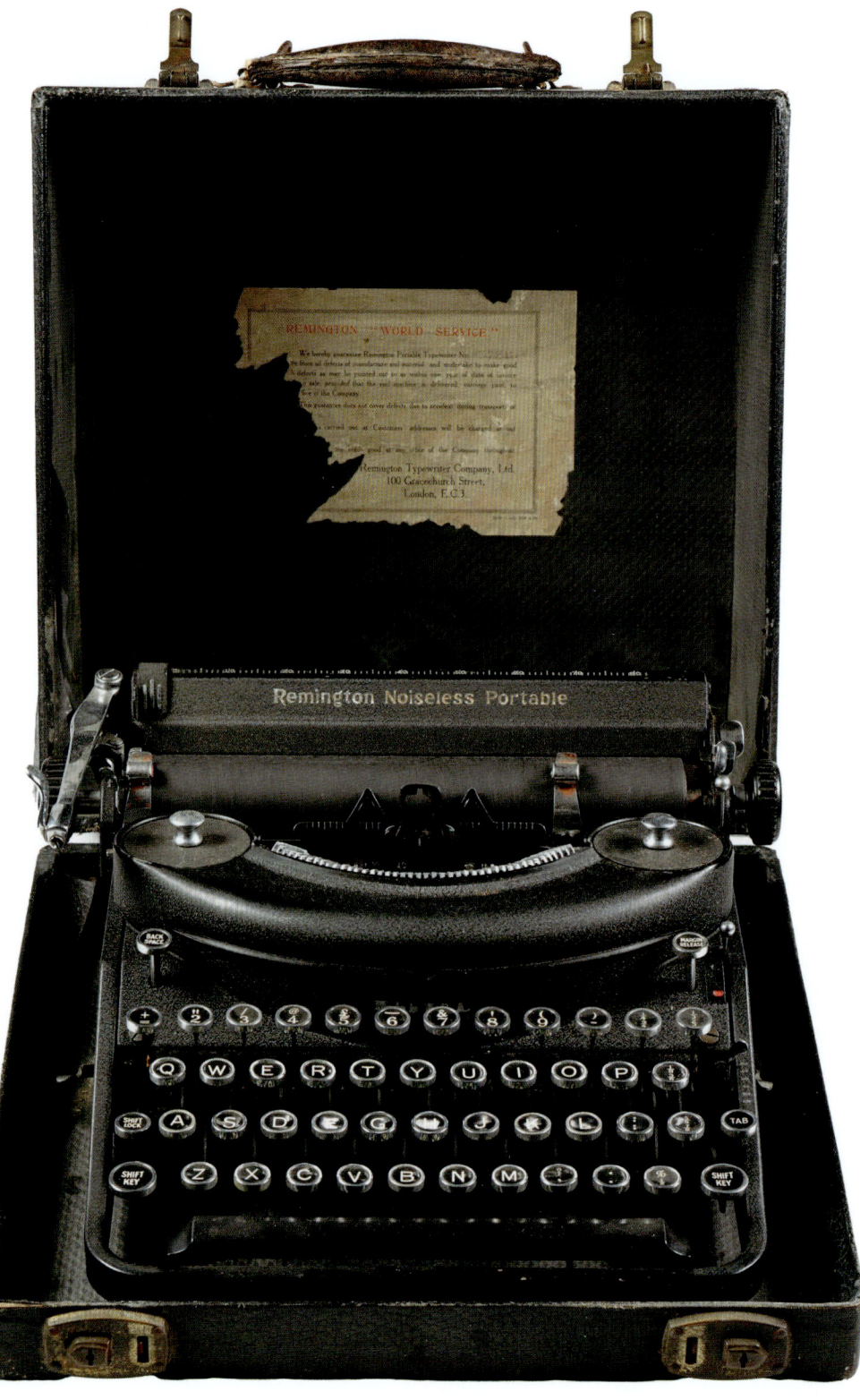

Arthur C. Clarke's portable typewriter (2010s)

49

Remington deluxe noiseless typewriter and case made by Remington, serial number ND173512, 1938–39. 16 × 33 × 32 cm.

Part of the Arthur C. Clarke Library, donated 2018.

Today's science fiction is tomorrow's science fact. From automatic doors to mobile communication devices, science-fiction authors have often been the predictors of the technologies of tomorrow. One of the most striking examples of this phenomena came from the mind of Arthur C. Clarke (1917–2008) in 1945 and was typed up on this unassuming 'Remington Noiseless Portable' Typewriter, which is part of the collection of Clarke's personal library of books and magazines held in the Science Fiction Collections at the University of Liverpool's Special Collections and Archives.

In his autobiography *Ascent to Orbit*, Clarke recalls writing a paper in late June of 1945 entitled 'The Future of World Communications'. In this essay, typed on this Remington typewriter, he outlined a system of orbiting geostationary space stations that could enable instant global communications by relaying radio waves around the Earth. He postulated that the entire globe could be covered by three space stations in geostationary orbit. The essay went on to be published in the October 1945 issue of *Wireless World* (pp. 305–08), which was the first significant journal dedicated to wireless communication. The editor renamed the essay 'Extra-Terrestrial Relays', evoking the science-fiction world that Clarke is known more for today. While the renamed essay might suggest correspondence with aliens, the extra-terrestrial objects it refers to correspond to what we know today as communication satellites.

Clarke's essay advanced the idea of using geostationary satellites for communication. His ideas were not considered realistic when first published, but 20 years later the first commercial geostationary communication satellite launched in 1965. Nicknamed *Early Bird*, it provided direct and instant contact between Europe and North America, enabling television and telephone transmissions.

Today, there are more than 500 active satellites in geostationary orbit, allowing us to send transmissions by radio, telephone, and internet. Aligned with the equator and 36,000 kilometres high, this orbit is the most distant from the Earth's surface and is now called the *Clarke Orbit*, in honour of the late science-fiction writer and his incredible vision of the future. A further honour came in 1995, when Clarke was awarded an honorary doctorate from the University of Liverpool, which was, fittingly, conferred over satellite link.

A far cry from the astronomic wireless technologies that it was used to describe, the mechanical workings of this typewriter allowed Clarke to type up essays that were sent by post to the likes of the British Interplanetary Society, an institution he later became the intermittent chairman of between 1946 and 1953. Though it embodies the old mechanical technologies of the Second World War, it represents the invisible, instantaneous communication of today. It is humbling to witness such an everyday object that was used as a vehicle to share such a world-changing idea.

Hannah Little

FROM THE ARTIST'S PERSPECTIVE (2020s)

50

Noir Rhythm. Hand-carved sculpture in unglazed clay by Halima Cassell, 2013.
7.6 × 61 cm.

Art Collections: purchased from the artist, 2023.

Born in 1975 in Pakistan, brought up in Lancashire and now living in Shropshire, Halima's varied, multi-cultural background is tangibly present in her work, fusing her Asian roots with a fascination for African pattern work and her deep passion for architectural geometry. (artist's website)

Inspired by music, *Noir Rhythm* is a hand-carved sculpture in unglazed clay from Germany. While I work in many different materials within my practice, clay is my first love. I am intrigued by how different clays bring their own feelings and challenges to the way you can work with them. Some clays might be great to work with, others might have the hue that you are looking for; however, each one has its own characteristics.

Each piece of work starts with an idea, which I call my 'shorthand of thought', that is drawn onto paper and worked through into my design book. Once I have finished hand-building the form from my chosen clay, I carefully map my design onto the piece. It is only when I start carving that I instinctively manipulate the form, working into the different parts of the design with varying depths, undercuts, and angles.

My work is grounded in strong geometric elements and recurrent patterns, and *Noir Rhythm* is no exception. However, in this piece the angles were inspired by the dramatic notes and pace changes in the classical music playing at the time I was making this piece. Music is often the backdrop to my day in the studio, and inspiration can come from the eclectic range I listen to – from the dynamic and soft expressive nature of classical and instrumental music to the words and rhythms of more popular music, which can all stimulate and move me.

Maths has always underpinned my creative process, having been one of my favourite subjects at school – alongside art, obviously. The link of maths and nature is something I see in all my surroundings; from sunbeams through cloud formations, ripples in water, rock and crystal formations, the unfolding of flower buds, the folds created in fabric, even to the flow of hair. While I am inspired by the geometry that I can see, it is also innate in everything around us, from our cells and plant formations to the moon cycles and seasons, and this number pattern and repetition in forms and shapes influences what I create and makes a connection with the world around us, that I want people to feel and experience when they view my work.

I have always been intrigued and attentive to my environment and inquisitive as to how things are made and constructed, as well as their link to the natural world, and draw so much inspiration from it. For example, the forms found in traditional architecture, such as cathedrals, mosques, synagogues, and other buildings of importance, are often drawn from nature. The role of such buildings was to draw people in with beauty, and art is the same, so it gives me so much joy if something I create has the same effect and makes people want to stop and touch and walk around it, enticed by its form and beauty. Like these beautiful pieces of architecture, which have inspired and touched people over the centuries, I want my work to be timeless. Without needing an explanation, I want a wide and varied audience to engage with, be moved by, and connect to my work in the same way now and in many years to come.

While working on *Noir Rhythm* in this black, German clay, which is one of my favourites, everything combined to give me a sense of freedom to playfully burnish some surfaces to reflect the light, while leaving others with textured surfaces to absorb it. In addition, with its single tone of colour, which dramatises the overall design, your eye is drawn in and around the twists and flows of the overall tessellations, adding to the feelings of mystery, intrigue, and sensuality. At different times of day, and with the ever-changing light, the individual elements of the form are highlighted or shaded, drawing the viewers into its intricate design.

The off-centred design of *Noir Rhythm* gives extra

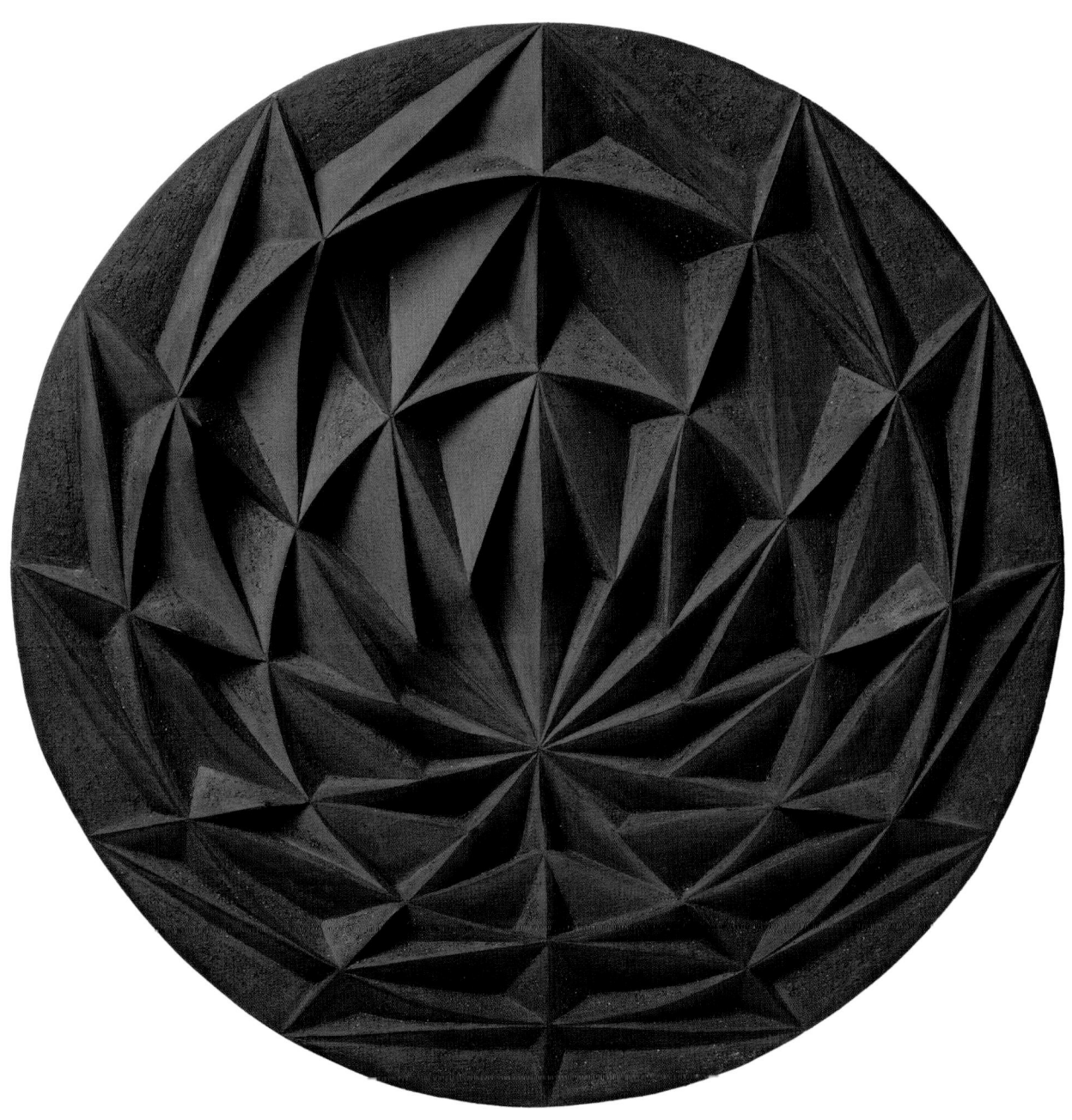

drama and a sense of movement. From the lines circling it to the individual carvings, shapes, and planes, the eye is drawn around the different contours and, when displayed as a standing charger, it invites people to engage from multiple perspectives, as the concave and convex elements accentuate the patterns to evoke a radiating, an opening of a starburst or flower.

Halima Cassell

UNIVERSITY OF LIVERPOOL ATHLETIC CLUB – OPEN FOILS CHAMPIONSHIP CUPS (2020s)

51

Sterling silver, with hallmark date 1936 by William Neale Ltd, Birmingham.
35 × 30 cm.

Gift of the Merseyside Open Fencing Tournament Committee, 2024.

Dorothy Knowles (1906–2010) is not a name that readily springs to mind for many of us in sport but she was a remarkable woman. A lecturer in French at the University of Liverpool (1934–67), Dorothy was also a major driving force in the local fencing scene, both at the University and in Liverpool. Her name is synonymous with these two trophies awarded for the event she helped to create.

In 1936 she had helped establish the Liverpool University Fencing Club. She inspired the creation of an open foil tournament in 1938; it took place for the first time on 12 February 1938, with 40 men and 20 women entering. Two trophies were presented, The Sir Frederick Marquis Cup for women and the Richard Armstrong cup for men, each named for their University donor: Sir Frederick Marquis (1883–1964, later Lord Woolton), University treasurer from 1936 to 1939, and Richard Armstrong (1874–1950), then President of Council.

Dorothy won this inaugural event, and the next event in 1946, when entry numbers were hugely increased, and many future instances of the competition. She was internationally successful in the Gisors challenge in France and, at the age of 59, at the Dynamo fencing club in Moscow. In 1968 she was still accumulating enough points to be ranked among the top 20 of Britain's female foilists – a sporting role model.

Dorothy, who lived to the age of 104, is just one of the many individuals who have helped sport at the University of Liverpool develop since its founding days in Victorian Britain and have contributed hugely to sport at Liverpool both within the clubs and the Athletic Union (AU), our collection of sports clubs.

The AU was founded in October 1884 as the University College Athletic Club, with Professor Herbert Augustus Strong (Chair of Latin) as its first president.

The Club's first treasurer, F.C. Larkin, and its joint secretaries, A.A. Kanthack and H.W. Nicholson, were all medical students. The first subscription was five shillings for active members and two shillings and sixpence for those less active. The original colours were light blue, navy blue and red. The red seems to have disappeared from our team colours.

Club and sporting activities started immediately. Some sports (which we now know as clubs) began their lives as an activity and grew into formally constituted clubs by the late 1880s. Local competitions were succeeded by competitions with Leeds and Manchester Universities in the Christie Cup: an ongoing competition and the biggest varsity competition, with over 190 teams. The Liverpool Varsity against our city rivals (Liverpool John Moores University) started in 1993.

The history of university sport competition owes the Christie Cup, the oldest university triangular, a great deal: the first national sports body, the Inter Varsity Board (IVAB), founded in 1919, was inspired by Christie sport. It quickly changed its name to the Universities Athletic Union (UAU) and continued proudly until 1994. Its first and last chairmen were Liverpool University staff and its only female chair was a Liverpool University lecturer. In addition, the initial meeting that created national sport took place in 1918 in our Guild of Students.

Since 1994 university sport has been served by two successor bodies: the British Universities Sports Association (BUSA) and, from 2007, the British Universities and Colleges Sport (BUCS). Over 130 higher education institutions are now members of BUCS. University sport is now a huge concern involving over 100,000 students competing in over 50 sports.

At Liverpool, the Athletic Union, after a strategic

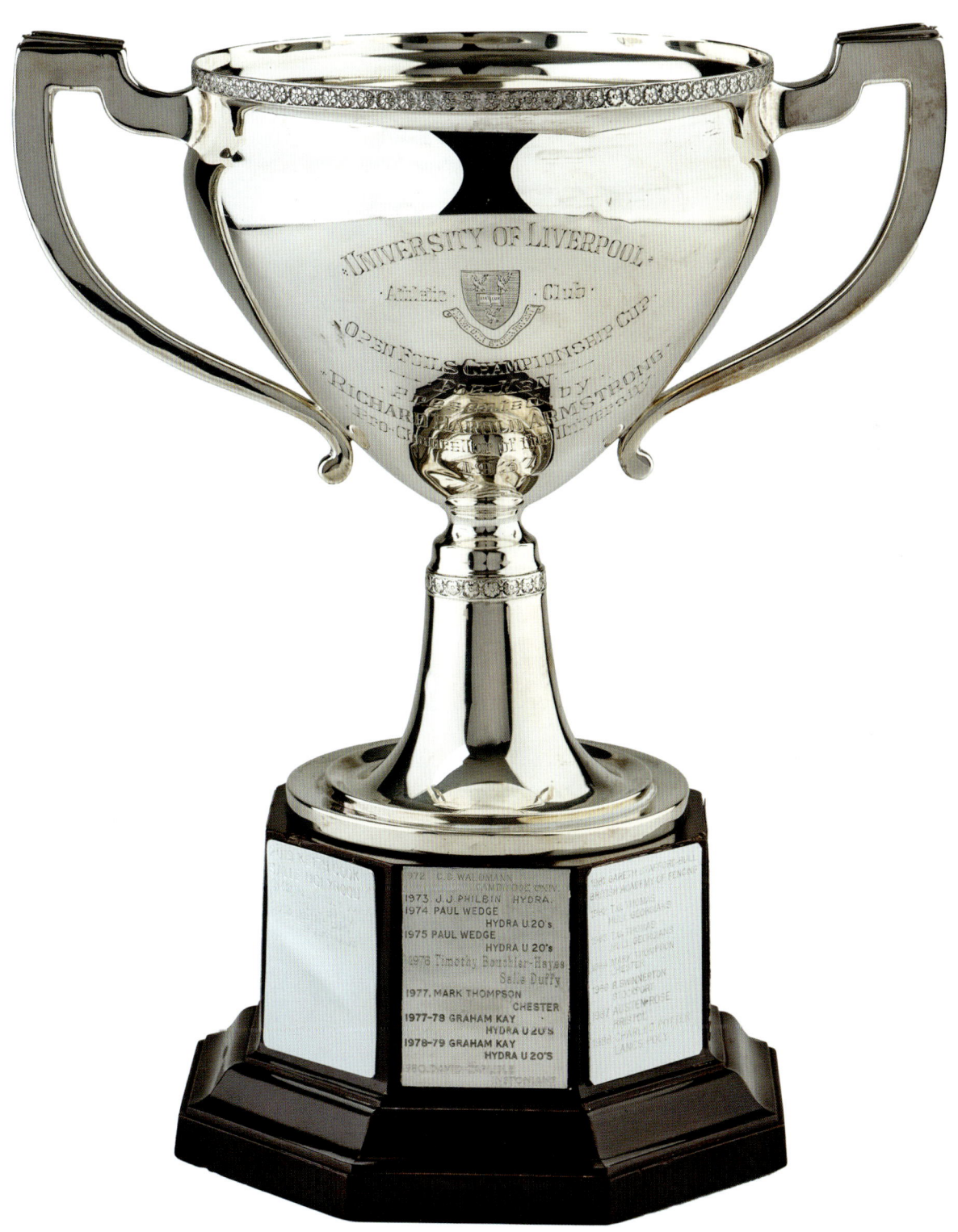

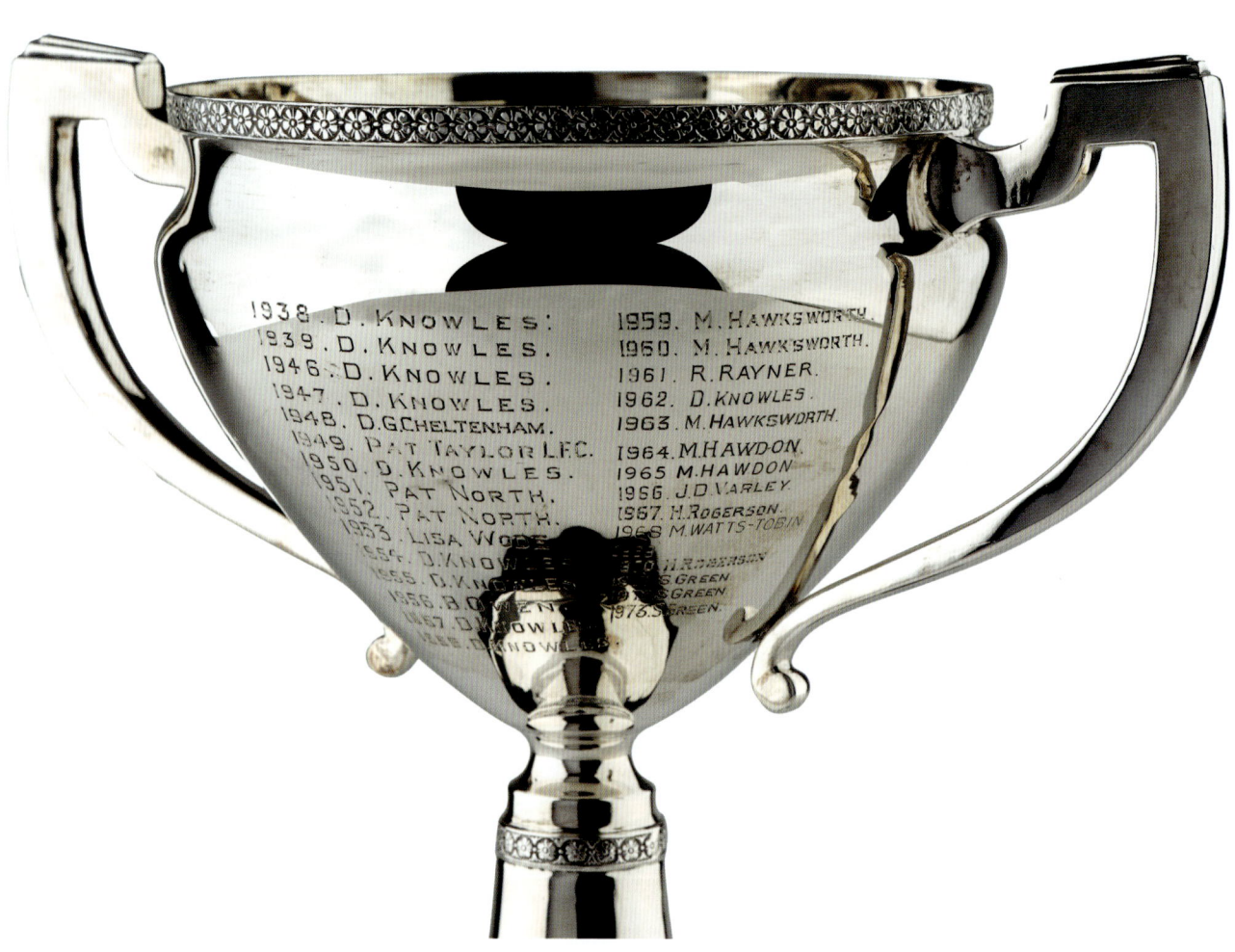

1938. D. KNOWLES.
1939. D. KNOWLES.
1946. D. KNOWLES.
1947. D. KNOWLES.
1948. D.G.CHELTENHAM.
1949. PAT TAYLOR LFC.
1950. D. KNOWLES.
1951. PAT NORTH.
1952. PAT NORTH.
1953. LISA WODE
1954. D.KNOWLES
1955. D.KNOWLES
1956. B.OWEN
1957. D.KNOWLES
1958. D.KNOWLES

1959. M. HAWKSWORTH.
1960. M. HAWKSWORTH.
1961. R. RAYNER.
1962. D. KNOWLES.
1963. M. HAWKSWORTH.
1964. M. HAWDON.
1965. M. HAWDON.
1966. J.D. VARLEY.
1967. H. ROGERSON.
1968. M. WATTS-TOBIN
H.ROGERSON
S.GREEN
S.GREEN
1973. S.GREEN.

overhaul in 2007, left the Guild of Students and became the heartbeat of the new sport department, Sport Liverpool. It was a successful move, as numbers have grown and we have moved from 41st in the BUCS performance table in 2007 to a consistent place in the top 25 in the 2020s.

We have continued to pick up national titles in most years in what is now the most competitive period in the university's sporting history. We have won 120 national student titles since 1919, with the 1970s our most successful decade, with 24 titles, and Water Polo our most successful club, with 17 titles.

Dorothy's story introduced us to this story of sport at Liverpool and she can take us out. She was an inspirational leader for our fencers for over 30 years. Her story and commitment encapsulate the essence of the role of sport for tens of thousands of our students since 1884. They have all experienced the AU and all that it has offered them for over 140 years.

Stuart Wade

SORBUS BULLEYANA, A LIVING SPECIMEN AT NESS BOTANIC GARDENS (2020S–)

52

Sorbus bulleyana. From north-western Yunnan, at the far eastern edge of the Himalayas. 300 cm.

Plant material collected by Keith Rushforth in 1993 and shared with Dr Hugh McAllister.

Sorbus bulleyana McAll. sp. nov a ceteris speciebus sectionis *Discolorium* foliolis magis numerosis, 9–11-jugis usque 30–42 × 12–16 mm et carpellis 3(-4) distinguenda. Typus: China, north-western Yunnan, Zongdian Gorge, top end (Xiao Zong Dian), 3200 m, 6 November 1993, Rushforth 2809 (holotypus LIV!).

Ness Botanic Gardens was founded in 1898 by Liverpool cotton broker Arthur Bulley (1861–1942) and was gifted to the University of Liverpool in 1948 by his daughter, Lois Bulley (1901–95). Arthur was passionate about plants – he was the sole sponsor of two of the most famous Edwardian plant collectors, George Forrest (1873–1932) and Frank Kingdon Ward (1885–1958), and established a series of garden areas at Ness close to the house he built, including a rock garden. The fields further from the house continued to be farmed.

In 1972 Dr Hugh McAllister joined the team at Ness as Botanist. Hugh set himself the task of investigating the taxonomy of several plant genera, including rowans (*Sorbus* spp.). Species of the genus *Sorbus* are found in Europe, Asia, and North America, and Hugh requested *Sorbus* seed from botanic gardens in these areas and occasionally visited sites himself, including Tibet in 1997.

Approximately 1,000 *Sorbus* trees were planted at Ness – together with many other genera – and the fields were slowly turned into an arboretum. In 2005 Hugh published a monograph on *Sorbus*. In it he notes that 'the long period of continuity [at Ness] gave me the opportunity to acquire species as they became available, provided me with space and the resources to grow them from seed to mature trees, and enabled me to carry out constant, detailed observations over more than thirty years.' In 2006 the *Sorbus* collection at Ness was registered as a National Plant Collection by Plant Heritage.

Hugh's research led to descriptions of new species of *Sorbus*, including *Sorbus bulleyana*, named by Hugh for Arthur Bulley. *S. bulleyana* was discovered growing in north-western Yunnan, at the far eastern edge of the Himalayas. There are living plants growing in the collection at Ness and the type herbarium specimen was deposited in the botany collection of National Museums Liverpool. It is still standard practice that every new species is given a Latin description. That of *S. bulleyana*, cited above from Hugh's *The Genus Sorbus: Mountain Ash and other Rowans* (2005), describes how the species is distinguished from other species of the *Discolores* section by the more numerous (9–11 pairs) short (to 30–42 × 12–16 mm) leaflets and 3(–4) carpels.

The living heritage of *Sorbus bulleyana* is a fitting memorial to its donor, Lois Bulley, described in her obituary by Peter Brinson for *The Independent* as 'a fighter against racism and for social justice and equality, especially for women, a philanthropist with a shrewd business brain, a national benefactor of applied plant biology and horticultural research … an exceptional human being'. Born into wealth, she sought to repay what she saw as a debt to society through political and charitable action on behalf of the low-paid and unemployed, championing mental health services in the newly founded NHS and establishing a trust in Nairobi to repay to Africa the profits from shares she had inherited in Motor Mart East Africa. The projects supported – water-sewage schemes, a mixed-race hospital for children, and a scholarship scheme for girls – were, at her insistence, administered by Africans. Her bequest to the University was one of the greatest legacies it has received.

Nick Lightfoot

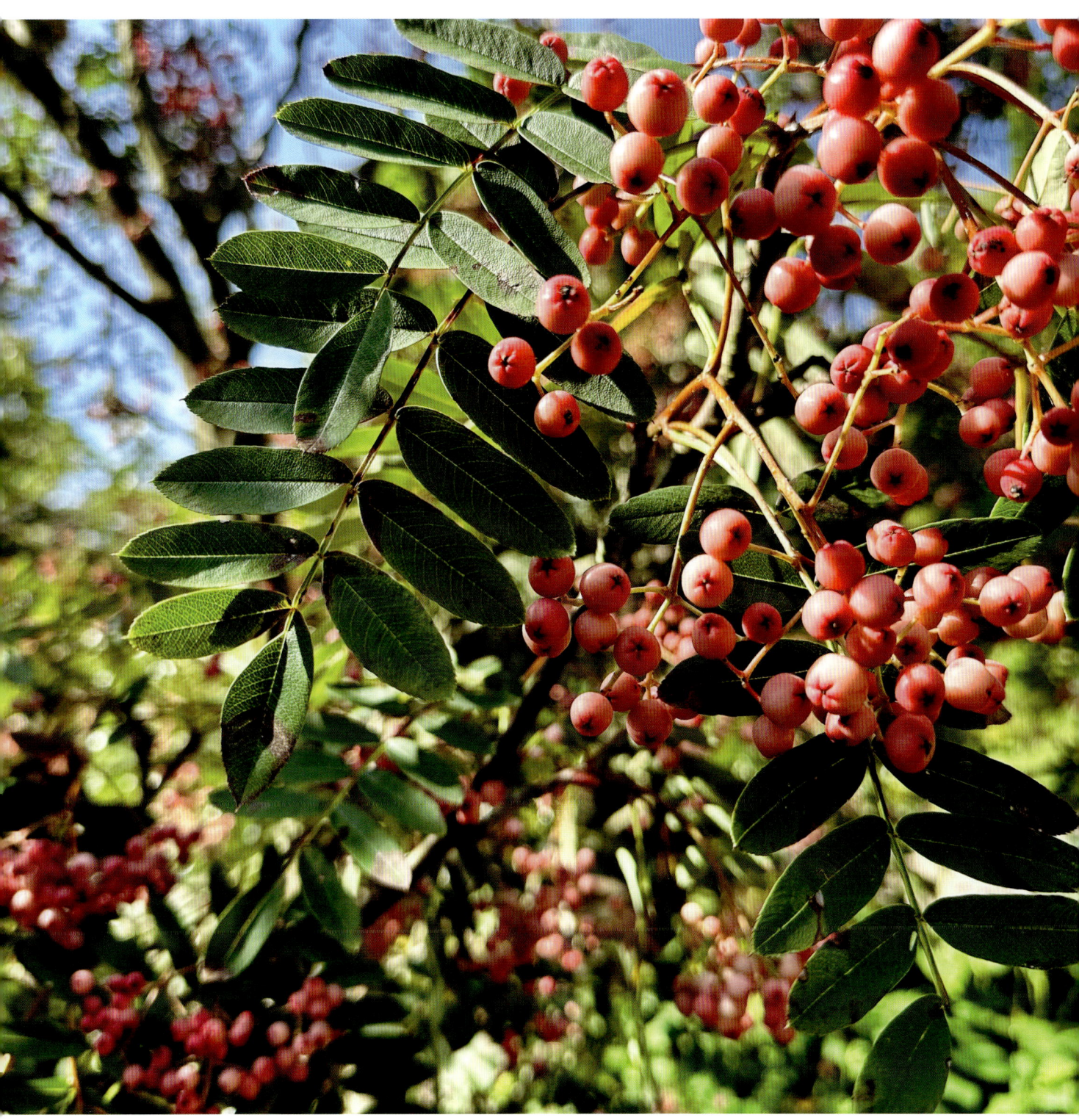

Notes on contributors

Brian Austin, Senior Lecturer (retired) in Electrical Engineering (45)

Lauren Aylward, PhD, Marine Biology (2024); scientific illustrator (3)

Paul Baines, Professor of English (21)

Richard Benjamin, Senior Lecturer in Contemporary Museum Practice and Co-Director of the Centre for the Study of International Slavery (37)

Alistair Bond, Senior Lecturer in Anatomy; Director, Human Anatomy Resource Centre (25)

Rowan Bradbury, Guild President 2024–25 (13)

Louise Bruton, Archivist & Curator (Popular Music), Libraries, Museums and Galleries (44)

Val Capewell, Student Partner 2023–24, Libraries, Museums and Galleries (42)

Halima Cassell, Artist (50)

Anna Chen, Chinese Language and Culture Advisor, Centre for Innovation in Education (23)

Lisa Colton, Professor of Musicology (27)

Ashley Cooke, Head of World Museum, National Museums Liverpool (16)

Gina Criscenzo-Laycock, Curator of the Garstang Museum, Libraries, Museums and Galleries (10, 16)

Diana Cullell Teixidor, Professor of Hispanic Studies (22)

Tinho da Cruz, Map Librarian, School of Environmental Sciences (6)

Niamh Delaney, Librarian, Special Collections, Libraries, Museums and Galleries (12)

Amanda Draper, Curator of Art and Exhibitions, Libraries, Museums and Galleries 2018–25 (46)

Paul Dunne, Professor of Computer Science (32)

Kelvin Everest, Emeritus Professor of English (29)

Joanne Fitton, Deputy Director, Libraries, Museums and Galleries (1)

Graham Gladden, Honorary Fellow, History and Libraries, Museums and Galleries (48)

Roger Hill, Freelance director, performer, arts and education consultant, writer, lecturer and broadcaster (41)

Aiden Ireland, Student, Earth, Ocean and Ecological Sciences (5)

Iain Jackson, Professor of Architecture (2)

John Jenkins, Senior Lecturer, School of Medicine (47)

Sophie Jones, Lecturer in Modern British History (11)

Janine L. Kavanagh, Professor of Volcanology (26)

Carl Larsen, Senior Lecturer and Director of Zoology (8)

Ken Lee, Alumnus, Lecturer (retired) Dept of Sociology and Anthropology, University of Newcastle, Australia (18)

Nick Lightfoot, Curator, Ness Botanic Gardens (52)

Hannah Little, Lecturer in Communication and Media (49)

Catherine Marcangeli, Curator and Art Historian, Université Paris Cité; Estate of Adrian Henri (38)

Esme Miskimmin, Senior Lecturer in English Literature, Theatre Liaison Lead (35)

John Moffett, Librarian, East Asian History of Science Library, Needham Research Institute, Cambridge (23)

Ekaterina Mulyk, Student Partner 2023–24, Libraries, Museums and Galleries (24)

Diana T. Nikolova, Collections Access Officer, Garstang Museum, Libraries, Museums and Galleries (7)

Sarah Peverley, Professor of English (14)

Paul Rakow, Reader in Mathematical Sciences (15)

Deryn Rees-Jones, Professor of Poetry (43)

Eve Rosenhaft, Emerita Professor of German Historical Studies (30)

Jill Rudd, Professor of English (20)

Pauline Rushton, Head of Lady Lever Art Gallery and Sudley House, National Museums Liverpool (39)

Gita Sedghi, Professor of Chemistry Education (34)

Leonie Sedman, Curator of Heritage and Collections Care, Libraries, Museums and Galleries (8)

Sally Sheard, Executive Dean, Institute of Population Health; Andrew Geddes and John Rankin Professor of Modern History (9)

Carl Sheridan, Senior Lecturer in Ocular Cell Transplantation, Eye and Vision Science (40)

Frank Shovlin, Professor of Irish Studies (31)

Dina-Leigh Simons, Postgraduate Researcher, Earth Ocean and Ecological Sciences (3)

Will Slocombe, Senior Lecturer in English (33)

Sophie Smith, McLua Project Archivist 2022–24 (31)

Pat Starkey, Honorary Research Fellow, Dept of History (36)

Mark Towsey, Professor of the History of the Book (11)

Stuart Wade, Sport Liverpool (51)

Elizabeth Williams, Archivist, Libraries, Museums and Galleries (30)

John James Wilson, Lead Curator Zoology, National Museums Liverpool (4)

Şizen Yiacoup, Senior Lecturer in Hispanic Studies (17, 28)

Callum Youngson, MBE, Emeritus Professor Health and Life Sciences Education Directorate (19)

Concordance and credits

1. *Keramic Art of Japan*: Printed Book collection (19c) SPEC H1.04/oversize

2. Victoria Building plan: University Archive A38/49/1 © John King Limited, Liverpool; photograph of the Victoria Gallery and Museum image credit: McCoy-Wynne

3. HMS *Challenger* specimen of *Neptheis fascicularis*: Heritage collections 61.4a.2. Image credit: Lyndsay Roberts; with illustration of *Neptheis fascicularis* by Lauren Aylward

4. *Birds of Asia*: Liverpool Royal Institution collections SPEC 300.4.1–17; Javan Trogon specimens: National Museums Liverpool, Zoology NML-VZ D2581 and NML-VZ D2581a. Image credit: John James Wilson

5. *Monandrian Plants*: Liverpool Royal Institution collections SPEC 301.5.1

6. Atlas of portolan charts: Thomas Glazebrook Rylands collection MS.F.4.3

7. Silver coin of Ptolemy I: Numismatics collection CC.299

8. *An inquiry into variolae vaccinae*: Medical Books collection SPEC M.1.17/C

9. Charles Thurstan Holland X-rays: Heritage collections XRA.15 and XRA.22

10. Ivory label: Egyptology Collection E5116; photograph: John Garstang collections JG/N/34

11. Catalogue of the Liverpool Library: Gregson Institute collections SPEC G39.03

12. Ben Jonson, *Songs*: William Noble collection SPEC Noble A.23.11

13. University of Liverpool Appeal poster: University Archive D937

14. Ranulf Higden, *Polychronicon*: Charles Sydney Jones collections SPEC Inc.CSJ.D03

15. Copernicus, *De Revolutionibus*: Early Printed Books collection SPEC EP.D06

16. Wooden sundial from Meroë: Sudanese collection E.8501; photographs: John Garstang Collections JG/M/E/7b and JG/M/E/8b

17. Islamic manuscript: Asian, Near and Middle Eastern manuscripts LUL MS.2.20

18. Photograph of Lazzy Smith: Romany collections SMGC 1/2/10/58

19. Porcelain teeth guide: Dentistry collections: B.230

20. Piers Plowman manuscript: Medieval Manuscripts collection LUL MS.F.4.8

21. Rushton, *Poems*: Rathbone collections SPEC H91.18

22. Press cuttings: Edgar Allison Peers collection Peers IX 1936

23. Feng Zikai painting in Album of Chinese paintings: Asian, Near and Middle Eastern manuscripts LUL Album/1/5 © Ziyun Yang for the family of Feng Zikai

24. Liverpool and Manchester Railway print: Charles Sydney Jones collections SPEC Y83.5.75

25. Vesalius, *De fabrica*: Printed Book collection (16c) SPEC H99.38/oversize

26. J.M.W. Turner, *The Eruption of the Soufrière Mountains*: Art collections FA.459

27. Dominican Antiphoner: Medieval Manuscripts collection LUL MS.F.4.13

28. Hebrew scrolls: Asian, Near and Middle Eastern manuscripts LUL MS.170–171

29. *An Authentic Account*: Printed Book collection (18c) SPEC GR8.4(1) and SPEC Y79.4.38

30. 1937 telegram: Rathbone collections RP.XIV/2/11

31. St Patrick Day's card: MacLua collection MLA/01/08/47

32. Allen, *LEO Computer Storage Unit*: Art collections FA.517 © Artist's Estate; Carbonora Ltd, photograph: University Archive P754/4/1 © 2024 Glenton Media, formerly Carbonora

33. Timelines: Olaf Stapledon collection SF OS/I 1/3 © Estate of Olaf Stapledon 2024

34. *The Boy's Playbook of Science*: Children's Book collection JUV.1033:2

35. *Peter Pan Keepsake*: Children's Book collection JUV 659:1

36. Portrait of Josephine Butler: Josephine Butler collection JB.2/1/7

37. Bowling, *Big Bird*: Art collections FA.802 © Frank Bowling. All rights reserved, DACS 2025

38. 'Love Is … ': Adrian Henri collection Henri/A/I/1(14); *Love Heart*: Henri/7/6/2 © Adrian Henri Estate, reproduced by kind permission of Catherine Marcangeli

39. Chaffers, Dragon bowl: Ceramics collection *Cer.311*

40. Riley, *Study for 'Ra'*: Art collection FA.1933 © Bridget Riley 2024. All rights reserved

41. *Merseysound* fanzine: Roger Hill collection IPM

42. Parody Beatles album cover: Institute of Popular Music collection IPM © Universal Music

43. Designs for Felicia Hemans medal by Elkington & Co. Ltd: University Archive P3/21; Bronze medal by Charles John Allen: Art collection FA.1486 © Artist's Estate

44. Photograph and audio cassette, Canto Libre event: Pring-Mill and Jan Fairley collections IPM © Estate of Jan Fairley; Estate of Robert Pring-Mill

45. *Radio-Craft* cover: Oliver Lodge collections: SPEC S/TK6540

46. Frink, *Front Runner*: Art collections FA.3582 © The Elisabeth Frink Estate and Archive. All rights reserved, DACS 2025

47. Forsyth, *Form A*: Campus Art FA.3700 © Susan Forsyth 2024. All rights reserved

48. Cunard brochure: Cunard Archive Langley collection: JGL/2/1/17/134

49. Remington typewriter: Science Fiction collections SF Clarke 2018

50. Cassell, *Noir Rhythm*: Art collections FA.3698 © Halima Cassell 2024. All rights reserved

51. Open Foils Championship Cups: Art collection MET.508 and 509

52. *Sorbus bulleyana*: Ness Botanic Gardens

Further reading, viewing, and listening

2. P. Arnell and T. Bickford, 'Introduction, James Stirling: A highly personal and very disjointed memoir', in *James Stirling: Buildings and Projects*, ed. by P. Arnell and T. Bickford (London: The Architectural Press, 1984).
William Holford, 'Ludwig Mond Lecture: Growth and Form in University Building', Special Collections and Archives, University of Liverpool, D147/LA19/13/1.
Charles H. Reilly *et al.*, *Scaffolding in the sky: a semi-architectural autobiography* (London: George Routledge & Sons, 1938).

4. Clemency Fisher, ed., *A Passion for Natural History: The Life and Legacy of the 13th Earl of Derby* (Liverpool: National Museums & Galleries on Merseyside, 2002).
Roslyn Russel, *The Business of Nature: John Gould and Australia* (Canberra: NLA Publishing, 2011).

5. HerbWeb – Nathaniel Wallich – Kew Gardens
liverpoolbotanicaltrust.org.uk/creation-of-lbg
A.B. Shteir, 'Gender and "Modern" Botany in Victorian England', *Osiris*, 12 (1997), 29–38.

11. c18librariesonline.org

12. Roderick Cave, *The Private Press* (New York: R.R. Bowker Company, 1983).
Marcella D. Genz, *A History of the Eragny Press 1894–1914* (New Castle, DE: Oak Knoll Press and London: British Library, 2004).

13. Thomas Kelly, *For Advancement of Learning. The University of Liverpool 1881–1981* (Liverpool: Liverpool University Press, 1981).

14. C. Babington and J.R. Lumby, eds, *Polychronicon Ranulphi Higden monachi Cestrensis*, 9 vols, Rolls Series 41 (London: Longman and Co., 1865–86).
Jane Beal, *John Trevisa and the English Polychronicon* (Turnhout: Brepols, 2013).
Graeme Dunphy, ed., *Encyclopedia of the Medieval Chronicle*, 2 vols (Leiden and Boston: Brill, 2010).
Lister M. Matheson, 'Printer and Scribe: Caxton, the *Polychronicon*, and the *Brut*', *Speculum*, 60:3 (1985), 593–614.
https://manuscriptsandmore.liverpool.ac.uk/?p=8427

18. Ken Lee, 'Visions of Esmeralda Lock: Epistemic Injustice, "The Gypsy Woman", and Gypsilorism', *Critical Romani Studies*, 5:1 (2023), 4–28.
Ken Lee and Jodie Matthews, 'Romani Rebel Writing: George "Lazzy" Smith's Entrepreneurial Auto-Exoticism', in *Rebellious Writing: Contesting Marginalisation in Edwardian Britain*, ed. by Lauren Alex O'Hagan (Oxford: Peter Lang, 2020).

20. Joshua R. Eyler and C. David Benson, 'The Manuscripts of Piers Plowman', *Literature Compass*, 2:1 (2005), https://doi.org/10.1111/j.1741-4113.2005.00132.x.
J.H.G. Grattan, 'The Text of *Piers Plowman*: A Newly Discovered Manuscript and Its Affinities', *The Modern Language Review*, 42:1 (1947), 1–8.
https://digitalheritagelab.liverpool.ac.uk/Documents/Detail/piers-plowman/80861

25. Dániel Margócsy, Mark Somos, and Stephen N. Joffe, *The Fabrica of Andreas Vesalius: A Worldwide Descriptive Census, Ownership, and Annotations of the 1543 and 1555 Editions* (Leiden: Brill, 2018).

27. J. Blezzard, S. Ryle, and J. Alexander, 'New Perspectives on the Feast of the Crown of Thorns', *Journal of the Plainsong & Mediaeval Music Society*, 10 (1987), 23–53.

    John Ruskin, *Part of the Chapel of Santa Maria della Spina* (1845), Collection of the Guild of St George, Sheffield Museums.

    https://digitalheritagelab.liverpool.ac.uk/Documents/Detail/dominican-antiphoner/81086

32. David Buckman, *Artists in Britain since 1945* (Bristol: Art Dictionaries Ltd, 2006).

37. A. Dixon, *Frank Bowling*, https://www.sothebys.com/en/digital-catalogues/london-an-artistic-crossroads/big-bird-frank-bowling-liverpool-university-museums (2022).

    Amanda Draper, *Big Bird Takes Flight*, https://vgm.liverpool.ac.uk/blog/2022/big-bird-takes-flight/ (2022).

    M. Gooding, *Frank Bowling*, Royal Academy of Arts (2021).

    Tate, *FRANK BOWLING: 31 May–26 August 2019*. Exhibition guide (2019).

    UCL, *The Centre for the Study of the Legacies of British Slavery*, https://www.ucl.ac.uk/lbs/person/view/1279385607 (2024).

38. adrianhenri.com, website created and administered by the Adrian Henri Estate.

    Adrian Henri, *Tonight at Noon* (London: Rapp & Whiting, 1968).

    Adrian Henri, *Selected and Unpublished Poems*, ed. by Catherine Marcangeli (Liverpool: Liverpool University Press, 2007).

    Adrian Henri, Roger McGough, and Brian Patten, *The Mersey Sound* (London: Penguin, 1967).

    Catherine Marcangeli, ed., *Total Artist* (London: Occasional Papers, 2014).

    Catherine Marcangeli, ed., *I Want Everything to Happen* (London: Ecstatic Peace Library, 2019).

40. https://www.tate.org.uk/art/artists/bridget-riley-1845

    https://www.theartstory.org/movement/op-art/

    https://chinati.org/exhibitions/bridget-riley/

42. 'Beatles album parody art? He loves it, yeah, yeah, yeah, yeah … ', by John Kelly for the *Washington Post*, published 9 August 2016, accessed 13 August 2024.

    'How Jun Fukamachi Became a Cult Figure in Japanese Ambient Music', by Aaron Carnes for *Bandcamp Daily*, published 24 August 2018, accessed 21 August 2024.

    https://whitenoiserecords.org/products/深町純-jun-fukamachi-sgt-peppers-lonely-hearts-club-band,

    Jun Fukamachi – Sgt Pepper's Lonely Hearts Club Band reissue listing, the description of which (author unknown) quotes a relevant article from *Billboard Magazine*, 9 September 1978. Date of publication for the listing unknown, accessed 21 August 2024.

43. The Poetry Archive https://poetryarchive.org/poet/felicia-hemans/

45. Sir Oliver Lodge Collection (LDG) on Wiley Digital Archives: https://app-wileydigitalarchives-com.liverpool.idm.oclc.org/wiley/collection-details?archive=BAAS&id=LDG

52. Hugh McAllister, *The Genus Sorbus: Mountain Ash and other Rowans* (Kew: Royal Botanic Gardens (2005), p. 232.

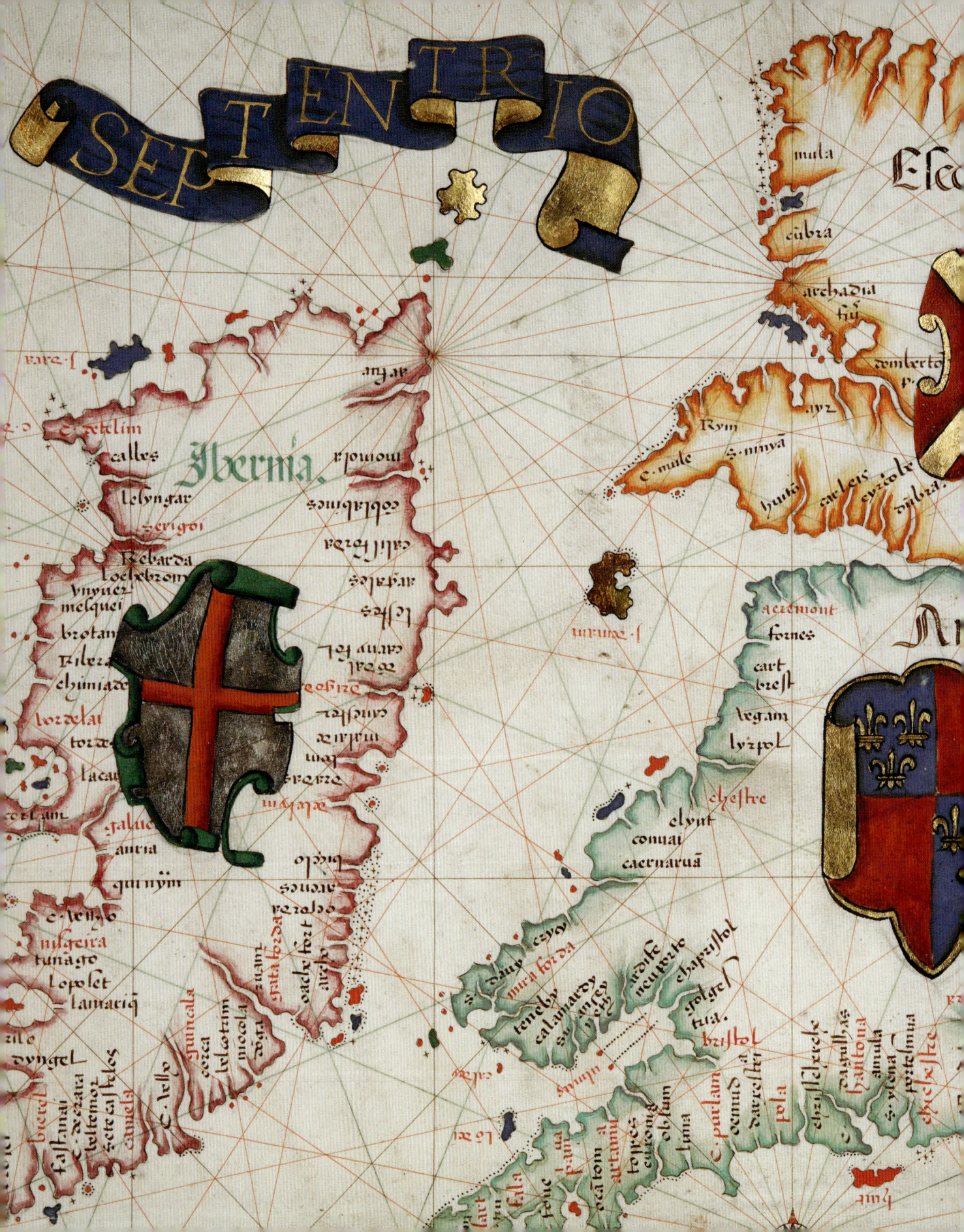